Advance Praise for *Italy Is My Boyfriend*

"Annette Joseph has written a sparkling book—full of humor and insight—about the cultural roadblocks to buying a house in Italy. Luckily, she prevailed, with her love for Italy intact, and has written a valentine of a book for all of us to savor. *Brava*!!"

—Tricia Brock, Director and Visionary Storyteller

"This memoir of memorable moments is a guide to making our own memories—a reminder to feel deeply, to love greatly, to dream big, and to notice the good, the bad, and everything in between along the way, whilst always holding onto the vision of finding the secret key to our own happiness. I so embrace Annette's generosity of spirit in sharing this guide to falling in love with and living in Italy. *'Fatene Tesoro!'*"

—Betty Soldi, Florentine and Creative Thinker

"If you've ever fantasized about buying a European farmhouse in the middle of a vineyard (and who hasn't?) you'll enjoy house hunting with Annette through the Tuscan countryside. We've worked together producing magazines for more than a decade, so I have followed the search from afar and once even spent a magical week at her home in Alassio. The Josephs' wildly entertaining tales of the crazy and often unwritten rules of real estate investing in Italy have made me laugh out loud, and now she's sharing them with readers. The book has the ups and downs of all good love stories. There's even a magic castle."

—Betsy Riley, Editor-in-Chief of *Atlanta Magazine*

Italy Is My Boyfriend

A memoir

Annette Joseph

POST HILL
PRESS

A POST HILL PRESS BOOK
ISBN: 978-1-64293-509-7
ISBN (eBook): 978-1-64293-510-3

Italy Is My Boyfriend
© 2020 by Annette Joseph
All Rights Reserved

Cover art by Ma Ni

Post Hill Press
New York • Nashville
posthillpress.com

Published in the United States of America

To my husband Frank

and

To my boyfriend Italy…

(not necessarily in that order)

Contents

CHAPTER 1

Getting to Know You

Rome was a summer romance, a first love, intense but brief. Perfect for any student in search of art and beauty. I spent an entire summer before college traveling, touring, learning, eating, and basking in the Italian sunshine. It was the best summer of my life, but, true to its time frame, it was over in a heartbeat. I have never forgotten my love for Rome, I just tucked the memories away and moved on to acquaint myself with all the other beauties the country has to offer.

My years here have revealed this truth: Italy in all its multifaceted, glorious history and culture has to be experienced in full. Over almost three decades, Italy has fed me, entertained me, confused me, excited me, lured me, promised me, lied to me, satisfied me, occasionally let me down, and utterly enchanted me. I leave, but I can't stay away; I always return. Always. Just like a beloved partner…

As you can plainly see, Italy is my boyfriend.

Years after that summer fling with Rome, I married my husband Frank and we had two children. Family summer vacations were spent on the Italian Riviera, always near the beach, renting a house by the sea for six weeks at a time. I cooked, we went to the beach, we painted, we read and napped, Frank biked all over the countryside—we lived *la dolce vita* with kids in tow. Most Americans opt for Tuscany, but our family was different, we liked the sea and the seaside vibe.

On our first family vacation to Italy in 1997, I found the Italian Riviera, called Liguria, through our dear friends Larry and Ole. They told us about a town called Santa Margherita Ligure on the east coast of Italy. Ole had vacationed there as a child from Denmark and loved it. So we went with them our first time, and it was immediate love for me. I had a sense that I had lived there in a past life; it felt very comfortable. That's where it began, my love affair with the Italian Riviera.

We rented a pretty pink house at the uppermost ridge of town. We had never rented a house; it was a first and with first times there are always a few nerves and the anticipation of things to come. But we felt pretty certain this would be an amazing summer. All the Ligurian seaside towns are built on cliffs with winding roads that lead down to the sea. We had a spectacular view and a yard with an exotic garden with kiwis growing on vines covering the pergola. We had most meals looking out at the sea beneath that pergola, heavily bowed with the furry, ripened fruit. It was a typical Italian house, two floors with a tiny well-appointed kitchen, big bedrooms, and a sitting room on the upper floor. The TV was big and we spent evenings watching soccer games (since that was the only thing we could understand in Italian). The best part of the vacation for me was the beach club. It was exactly what I pictured an Italian beach club would look like—red-and-white striped cabanas, striped chairs, and a wonderful little restaurant where we had lunched every day. Lunch consisted of heaps of salty fried calamari, fresh pesto pasta, and—always—the chilled house white wine.

The beach club at Paraggi Beach, located between Portofino and Santa Margherita, was a daily ritual that made me love Italy even more. The kids played on the beach all day, and at day's end we would shower them in the camp-like shower stall at the club, and dress them in tiny beach robes I had bought in town. The memory of their shiny, tan little faces eating an ice cream bar at the end of the day still makes me smile.

While we loved our little beach club and seaside garden in Santa Margherita, in 2000, we rented a house in Levanto to experience another seaside town. It was sort of like dating around; we wanted to see how it differed and if we liked it as much. It was a renovated farmer's house situated just below a very large villa. At one time, the farmer had lived there and worked the land for the proprietors of the villa. The villa even had a tiny church right next to it—a family chapel—that fascinated me.

A family from Turin lived in the villa, which had been in the family for generations—many, many generations, as Italians would insist. Which again is quite common in Italy; in fact, it's the rule and not the exception that large estates are passed down to all members of a family.

We met the family upon arrival—young parents like us, with five boys, ages four to eleven. For Levi, our son, this was a wonderful development; he was seven at the time and ready for anything, and was especially thrilled he would have a pack of boys to pal around with.

The rental farmhouse was quite comfortable and beautifully decorated in a rustic style, with five big bedrooms and a huge terrace that cantilevered out over the cliff affording insane sea views. I figured we would be living on that terrace, and I was right. Last but not least, the country kitchen was perfection. It had open shelving, a rudimentary gas stove from the 1960s, and thick Carrara marble tops (that I would later harken to when I was building our own country kitchen); it was simple and functional and to me it was beautiful. I cooked all our meals there with immense pleasure.

And I had a lot of meals to cook that first summer, too, as we had lots of visitors over our six-week stay—and I mean LOTS; five families joined us that summer, about twenty-five people in all. I had felt confident that our friends would love the Italian Riviera as much as we did, so I invited everyone.

I'm not kidding. Whenever I told our friends that we were renting a house for the summer at the Italian seaside, the next thing out of my mouth would be, "Why don't you come visit?" I learned that when you say that to people, they actually *will* show up. I didn't realize that

I needed to be educated on hosting a crowd of houseguests. Even now, having entertained summer guests for twenty-five years in Italy, there are always funny stories and some surprises.

In Levanto, we settled in before the onslaught of guests. Levi quickly found that there were two donkeys in the field next to the house. He was thrilled to feed them carrots and apples every morning, and he would trek up to the villa to play with some newfound Italian friends. Even with the language barrier, they had a grand time running around the yard and tromping all over the place.

Francesca, the new friends' mama, was tall, lean, and not at all how I pictured an Italian mama. She was blonde and dressed very preppy. In fact, she looked like a model from an Italian J. Crew catalog. I later learned that this was the popular look of the women of Turin. The coast-line was inhabited in the summer by city folk from Turin and Milan; it was the go-to vacation destination for these families in this part of Italy. Women like Francesca chose to dress in a more buttoned-down Swiss style since Turin shares its borders with the Swiss. This nugget of style info was the beginning of my learning how different all the regions in Italy are, and what makes the inhabitants of each region and city so unique. I had been stereotyping what Italians look like based on Sophia Loren and, of course, I was way off. Each region has its own special style—not just in the food realm, but also in fashion and demeanor.

Every morning Francesca and her boys packed themselves into her little vintage Fiat 500 and puttered down the hill, bumping along the curvy back road from the villa, to pick Levi up. They would all to go to their private beach club, and Levi was in heaven. Our daughter Alex would read to her heart's content and help me prepare lunch each day. It was pretty much perfection…well, to be truthful, not completely. There were chores that Alex was less than enthusiastic about, but would begrudgingly help me with.

Frank brought his newly purchased American bicycle packed in a box that summer—it was literally a bike in a box. Frank had decided back in our hometown of Atlanta that assembling a bike in Italy was a good decision. In a country that builds bikes, and virtually lives on bikes, how could a bike in twenty-five pieces seem like a great idea, I wondered? I thought it would be easier to just buy or rent a bike in Italy. So I was not completely on board with it, but this was his vacation too, and I was not going to rain on his parade.

Here's how it turned out: Frank, who is a very adept guy, unfortunately had no luck building his twenty-five-piece packable American bike. After two hours of trying to make a bike, we loaded the rental car with bike bits and headed down into town to find a bike repair shop. We found one, but the sweet little Italian bike repairman just scratched and shook his head simultaneously when he saw Frank's bike parts. Somehow, with my (then) shitty Italian and Frank's fairly good Spanish, the three of us got the bike together, back into the rental car, and returned home in an hour's time.

Frank took the bike for a spin the next day and came back with a brand-new Italian bike he'd rented in town. I did not say a word, and I still don't know what happened to the packable bike, but I thought the whole thing was pretty hilarious in the end.

Frank loved biking all over the town, into the hills and mountains behind us. He'd come back just in time for lunch and an afternoon nap. It was pretty much the best daily routine ever, and the thing we all loved most about Italy. I like that it's referred to as *pausa* (the pause) in some parts of Italy. The *pausa* consists of lunchtime and a nap, and lasts for three hours every day—something, I will say, we got used to quite easily. To this day, our American guests struggle with what to do during *pausa*—the idea that the whole town shuts down for four to five hours blows their minds.

That summer in Levanto, Judy and Robby Johnson—parents we had become friendly with from Alex's school—and their daughters Mindy and Maura arrived with their large suitcases.

I loved cooking for everyone and taking all the girls to the local flea market on Sunday. Sunday Market in *Forte dei Marmi* is insanely fun. Imagine every Italian product, from home to fashion, in one large *piazza*. It's the best market on the Tuscan Riviera and has become one of my favorite places to take girlfriends when they visit. We had a blast there: both families ate at the local pizzeria, gobbling tons of *focaccia* and *gelato*. We were having a grand old time in our country house as the days passed, until one night we came back from dinner and discovered we had been robbed. Apparently, the fantasy of the Italian countryside came with a warning of thieves. I had missed the memo.

> *Tip # 1: Even though Italy is mostly safe, residences*
> *are prone to thieves. It's not an epidemic but one*
> *should be mindful and not pack expensive jewelry.*

When we arrived home, our guests went to their room and quickly discovered Judy's jewelry was missing. All of it. We were all upset, but I always try to look at the bright side. A: No one was hurt. B: The Italian policemen were super handsome and wore really spiffy uniforms. So, at midnight, two fashionably-uniformed policemen showed up at our door. Right off the bat they suspected that the maid and an accomplice were probably responsible, since nothing else was stolen. We shared a bottle of wine with the officers and had a nice little chat, and then they were off into the night and we headed to bed.

> *Tip #2: In Italy, one should offer a country*
> *cop a glass of vino, or at least an espresso.*

Our next set of guests were great travelers; in fact, they could not sit their butts down for a second, constantly needing to be occupied. Sometimes these can be the best guests, the kind of guests that will make you breakfast and coffee, and play with your kids. Our friend Micky and his boyfriend Bill fell into this category—they were energetic guests. Always moving, never relaxing—hiking, biking, swimming, and playing with Levi nonstop. In fact, sometimes Micky's manic energy was downright scary.

Micky loved the beach club and the water; we all did.

A little about beach clubs: one has to join a beach club in town, or you can pay on a daily, weekly, or seasonal rate, but it's not cheap. Beach clubs are all very professionally run. In most cases these clubs are family businesses; I mean generational, much like most businesses in Italy.

Beach clubs are the summer vacation destination for most Italians, especially in Liguria. Italians will come to the same beach club for a lifetime. I find it interesting, that one could go to the same spot every summer for a lifetime. In fact, some families have had the same cabana for generations. Let me explain what a cabana is. Some of you might be thinking that you know what a cabana is, but in Italy it is something quite unique.

At the beginning of summer, one brings a season's worth of beach supplies to the club and stuffs everything into a rented cabana, a little wooden hut with a number on it, and locked with a key with a coinciding number on a key fob. There are hundreds of these little huts that line individual beach clubs. Italians love to go to the beach club dressed in street clothes, change, and then when they are ready to leave, they shower and get dressed in street clothes, and usually head for an *aperitivo* at the club bar or nearby bar with their friends from the club.

The first day at the beach, I said, "Micky, don't break my kid." He just laughed, but sure enough, I was just about to doze off when I heard footsteps running towards me. I opened one eye to see Micky, carrying a bleeding Levi, not knowing where to take him.

"Micky!" I yelled. "Take him to the lifeguard station."

Lifeguards at the beach clubs are pros, surfer boys, or studs, and they are trained in first aid—I mean, as well-trained as a doctor. I pointed Micky to the lifeguard station, and ran behind to see the damage he had done to my boy. Fortunately it was nothing serious, just a cut on the arm from playing on rocks covered in sharp mussel shells. It healed quickly.

Micky was a great guest and my kids loved him, but Micky never lived down the fact that it took him less than five minutes to break my kid.

Since we had fired the maid thinking she must be a crook, it was up to Alex and me to run my self-proclaimed B&B. Laundry is an issue if you've invited a million people to stay with you in the Italian countryside—imagine that! It seems that most Italians hate clothes dryers, so we didn't have one. There was no dryer, but we had full access to clotheslines strung up in the garden.

My most vivid memory of Alex that summer was our hanging out hundreds of sheets and towels to dry on those clotheslines. We hung and folded laundry every single day. We wrapped our heads in scarves to protect us from the sun beating down. (Did I mention it was one of the hottest summers on record in Italy?) We were bitten by mosquitoes, scratched by thistles, and were generally miserable. We pictured ourselves looking like quintessential Italian mamas—kind of how I pictured Francesca before I actually met her.

I think I scarred our daughter that summer; she's still not keen on coming to the Italian countryside for fear of hard labor. Turns out those pretty pictures of Italian laundry floating in the breeze are really pretty hard work. Like everything in life, it's usually not as easy-breezy as it looks.

Our funniest and least-traveled guests were the last to arrive that summer. They were dear friends, a newly married middle-aged couple who had asked to visit. Of course I said yes. The funny thing about people that don't travel much is that sometimes they don't ask questions up front and end up making some wonky travel decisions, which was the case here. I like to call them "timid travelers."

The day they were to arrive, we headed to the beach in the morning. Their arrival time was planned to be around 6:00 p.m., just in time for *aperitivo* and supper. Like most days, we had a great time playing in the sea all day. We headed back up the hill to the house around 5:00 because I wanted to get the kids bathed and myself ready before their arrival. As we walked towards the house, we noticed a tiny car parked in front, with the windows rolled down.

We figured correctly that our guests had arrived early, and we walked into the house to discover Rick and Maren passed out in the front room, sound asleep. They must have heard us come in, because they rallied and sat up.

"*Ciao*," I said. "You're here. Welcome."

Rick responded with a grunt, and mumbled, "That damn car was a stick shift. It took me a half hour to remember how to use a manual car. And the damn thing does *not* have air conditioning."

"What?" I said. "That's impossible."

"Nope, these damn I-talian cars don't have anything," he complained. Maren agreed, shaking her head and rubbing her eyes. She said, "We almost died coming here; it was boiling hot and there is no radio!"

Knowing this couldn't be right, I insisted, ""Wait a minute that can't be, let's go have a look."

"Well, we really almost died of heat," Maren insisted.

We all made our way to the tiniest car in the world and right there on the dashboard was a snowflake icon. I asked, "Did you try pushing this? It's usually the symbol for frozen air."

Maren went pale, and asked, "You mean we drove all the way down here on the *autostrada*, for three hours, sweating up a storm, with the windows down, and all we needed to do was push this button?" We all had a laugh, then a shower, and spent the evening on the terrace talking and eating and drinking *vino* into the night.

CHAPTER 2

Looking for The Right One

bout the time Rick and Maren arrived, I kept having thoughts about buying property in Italy. One night before dinner we were drinking wine on the terrace and Francesca came down from the villa to check in. I asked if she'd like to have a glass of wine with us. Since I knew absolutely nothing about her, I thought it might be nice to get to know each other.

She shared that she'd grown up with the villa as their summerhouse. Her father was an oil painter, which was wild because so was my father. Of course, with that in common we had an instant connection, which was nice. Her husband Enrico and she lived in Turin with their five boys. Enrico was an architect, which I figured out much later was a descriptive used in two different ways in Italy, both as an actual architect as we think of them in the US, and also as an interior designer.

He was the former, which explained why the farmhouse was so well-designed and well-appointed. We chatted about children, travel, and cooking.

At this point I felt comfortable enough to ask her if she knew of any real estate for sale in the area. The reason I was hesitant was not because

I did not know her, it was because I had not even broached the subject with my husband, Frank. But it couldn't hurt to look right?

Frank was off with the kids on a mini trip to Germany to visit his aunts, seventy-year-old twins. So I felt comfortable gathering information without Frank rolling his eyes at me. Rick, however, was so in; since he was a builder in the US, the prospect of house hunting in Italy intrigued him. Francesca said she would ask around and get back to us. Frank arrived later that evening after dinner and Rick brought up the idea of looking at some real estate, so I was thankfully spared the eye-rolling (that would come later).

The next day Francesca barreled down the hill from the villa to pick up Levi up like she did every morning. This time she rolled down her window: "I think I have a property for you to look at about thirty minutes away. How about we go after lunch?"

"Of course," I said. "After lunch is perfect!"

After a yummy lunch of fresh seafood pasta, arugula salad, and slices of pineapple for dessert, we headed to the car where Francesca was waiting for us. "Follow me," she said.

Frank, Rick, Maren, and I jumped in the car and drove closely so we would not lose Francesca. About a hundred meters down the road Francesca stopped; apparently there was a minor issue at the villa, so she gave us directions and told us she would meet us in the driveway of the house that was for sale. The directions seemed simple, and doable, so we agreed that we would meet there.

I was driving and Frank was the navigator. Since I had spent so much time in this area I knew it well, so I felt confident finding the exact location would not be an issue. We drove the winding roads for about a half hour before arriving at our destination—"the driveway right before the railroad bridge," as Francesca had said. I pulled into the driveway, and we all got out to assess the situation.

Maren and I decided that we would blaze the trail and head towards the house, which looked to be miles down the driveway. The guys would stay behind and drive down with Francesca when she arrived. As we began wandering down the drive, we could not help but be very curious and excited about what might lie ahead. We walked for what seemed like hours, down the magical forest path. Birds chirped, frogs croaked, and I could swear I saw wood nymphs playing among the trees.

I looked at Maren and said, "Wow, this is amazing. I am so excited! Could we be so lucky to find *the one*…so easily?"

Maren, who was equally mesmerized by the beauty all around us, said," I wonder what this house looks like, if this is the entrance?" Keep in mind the price Francesca quoted was very affordable, so we were both a bit perplexed by how this could be the right setting.

We finally arrived at the clearing at the end of the driveway, and we found an enormous golden villa, flanked by its own chapel. (There was that personal chapel again!) I decided right then and there I needed a chapel in my life, which is funny since I am Jewish, but in any case, this had become a personal non-negotiable in my house hunt. My stomach was doing back flips; it was hard not to jump up and down and squeal, which I am pretty sure I did. Maren looked at me in awe and said, "Whoa, this is amazing. It's perfect." I noticed a car in the driveway, then wandered around to the chapel side and looked in a window. Suddenly I was struck by the realization that this was not the right house. Francesca had said it was abandoned, and this villa was very much lived in.

Horrified that we had just trekked down someone's private driveway, I told Maren, "This is wrong. This can't be the right place!"

"What?" she whispered.

"This is someone's private residence and we are clearly trespassing!" We really did not know whether to laugh or bolt up the driveway. We chose to do both, laughing hysterically all the way up the driveway. When we reached the top, Frank and Rick were smirking; Francesca stood behind them with a startled look on her face. It turns out that in Italy, most folks in the country have guard dogs, and we were lucky we did not get mauled that day. Needless to say, we had a good giggle and headed to the right location to look at the abandoned villa. I still had high hopes, and even though the mistaken magical villa was not the one, I was feeling lucky.

We all piled into the car once again and headed up the road right behind Francesca's car, careful not to lose her. She pulled into a driveway on the right, up the road and around the corner from the villa with the chapel. We noticed that the driveway needed some work. We parked the cars and all followed Francesca down, down, down to a platform made of wood and covered in black tar and tarps.

The view was spectacular; in fact, we had an amazing overview of the beautiful villa we had just trespassed.

Frank asked Francesca, "Where's the house?"

"We are standing on the roof," she responded. We all looked down, then up again at each other in disbelief. This was not a house; this was a mess, and it was indeed abandoned—not only abandoned, but invisible.

Frank politely asked, "How much do they want for this?"

"500,000 Euros," Francesca responded. Silence, then we all broke out in laughter, looking around this pile of rocks and trash. Standing on the roof of this disaster, we laughed so hard that we cried. Francesca seemed a bit insulted that we thought this real estate prospect was so funny. We tried to stop laughing, but the more we tried, the harder it was to stop.

I said to Frank, "This is perfect! If we buy this, we can sink a ton of money into it and *still* not have the beautiful villa we just saw. Plus, I can be tortured everyday with the view of the beautiful villa and the chapel of my dreams."

As we continued to look at properties over the years, we would find that this was not unusual at all. In fact, showing Americans impossible projects that an Italian would not touch with a ten-foot pole was the norm. As an Italian would say, this was a *Bruta Figura*, which loosely translated means "a bad thing" and it marked the beginning of our house hunt in Italy.

Back in the car, Frank said he was on board with finding a home in Italy, but we both agreed it needed to be the right fit, in the right location. Looking for the right one would take time and perseverance, and luckily, we had plenty of both.

Frank headed back to the US a few days after our house-hunting adventure, while I stayed on with the kids for a few more weeks. I continued to cook, walk into town to do the marketing, battle the army of ants that had taken up residence in the kitchen, clean, and do the laundry. Alex and I continued to hang laundry on the clothesline next to the donkeys that had little interest in us if we did not have a carrot in hand. Levi continued his having fun-filled days playing with the boys from the villa all over town.

One night not long after Frank left, I took a break from cooking, and we walked down the hill into town for dinner. There was a charming family-owned spot that served seafood and pesto pasta, like all the other places in town. We liked this one because it had a terrace on the seaside and we could dine while watching the seagulls play. Levi loved pesto pasta. I swear, he ate it every day for lunch and dinner that summer. Alex and I shared a piping hot Margherita pizza.

After dinner we took a stroll on the boardwalk with gelato in hand. We passed a beautiful villa that overlooked the sea; this villa had the most amazing formal gardens and a stunning iron gate with a crest of some sort in the middle. I said to Alex and Levi, "I would really love to see the inside of that place and meet the people that live there."

Levi piped up, "Oh, I was there yesterday with Francesca and the boys. It's really pretty."

"What?" I said, surprised. "Are you kidding me? You got a tour of that place?"

"Yeah, the owners are good friends of Francesca's family," he answered.

I shook my head, "You lucky duck. I can't believe it. Pays to know the right people, eh?"

As we walked on toward the marina, Levi pointed to a large sailing yacht and said, "Yeah, a couple days ago I sailed on that boat."

"You did not," I said in disbelief.

"I did, and I jumped off the cliffs out there, too, " he said, pointing to an outcropping of rocks in the water.

"Wow, Levi, you're having the best vacation of all of us!" It was true; Levi had the best summer hanging out with the locals. Every day Francesca would take Levi along with her brood to experience what was their typical family summer, but there was nothing ordinary about it. Levi was truly a lucky little duck.

Near the end of our summer vacation, we were sitting on the terrace, finishing up dinner, when a big, dark storm cloud rolled in over the sea. You could watch the cloud make its way across the sky like a slow-moving train. While we ate dessert, we watched lightning bolts dart across the sky and crash into the sea, and soon the rumble and boom of thunder claps across the horizon grew so loud that we all jumped out of our seats simultaneously to run inside for cover.

The sky became pitch dark within moments, and then the rain came down. One of the things I have learned over years of living by the sea is that the weather is ever shifting and changing, always surprising, and sometimes very frightening. This storm was all those things.

We headed to bed to read our books and I soon dozed off, only to awaken to the loudest and angriest thunder I've ever heard, along with howling winds. I was convinced the house would blow off the cliff. The kids ran into my room to hide under the covers. Frank was already back in the States, so we were on our own, alone to weather the storm.

All of a sudden, the guest room window in the room next to ours blew open. Alex and I jumped out of bed and rushed across the hall to try to close and latch the gaping window. The winds were so intense it was raining sideways, and as the rain hit the window sash it soaked our nightgowns and chilled us to the bone. It was like something out of a horror movie. After struggling for a few minutes, we finally latched the window and headed back to Levi, who was hiding in bed under the covers, scared to death.

The electricity went out, and the storm continued for several hours. I kept the kids quiet by playing a movie on our portable DVD player and hoped the battery would hold out until the storm abated. It was hard to sleep, and I kept thinking about fishermen at sea, and how afraid I would be if I were on a boat in the middle of the storm that night.

When we woke in the morning there was no sign that there had been a violent storm during the night! Just like every day, the sun was shining and the sea was beckoning us to its sandy shore. We packed up and headed into town to grab a breakfast pastry and head to the beach club to enjoy the last days of our Italian summer.

We ended our summer on a high note. Francesca invited all of us up to the villa to meet her Mama. Mama had made fresh mussels with garlic and wine and plenty of homemade *focaccia*; a salad of wild greens picked right from the garden, with homegrown olive oil; briny sardines mixed with homemade pasta and tomatoes; roasted lamb with capers and onions; and afterward, strong espresso and *biscotti* and *gelato* from our favorite place in town. A typical Italian meal! We drank local wine and talked into the night about the town and about the boys and about our great summer. It was the summer we decided to buy a home in Italy, we had been toying with the idea. Now we had to begin the real hunt in earnest.

The kids and I flew home at the end of August; school was starting and I was back to booking styling jobs and producing features for magazines.

I felt a little sad that it was all over, more that summer than ever before. That little rental house in Levanto had won my heart and I wanted to go back again next summer. It was like the heartache of a summer romance, and I had it bad. Frank was very understanding and supportive of my feelings, as well as my quest to find us our own place in Italy. So where to begin? I soon found that I knew nothing about looking for a house in Italy. I read books about expats that had found homes there; I scanned real estate sites about how to buy property in Italy. It all seemed very daunting to me. Looking for a house in Italy was like looking for a needle in a haystack.

I read book after book, article after article. I even re-read *Under the Tuscan Sun*! Looking for a house in Italy was more like "Under the Tuscan Nightmare." I culled the internet daily for some insight about the best approach. Traditional real estate agencies were of no help. I would email them and hear nothing back. I researched for a year before stumbling across a site that held some promise. I found an old olive mill; it was a wreck, but, as they say, had good bones. The mill was in Liguria, the region we had been vacationing in for five years. A tiny sparkle of light at the end of what seemed like a very dark long tunnel was before me on my computer screen. I tapped the keyboard and typed a note to the agent selling the property, hit send, and hoped for the best.

By January 2001, we began making plans to rent a house and spend the summer in Italy yet again. This time we would go to the town of Alassio in Liguria, and spend eight weeks by the sea. It appealed to us because it had a vibrant boardwalk and one of the longest sandy beaches in Italy. It was the quintessential Italian Riviera town and, most important, there was lots of real estate for sale there, so we would give it a try and see if we could find anything to buy. Although I had fallen in love with the farmhouse in Levanto, I thought it was a good idea to try some other locations as part of our research; we were on a mission.

Back in Atlanta, it seemed like forever until summer; the winter months went by much slower than usual. The only thing that made it easier is that I finally contacted a woman from a German real estate agency I found on the internet that had the olive mill for sale—a great find! As we chose our house to rent and made plans with various friends to visit, the days ticked by.

Flying across the ocean to stay in a house in the Italian countryside had always been very exciting to me. I am not so sure the rest of the family felt the same way. The kids liked Italy, but they wanted to hang with friends in Atlanta; Frank enjoyed Italy, but was always worried that the house would not be up to his standards—people always think Frank is chill, but the reality is that he is a bit pickier than me. I call him the Prince; he's pretty fancy. I must admit I was the only one in the family that was super excited to head to Italy again for the summer. But my family was very tolerant, and all-you-can-eat *gelato* and non-stop pesto and *focaccia* were a big selling point for Frank and the kids. Truth is that I am the adventurer and they are the homebodies.

CHAPTER 3

Internet Dating

The place we rented in Alassio was an apartment in a very lovely seaside town just on the Italian side of the French border, which made it easy to drive through the south of France, an area called Provence. We settled into our four-bedroom flat with ease—after all we were professional renters by now.

The kitchen was quite large. It was the biggest kitchen we had ever seen in Italy, and of course I was thrilled to have a chance to cook there. It had an open fireplace—for warmth, not cooking—and a well-worn kitchen table, where we spent many mornings reading and sipping strong espresso. It amazed me that the kids still insisted on eating a traditional American breakfast every morning. I had to scour the stores for cornflakes or some form of American-style cereal. They were not interested in the warm brioche I toted upstairs every morning; they wanted sugar pops. The best I could find was corn flakes, to which my response when they moaned that corn flakes were awful was "just put lots of sugar on it and enjoy."

Each morning I would stop at the bar next to our building and grab a quick espresso. Even after all these years I find it fascinating that

Italians consume their espresso in one big gulp. Like addicts, they line up at the bar and throw back the smooth black brew. I, too, am a *caffe* addict, (espresso in Italian is a *caffe normale*) and I have learned to finish my espresso in one quick sip, like a local. This practice was not hard for me to conquer; I can't get enough of the stuff. Once I threw back my *caffe*, I was ready to explore the town and find new and exciting shops and resources.

Another important thing we do when we would hit a new beach town was to check out the beach clubs. Lucky for us, there were many to choose from in Alassio. So many, in fact, that we literally went to a different beach club every week for eight weeks without ever repeating one!

The thing to know about Italian beach clubs is that personal space is at a premium. Understand, you will be lying on the beach within an arms' reach of your neighbor. You will jostle with other beachgoers for places to sit at lunch, and stand in close lines just to grab a bottle of water. These clubs are very effective in using every square inch to turn a profit. It's something I have gotten used to over the years; however, when we moved to Italy later, we opted for a more generous beach club with more elbow room.

As we settled into our everyday routines of breakfast, beach, and napping, I started trolling the internet again for possible houses for sale in the area. I finally began to get return emails from Italian real estate agencies, and the German agency with the olive mill wanted to connect and perhaps have us visit the mill. However, we had a roster of guests arriving, so house hunting was put on the back burner for a month.

Before the guests began arriving, Frank and I were busy planning a family trip through the South of France. We love road trips and Frank loved picking the route and itinerary. Frank is of German heritage and tends to be a more rigid planner, whereas I really love getting in the car and seeing where the road takes me. As you can imagine this combination of personalities does not always work, but we make it work… with only a little screaming in the car thrown in. Our good friends love coming with us on road trips in Italy just to see the fireworks. I guess it's entertaining, but it's just our way of communicating. Hey, it's worked so far, so what the heck?

The South of France is about a ninety-minute drive from the Italian Riviera. We rented a comfortable car, loaded our suitcases into the boot, and off we went to the see the South of France with the kiddos.

About an hour into the ride I decided I wanted to detour—already you can imagine the look I garnered from Frank.

"What, where?" he asked.

"I want to go to buy perfume in Graz. It's about two hours north from here," I said.

A big groan from the peanut gallery in the backseat prevented me from altering the route. So onward we went. Lucky for me, our first stop was L'Isle-sur-la-Sorgue, a small French town known for its amazing antique shops. It was my first time, and I was, as you can imagine, beyond excited.

This market in Provence has been around since the sixteenth century. We arrived and parked without a hitch, then headed into the main market plaza—a giant park chock full of the most ridiculous and fabulous wares I had ever laid eyes on. Heaven on earth for a prop stylist! I wanted to devour and buy everything, and as my family took it all in our eight -year old said, "We're going to be here awhile. I hope there's ice cream." Frank and Alex agreed, and we decided to meet back at the park entrance at noon.

I was left to my own devices, and, boy, did I have some fun. I started with the linens kiosk and bought about seventeen different pieces of antique linen, figuring this would be easy to pack. But as I continued looking I started getting overwhelmed. What about all the furniture and the paintings and the amazing vessels, plates, and pottery? I wanted it all, which is something that rarely happens to me while shopping. I am pretty much like a laser when it comes to picking and purchasing. But today, in this special place, well, I had to take a deep breath and remind myself that this was the first time here, and I promised myself I would come back, again and again.

Although it was shopping heaven for me, our family trip though the South of France was not exactly family friendly. I had to face the fact that our kids were pretty bored that first day. We stayed that night at a very funky hotel near Aix, and the kids went to the lobby in search of Coca-Colas. They returned with a stack of travel brochures with family appropriate activities in the vicinity. These are the kid-approved activities they presented us with convincing zeal: a water park, a McDonalds (which seemed strange since we never dined at McDonalds in the States), and the Haribo Candy Factory.

Frank and I looked at the brochures, looked at each other, and in unison announced, "The Haribo Factory." The next day, brochure map in hand, we drove to the Haribo Factory on the other side of town. I spotted lots of antique warehouses on the way and was dying to stop, but for the sake of the children I bit my lip and we headed on down the road to Haribo.

For those of you unfamiliar with Haribo, it's a European candy company, best known for inventing the gummy bear. Levi and Alex were both excited—it was the happiest I had seen them since we began this road trip—all smiles and jumpy, just dying to get their hands on some of the gummy bears. The factory tour was set up much like the Vatican tour. If you've even been, you know that you have to slug through an enormous museum before you get a look at the Sistine Chapel—sort of a Catholic "bait and switch." This tour was not much different. You had to visit floor after floor, reliving the history of the gummy bear, before you got your hands on the goods. At the end of the history lesson, we were dumped into what seemed like a Willy Wonka workshop. Alex and Levi were handed big bags that they could take to a row of big funnels and a pipeline, all filled with as many Haribo candies as you could imagine. Frank and I even got into it, helping them fill their bags. We left full of sweets, happy and completely sugared out. The rest of our trip to the South of France was really beautiful. We ate some amazing food and visited a lavender field outside a picturesque monastery. But I must admit, the Haribo factory is my fondest memory. This would be the first of many trips. I would return to the flea markets in the south of France to buy things for our home in Italy.

We had fewer guests that summer. So we were free to schedule a little house hunting. I managed to get the German real estate lady on the phone, and she was game to set up some viewings later in the week. We were really excited to start our search!

Friday rolled around and we agreed to meet the real estate lady in the street in front of a popular hotel in town. Frank and I headed over, leaving Alex to babysit; she was perfectly happy reading on the sofa while her brother watched a soccer match and ate corn flakes out of the box.

The real estate lady, Maura, brought her husband Marcus. They were a middle-aged couple who had lived in a small town up the coast. They owned the agency together and were professional and friendly. They had lived in Italy for more than fifteen years. They also had great command of the language and local customs, and, according to their website, boasted great connections in real estate. We felt like we were in good hands as we piled into the back seat of their big black Mercedes.

We sped off to look at property. The olive mill that we had originally seen online was about thirty minutes west of Alassio, up in the hills in an olive grove above the sea. Marcus drove like a crazy Italian, ninety miles an hour up the narrow roads carved into the mountains; truth is, I feared for our lives. I was pale, my heart beat out of my chest, and I held Frank's hand so hard that he lost circulation for most of the drive. I became very religious as I prayed that the car not careen off the narrowest roads, thousands of feet above the sea. You can imagine how relieved I was when we finally reached our destination alive, so high in the mountains that the ocean was just a shiny sliver in the distance.

"This property is terraced," Marcus said in his thick German accent. "Many olive trees, so can have your own olive oil."

That sounded fantastic to me. I am sure my mouth gaped open in disbelief at the thought that I could own an olive farm in Liguria and make my own oil. It sounded like a dream. We walked all over the property, and up over the hill we came to a rubble of a building with no roof and a broken door that was standing half open. The building could not have been more than a hundred square feet and it was a mess—with rocks scattered everywhere on the floor and trees growing out the middle of it.

"This is the mill," said Maura. "This would be the house you would renovate."

Frank and I looked at each other and we were speechless. It seemed like our house history in Italy was repeating itself. My first thought was that this was not a mill, and that it sure looked bigger online.

Frank spoke first, "So if we bought this property we could repair this building and then add on to it as well?"

"Well, not exactly," said Marcus. "You would need to get permission from the community to add on to the house. Right now it is only zoned for this square footage; if you would get permission then you could add on to the original footprint."

I was afraid to ask about anything in else; I was still in love with the idea of making my own olive oil. In silence, Frank and I explored the property again. We loved the olive trees and the way the sun streamed through the grove. We loved the terraces and the feeling of being on top of the world. The downside was that this property, as we would find with many properties in Liguria, was so secluded and high up in the mountains that it would be tough for our guests to navigate, and harder to run to town for a carton of milk. In the end, we realized we desired something closer to a town or a village.

We spent the next two days with the help of the Germans looking at other properties on which to build our dream home. The last property was just above Alassio, up some dizzying curves of road. I had no idea how we would ever find this property on our own without leaving breadcrumbs. Up, up, up we went, sliding back and forth in the back seat of Marcus's Mercedes, until finally we arrived at a plateau and could go no further.

This property had great potential. With two *rustici,* or run-down cottages, it was only fifteen minutes from a major beach town. We walked around the property for about an hour. It had the most beautiful view of any land we had seen, and the two cottages would allow the footprint we needed to build a house that would be large enough for our needs. Frank and I decided that this property would go to the top of our list. We drove back into town with Maura and Marcus and bid farewell with the promise that we would be back the following year and would be in touch about the property above Alassio.

CHAPTER 4

Reunited, and It Feels So Good

ight around the same time we started our serious house-hunt on the Italian Riviera, I attended a birthday party in the US for a friend. I was standing at the bar waiting for my cocktail with one of the other party guests, Betsy, a dear friend of the birthday girl and someone I always saw at these events. We chit-chatted while the barman made us our drinks. "I hear you're house hunting in Italy," Betsy said.

"Yes, we have been looking for a year now and I think we may have found a piece of property," I said.

"I have a dear friend that lives in Genoa. I love that area of Italy," Betsy replied.

"It's not that well known to Americans," I said.

"My friend's partner is a prince of the region," she added.

"Wait a minute," I said, "…you're not talking about Rupert Spitzmiller, are you?"

"Do you know him?" Betsy asked.

"Oh my God, I have not seen him in seven years. I thought he was in Florence," I answered.

"The prince is from Genoa so they moved there about five years ago," Betsy said. "I can't believe this. We both know Rupert! I need to connect you two immediately. Maybe he can help you with your house hunt." With that, we clinked our glasses. Neither one of us could believe the kismet that had just presented itself.

The next morning, bright and early as she promised, Betsy reconnected Rupert and me, and just like that we were destined to share a great adventure in Italy.

I was so excited to reconnect that I immediately called Rupert on the phone instead of emailing him. He answered and was pleased that Betsy had intervened and brought us together again. Rupert and I first met in the 1980s. We were both working with a major department store—actually, helping to open the store. He was Director of Men's Couture and I was the Visual Merchandising Manager. We always joked that we bonded over cigarette breaks while working our butts off in our youth. It was one of my first jobs—and the same for Rupert—so we were overworked and stressed out. Nothing bonds you more.

About two years after we met, Rupert announced he was moving to Italy. I seriously thought he had lost his mind. I was shocked when he informed me he did not have a job there and did not speak Italian. Now, that's gutsy...which is my best description of Rupert to this day. After living in Italy for two years, Rupert had become a shoe designer, But the really great thing was that Rupert had a degree in interior design and had started doing some renovation projects in Italy.

Frank and I made a plan to meet Rupert in our hotel in Alassio. We were going to be back in Italy in the winter, when there would be fewer tourists and the seaside town would be more restful.

Rupert barreled up the stairs through the lobby when he saw us. He's a big bear of a man, so there were big hugs all around, and Frank and I were happy to see him. We all ordered drinks, and Frank and I described the property we were excited about. We explained visiting the first property so far away—the old olive mill I found on the internet that turned out to be a shack, hardly worth saving. Then I described to him the second property they showed us, the one we loved with two stone cottages and the spectacular view above Alassio. We told him how nice Maura and Marcus were, how they had invited us to their house for lunch after viewing. We described the view and the precarious ride up the mountain to the property. We shared our ideas about enlarging the little fallen-down stone houses into one beautiful stone farmhouse, about the pool we envisioned, and the olive grove where we would produce our own olive oil. Rupert listened intently, and we decided to meet and go up to the property the next day. We had a lovely dinner at a local place with fresh seafood and pesto and plenty of wine. That night, I drifted off to sleep thinking about floor plans and vegetable gardens.

After a quick espresso and warm brioche the next morning, we met and headed up the mountain to survey the property Frank and I were interested in buying. That day the sky was gray and there was a chill in the air. Once we navigated the narrow and winding roads to the bluff, we eagerly parked and hiked to the top of the plateau that was to be our new home.

"Wow," Rupert said, "what a view."

"I know. And the sliver of sea is so pretty, right?" I asked.

"I think this place has distinct possibilities," he replied.

"We would like the pool to sit right here on the edge of this drop-off," Frank explained as he pulled out the land plat the agents had supplied. We spent the early afternoon plotting and planning our new project, then headed down the steep hill back into Alassio for a bite to eat. We walked to lunch, a chill in the air, we were enveloped by the warmth and lovely smell of local dishes at a local *osteria*. We sat down at the wooden table and ordered. We all devoured heavy plates of spaghetti *Bolognese* and oodles of fragrant *focaccia* and drank house red. After what seemed like hours of eating and talking, we had a plan for the house.

My head spun with too much wine and too many design possibilities. So it began, this great big Italian house adventure—with Rupert in tow. Frank and I thought it would be a great idea to hire him as our consultant and then project manager (once we had a project to manage). Rupert agreed this would be a fun project and he would love to work with us on this. We shook on it. Rupert headed back to Genoa and we headed to our hotel for a nap.

The next day, we headed back to the States, and since we had just finished building our home in Atlanta, we decided to skip Italy that summer and concentrate on moving into our home in Atlanta. I continued to communicate with Maura and assured her we were interested in the property and would return the next year to revisit buying the property. Since everything moves at a snail's pace in Italy—especially real estate—Rupert assured us that the property would be there. There is something to be said for taking your time. Italians get this concept like no one else.

Good Boyfriend Versus Bad Boyfriend

Frank and I revisited the property with Maura and Marcus again in early spring. With support and counsel from Rupert, we decided that we would purchase the olive grove and build our dream home there.

The first thing that Rupert did was to introduce us to a *notaio*, something we do not have in the US. We do have a notary, which is the exact translation, but the *notaio* in Italy and the notary in the US couldn't be more different. A *notaio* is someone in the Italian legal system that literally only deals with property, since the buying and selling of property is beyond complicated—as we learned. A *notaio* is the buyers' ally and can make the purchase of a property much easier and, most importantly, legal. All property goes through the hands of the *notaio*. Rarely is money exchanged directly between sellers and the buyers without the services and the expert advice of a *notaio*.

Maura was happy to walk us through the buying process, including introducing us to her *notaio*, who would be writing the contract for the sellers. She quickly let me know that we would need to apply for an Italian identity card known as a *Codice Fiscale*—the Italian tax code card, similar to a Social Security card in the United States. This card serves to unambiguously identify individuals residing in Italy, irrespective of their residency status.

The *Codice Fiscale* would make all transactions seamless, according to Maura. I gave her our information and a power of attorney just for this document, and she promised to file everything for us. I loved the German precision Maura applied to all tasks.

The efficiency and ease with which Maura took care of everything and answered all of our questions seemed remarkable; she was friendly, available, and always patient, walking us though everything we needed to know. She gave us the land plat and informed us that the owners were excited to sell the property to us.

Another benefit of using Maura and Marcus was that Marcus was a contractor. They had taken us to a couple of projects he had built and they all looked beautiful and well-constructed. Maura gave me an extensive list of references and even made email introductions for me. I followed up on all of them—due diligence is my middle name.

Around this time I started working with Maura's assistant Maria. We met her at lunch when we dined at Maura and Marcus's home once again. It was a lovely lunch at their country house, with their daughter and one of their sons present—it was all very Italian-family style. We were pleased to be included and had a great time. Doing business in Italy was fun! It reminded us of the movie *Under the Tuscan Sun,* all friendly and warm and embracing.

At this lunch she presented us our *Codice Fiscale* cards. Maura told me to go ahead and start the design of our house around the small structures on the property and they would get all the approvals done for us.

She shared the information that we could only add a 30 percent addition of the total footprint of the original run-down cottages. On the plat, the cottages totaled 2900 square feet. It was a little smaller than we had imagined, but it was Italy and I assured myself that everything was a little smaller scale here in Italy. We said our goodbyes, and I told Maura we would be in touch soon. We stayed and enjoyed Italy for a few more days and then flew back to the US, designing our new digs in Italy on our minds.

When we got back home, we decided to hire our Atlanta architect Jamie—the same one that had designed our home in the States—to work with us on the Italian property. Imagine how excited Jamie was when I told her we would be designing our home in Italy together! Every Tuesday morning for four months we worked on the detailed plan for our dream house high above the sea. Once the plans were complete, we sent them to Marcus and Maura to look over. They loved the plans and said that they did not see any problems getting permissions.

Then, to our surprise, we received an email from Maura's assistant containing a whole new plan. When I got the letter, to say I was confused was an understatement.

After receiving and initially approving our plan, Maura promptly threw it out the window and sent us their plan of what could realistically be built on the property, with strict instructions that if we wanted to build our dream home in Italy we would have to do things their way, the Italian way. Honestly, in hindsight, it should have been a red flag and a reason not to buy the property, but when you want a house in Italy—and you're in love—sometimes you're just not thinking with a cool head. Frank said, "Do as you wish Annette." Quite honestly, he let me have my way. Frank trusted me and I was leading the way at this point in the process. So I went along with Maura's instructions.

Here's what Maura had her assistant Maria write back after Maura originally told us it would be no problem getting permissions on our US architect's plans. It made no sense, but, as I would find out, this was the Italian way.

July 2002

Dear Annette,

Hope your jet lag is gone by now. How long did it take to get over? I am really not looking forward to it! I missed the bank question, sorry! It is better if you can get financing from your local bank or at least from the US to insure the best rates and fastest service. You won't need to translate anything and can talk to them directly without intermediaries. If you can't get a loan at your local bank, Maura will help you get something here.

Included are Maura's sketches.

- The top sketch gives you a side view of the home with the max dimensions allowable.
- You can have a max size of 280sqm. but naturally can make the home smaller. Up to 100sqm on the upper floor and 180sqm on the lower floor which is "*interrato*," in the earth. The *interrato* is placed on the lower of the two terraces of the plot while the top floor is found on the terrace with the large tree (also in picture). The main entrance would face north towards the rear of the home, leaving the south facing area in front of the upper level as a terrace. The pool, half in/half out with a height of 2 meters - extends from the lower level. The lower level has 12 x 15 x 2.70 meters - also on the sketch.
- The lower sketch gives you a front view.
- The lower level must be lined with stones. You may have a maximum opening of three meters (window doors) within every 5 meters

but no more. Meaning, you may not have 9m of continuous opening. It must be separated as shown in the picture.

- The top sketch shows the side wall without any windows. This is another one of the rules - only the front facing side of the *interrato* may have openings. So, what we do is prepare the walls with the openings for windows anyhow and then fill them with a thin layer of stone/bricks so that we get the approval from the inspector. Then we knock out the stone/brick filling and place the windows in. It's a matter of 1-2 days' work. However, the windows may only extend from the edge of the top level towards the front. From that border towards the back you'll still have rooms without views. You can use these as storage, laundry, gym etc.

Let me know if you have any other questions. Maura doesn't have a map of the topography on hand but will look into getting one but the whole process can take 1-2 weeks because it's a tiny office that works by appointments.

Have a great day,
Maria

This was not exactly our plan, but I felt it was something we could work with, so I determined, with Frank's agreement, that now was the time to buy the property. I had read about how to buy a property in Italy, so I was aware that Frank and I would have a *compremesso*, the first closing to seal the deal—it's where you officially own the property—and then the final closing thirty to sixty days later, called the *atto*. I was aware that at the first closing we would have to put money down, or as we say in the US, put the down payment into escrow. How much, we were not sure, but Maura said she would fill us in.

After waiting a couple of weeks, Maura called to say we only needed to put 10 percent down and we were good to go. Great news! Maura had us transfer the money into their business account for safekeeping, and we were in business. At this point, we were scheduled to come for the final closing in three months, after the holidays in February 2003, and Maura assured us that the sellers would be there for the *compremesso*.

CHAPTER 6

Say What Now?
A Bad Breakup

Jamie and I occupied ourselves for a few months with finalizing the design of the house, with Maura's plan in mind. Maura and I would speak once a month about the progress of the final contract, the *atto*. I had the first contract in hand but the *atto* would be the final paperwork that would make the property ours for good. There was one problem that Maura brought to my attention. In Italian law there are provisions for access roads. This means that there was a road on the plat that our neighbors could use, and we had no way of preventing this. I was a little perplexed as to how this would be resolved, but Maura assured me they were working on it with the land surveyors and would have a plan by the final closing, not to worry. If we had to meet with the Mayor of Alassio, we would do it; they had a good relationship with him and, after all, in Italy who you know is important.

I heard from Maura, who said that she had given our plans to a *geometra*, who just happened to be the Mayor of Alassio as well. In Italy we came to find out that no construction can get done without a *geometra*, who not only oversees construction but also acts as the liaison between you, the contractor, and the community. It's a major deal. Your entire project rests on the quality of the *geometra* you hire. We were told that he can be your best advocate, or your worst nightmare. There's not much choice in who you get—usually there are only a couple in each town. This person is a vital part of your project and you cannot do without one. Since the Mayor was the *geometra*, we felt sure that we'd have no problem with community officials and everything would be easy. Lucky us.

I had very little contact with Maura after the holidays. I had spoken to her early in November and nothing in December. I found out why the silence in January: Unfortunately, Marcus was diagnosed with cancer and they had spent the winter taking him to specialists. She was MIA most of the winter. When I pressed her for the first closing date which was supposed to be February, she would not give me an answer, but would instead tell me about how stressed she was and how sick Marcus was. They ended up in Germany for some treatments in February. In the meantime, I did not want to bother them at this great time of stress and health issues. I guess our closing would have to wait. I heard nothing for weeks. I was perplexed, but did not want to bother Maura since her husband was so ill.

I was on the phone with Rupert quite regularly at this point asking his advice, since everything had stalled. But it was Italy, after all, and everything takes much more time than you would think, so I was trying to be patient. Finally, after a few months of back and forth, Rupert asked that we talk to his *notaio*, Ilario. I thought this was a great suggestion. Rupert and he were close friends and our property had been a topic of conversation at a few dinners. They both thought it was a good idea that Ilario intervene on our behalf. I sent Rupert all the information, the plat for the land, the initial *compremesso* (contract), which included the 10 percent deposit towards the first closing we had given Marcus and Maura. The contract also had the owners' information included. I thanked Rupert. Then we waited.

I will never forget Rupert's phone call to me. I was heading to a photo shoot and my phone rang. Rupert asked that I sit and listen, so I pulled my car over. He sounded very serious and all of his words were weighted. "Annette, I have some news about the property you and Frank are buying," he said.

"Please listen carefully." He said Ilario had looked up the plat and the owners' information (*notaios* have access to all sales and land deals in the region). "Annette," he said, "the property you want to buy is not for sale."

Say what now? *That's impossible*, I thought, and told him so.

"Well, Annette, these agents have no right to sell this property. It is owned by three siblings and they all have to agree to sell. The sister wants to keep the property and the two brothers want to sell. In Italy, the siblings all have to agree. Ilario says that you will never own the property unless you convince the sister, and that could take a lifetime," he said. "Maura and Marcus knew this and took advantage of you not knowing the laws in Italy and not having your own advocate here. Ilario is worried," he said finally.

I hung up the phone and told Rupert I would call him back. Now what to do? I needed to think. We had wired money into Maura's account and it was sitting there. I needed to talk to her about how we should proceed with the sister. I had to think.

The next day, when my head was a little clearer, I emailed Maura that we needed to talk soon. I did not want to spook her. I had a bad feeling that we might be in over our heads—and I began to think there was a small possibility we may have been duped. But being a person that never thinks ill of anyone, I was optimistic that this would all turn out fine, and this glitch was just part of the real estate drama that was Italy.

Maura emailed me back immediately and said that we should definitely talk on the phone, not to worry, and that she would be back in the office in a week. Marcus was undergoing some procedure, and they would both be available the following week.

Sometimes my red flag radar doesn't work (especially when love is involved—and I loved Italy), but this time it was working overtime. I asked Rupert to employ Ilario, and I told him to have Ilario start working on our property. I needed an advocate, someone in our corner. Frank and I decided that we needed to be realistic about the likely possibility that Maura and Marcus were not on the up-and-up.

By this time it was early March 2003 and we had no word from Maura after our brief phone call; in fact, her assistant even stopped emailing us. I had previously booked a trip to Alassio for early March, assuming we would be closing on our property, and I had been planning on meeting the Mayor as well about the status of the building project. I decided to proceed as if everything was on schedule.

In the meantime, Rupert took it upon himself to consult an architect friend who was doing several projects in Alassio to do a little research on the property we were planning to buy. Carlo was a sweet man, and someone very connected in the community. He would have a good idea about the property, the plat, and the plan. He knew the Mayor well, and told us that the Mayor was corrupt—out for his own benefit—and someone to be wary of. He was possibly connected to very bad people in Italy. This was all rumor of course, very hush-hush. But it led me to believe that I could not depend on the Mayor for help.

I arrived in Alassio and checked into the hotel—the very same hotel where we had reconnected with Rupert. The next morning, I called Maura—no answer. Not even a message. I had emailed her several times that I was coming to Alassio and wanted to talk to her about our property and the closing date. No word. Of course, I was panicked but trying to keep my head straight. After three days passed and we heard nothing, I met with Rupert and the architect Carlo in Alassio. We took the plat to the Mayor's office to go over the property lines and talk to him about the owners. After about an hour spent pouring over the official plat, Carlo concluded that the property was, in fact, owned by three siblings. We had their names, and a quick phone call confirmed very unceremoniously that the property was not for sale.

I immediately drove myself to Maura's office to confront her and get our deposit refunded. As I wound up the curvy roads to her office, I grew more and more angry. I could feel my face flush, and my hands were shaking on the steering wheel. I pulled into the parking lot across from her office, located in the center of a tiny hilltop village about thirty minutes from Alassio. She was sitting in the office on the phone (yet she could not return any of my phone calls!). Marcus was there too, and he looked fit and healthy—which led me to believe they had been scamming us all along. The realization that we had been conned by con artists…I could not wrap my head around it. I always regarded myself as a savvy person, street smart, but these two were good; they were very good. It hit me like a brick when I saw them sitting there conducting "business," relaxed, all smiles. I am not a violent person, but I swear I wanted to punch those smiles off their faces.

I walked in without knocking and Maura could tell I was about to let her have it. She smiled and said, "So nice to see you, Annette. What can I do for you?"

Her assistants stood there staring, mouths agape, as I proceeded to ask in a firm but calm (angry) tone, "Why have you not answered my calls or emails the past month? Marcus is here working, not recuperating in Germany, so I am confused."

Maura looked at Marcus, and he looked angry, very angry. "Maura, let's talk about this outside," he said.

"I think we can talk about this here in the office, with everyone around," I quickly responded. I was not going anywhere.

"We have nothing to say," Maura spit out, "and we would like you to leave. You are obviously very upset, for no reason."

Now I am usually a very intuitive person, and my intuition was telling me to leave before this confrontation escalated. I had come alone, and these were not good people. I decided then and there that I would have to get a lawyer involved and sue them. I would need to take them to an Italian court and retrieve my deposit through the legal system. I got in my car—I was so shaken that it took me a minute to figure out how to leave the city center. I rode down the road and pulled over and started to cry. We had been duped. Bamboozled. How could this happen? I calmed down, went back to the hotel, ordered a gin and tonic from the bar. I called in the troops—our *notaio* and our friend and advisor, Rupert—to see if we could get our money back. Before I headed back to the US, we hired an Italian lawyer and started the process of suing in Italy, and perhaps even putting Maura and Marcus in jail.

A few months passed—with no word from Maura, of course. Our lawyer investigated Maura and Marcus and found that Marcus was under house arrest, which explained the lie about his absence due to "illness" that past year. He had been arrested for tax fraud, and he and Maura were well-known con artists in the region. We would have to wait in line with many that had been duped by them.

After almost a year to the day in February 2004, we went to court in Italy to plead our case. The suit was heard at the San Remo Courthouse, and it was a very formal and very wordy trial. Maura and Marcus had no representation, and they didn't show up in court. So the judge ordered that they pay us back, but in truth that was never going to happen; however, they did have a warrant (or the equivalent in Italy) on their head. Of course, we all thought they were most likely on the run and no longer in Italy.

The final outcome was that we won our suit, but would never recover our deposit since we were part of a crowd of victims that were owed money for the same reason. Bottom line for me: the satisfaction of knowing that they were fugitives and their bank accounts were frozen gave us some solace. We were given the names of people that had been victims, and were encouraged to spread the word about these criminals.

At the end, we had learned painful lesson, one that would serve us well in our future real estate dealings in Italy. It stung for a few months, but then we decided to move on and keep looking for the right house in Italy. One must be well taken care of in Italy, there are lots of pitfalls, unlike *Under the Tuscan Sun*; one needs real representation and my advice is to live here for a while, make real Italian friends, learn the language, and cover your ass.

Life in Italy is not a movie—it's real life. We learned this the hard way.

CHAPTER 7

Considering a Monastery

Even though Frank and I had learned a very valuable Italian real estate lesson, it did not stop us from wanting to find a great place in Liguria. In fact, it made us even more resolute. We were both in agreement that we would not let this get in the way of our vision and our happiness. Plenty of people take a bath with real estate deals, and this lesson had made us stronger and wiser.

Rupert talked us into looking at houses in a region that he was interested in. He was seriously considering buying a country home in the Lunigiana, a region that is in northern Tuscany, about two hours north of Florence—near Carrara—and one hour west of Parma. It was a region we knew nothing about. Even after all the years we spent in Italy so close to this region, we had never heard of it. It is a beautiful area, green hills, winding roads, and nestled in the Apennine Mountain range.

One rainy Saturday with an Italian real estate person in tow, we decided to have a look. It is fair to say this real estate guy showed us the saddest, most unappealing homes in his repertoire. However, there was one glimmer of hope when he showed us a villa, plopped on an incredible piece of land that had a mountain view. It was massive and needed tons of renovation, but it was charming and held our attention…until he quoted us the price: one million euro. Laughable. And with that, we abandoned the Lunigiana and moved on to Liguria, where we knew the score.

After our failed excursion with no house prospects in the Lunigiana. Rupert and I decided to meet with Carlo the architect again in Alassio. Carlo had mentioned that he had been working on a project there and we thought we should check it out. Rupert and I invited him for a *caffe* at a local bar in the square. We sat down, ordered our espressos, and Rupert promptly excused himself to use the *bagno*. With my very, very limited Italian, I was left to fend for myself with Carlo, who only spoke Italian. Finding my words, I asked him how his work in Alassio was going. By the time Rupert returned, I had learned all about his big project—the monastery he was renovating for a developer in Milan, to be turned into vacation flats. My ears had perked up, and I said to Rupert, "Well, we should have a look, don't you think?" With big smiles on our faces, we headed to Carlo's car and drove to his new project.

Riding down main street, we took a sharp right and headed to the outer rim of the city. We drove through big old iron gates, followed the driveway as far as we could go, and parked close to the heavy machinery on the building site.

The monastery was breathtaking—it had originally been a villa that had then housed a monastery, school, and nuns in the past years. The villa perched on a hill; it was an amazing site. There was a beautiful botanical garden in front of the villa. We walked to the top of the hill and entered what was a temporary sales office on the ground floor. Here we were introduced to Stefano, the on-site manager and a sales and construction foreman all rolled into one. He was a small, well-built man with a nice smile and sort of a "hey, baby" vibe (like most men in Italy, that "hey, baby" is always around). He grabbed some floor plans, and Carlo and Rupert and I followed Stefano up the staircase to the first floor to have a look. The villa had four floors—a ground and then three above. The Milanese developers had already claimed the top floor with terraces and an insane view of the sea.

The ceilings were extremely high and the hallway was impressively wide. We walked to the far right-hand corner of the floor and began the tour. The floors at this point were wide open—and by wide open, I mean there were no dividing walls. The walls had been ripped out to allow potential buyers to stake their claim and buy whatever configuration they desired or could afford. I loved this tactic. I walked all over the space. There were charming unearthed frescos and columns that had been salvaged. This place had some really attractive elements that were highly desirable to a potential buyer.

Truth is, I had never thought about buying a flat; we had mainly focused on free-standing houses. However, it is always important to keep an open mind. Not to mention that our last real estate experience had left me a little gun-shy about real estate agents. This property was being marketed by a big developer out of Milan—a real company. Plus, a lock-and-leave situation was probably a good idea for first-timers in Italy.

We continued the tour and wandered to the opposite far corner of the floor. Mind you, these floors were huge—about 8,000 to 10,000 square feet. In the far-left corner, was *the view*—an incredible view of the Gallinara Island off the coastline of Alassio, the sea, and terraced olive groves. Just spectacular!

"Whoa," I said to Rupert. "This is gorgeous and the lighting is perfect. What do you think?" Rupert smiled and said, "This has distinct possibilities."

"Yeah, I think so, too. It is pretty cool here." We walked the rest of the building and the higher we climbed, the more beautiful the view became. When we hit the penthouses (which was owned by the two developers, each having a separate penthouse connected by the rooftop terrace), I was pretty convinced this had been dropped into our lap as a reward for the world of hurt we had just experienced with our last venture into Italian real estate. We went down to the office to discuss possibilities, because this project had just that—distinct possibilities.

After about an hour-long discussion, we decided on the southern corner of the building on the second floor, which faced west towards the sea and had the most incredible views. We planned the square footage to include two bedrooms, two bathrooms, and a big kitchen with a smaller sitting area. Since it was the only spot that I fell in love with, I needed to make a fast decision, because my trip was coming to an end. Also, I was feeling some pressure since our last year-and-a-half had been an epic failure. This apartment made sense: it was beautiful and in a great location, I could walk everywhere, and—most importantly—it had an underground parking space. To hold the spot would only cost a hundred euros, so how could I not, right? Rupert agreed, and we were both were pretty excited about the prospect of working on this project together.

By this time it was noon, so Stefano excused himself to head home to lunch and suggested we meet later in the afternoon to discuss specifics.

You gotta love Italy. No one in their right mind in the US would ever leave a meeting when they were about to close the deal. But there, which is why I love it, family and quality of life come first, and business can and will wait. You may say this is why Italians are always in a financial crisis, but you'd never know there was any crisis when you see Italians enjoying lunch. Is there a lesson here? I think so.

We said *buon appetito* and adjourned for lunch. Rupert and I ended up at a seaside *trattoria* sipping *Vermentino* and nibbling on grilled octopus with a crisp green salad and plenty of salty *focaccia* soaked in olive oil. We chatted about the flat and Villa Fiske (the name of the development). Rupert and I agreed I should hold the space on the southern corner of the building with the amazing views, and that way Frank and I had a couple of weeks to think about it and it would not get away. The way our luck had been running, the safer the better. Around four o'clock we headed back up the hill towards Villa Fiske and our certain fate. Stefano was already there to greet us.

What happened next is pretty typical of how Frank and I interact on decisions. I jumped on the phone and called Frank. With the time change (six hours earlier in Atlanta), he was just starting his first case.

He's a surgeon and when I called him, he informed me that he was scrubbing in so I should make it fast, because he would need to scrub in again after our phone call. I wanted to let him know I had found a great place for us to buy in Alassio, and that I was going to put it on hold. It would take a bit more explaining than usual.

"Tell me," he said, "What's happening?"

"Oh *ciao*, sorry, I forgot you're operating today," I replied.

"Yeah, well, what's up? I'm in the middle of something here. Can I call you back?" he asked.

"I will make this fast," I said. "I found an amazing place for us and I am putting a down payment on it today. I can tell you all about it later, but I need to get this done since I am leaving tomorrow."

"What the hell is going on? Are you insane, just putting a down payment on a flat without a conversation first?" He sounded mad, and he's never mad.

"Calm down," I said. "It's just a hundred euros to hold it for us for two weeks so we can talk about it." I was pleading at this point.

"Why didn't you start with that sentence?" he asked.

"Oh yeah," I said. "Sorry, I always bury the lede." He quickly hung up the phone and headed back to scrub in again and I carried on with the business of holding the flat, then packing to head back to the US.

Rupert and I said a fond goodbye until next time, which would be sooner rather than later in order to start work on the flat.

In the end, we wound up with the flat in Villa Fiske. Living there and renovating it would prove to be a wonderful adventure.

CHAPTER 8

The Villa Fiske

When I got back to the States, life carried on as usual. I was crazed with the kids and my work. Frank was busy with his work. We chatted about the flat briefly, but, in true form, Frank left it to me to make the ultimate decision about the flat. He has always trusted my instincts—he is wonderful that way. I spent many hours emailing and consulting Rupert.

We all decided this flat would be a good, safe purchase and would serve our purposes. We could dip our toe into international real estate and live in Italy part-time. After many months of contractual correspondence (six months), our *notaio* Ilario in Genova proclaimed we were ready for the first closing, the *compremesso*. We set a date for February (one year after our misadventure with buying property) and all parties were copied. I had to pinch myself that we actually did it: after three years of looking we found our place by the sea and were about to put our money down.

With a little trepidation, we set a date to put down the first installment of payment. With everything that had transpired, this was no small feat. It made for many sleepless nights. But, in the end, we felt that this was going to be the right choice and everything would work out. We had learned our lesson and knew this was the proper way to buy real estate in Italy. Thank God for Rupert—who turned out to be not only our advisor and friend, but also our savior—and our incredible *notaio* Ilario.

I was inclined to do a search about Villa Fiske, mainly because the name was not an Italian surname. While I had some time at home to research the villa, I headed to the internet to see what info I could come up with.

I typed in the name John Fiske, Alassio, and immediately I came across his bio. From 1863 to 1864 he worked as a deputy clerk in Albany for the New York State Senate. In 1865, he was a private tutor near New York City. In October 1867, he was nominated by President Andrew Johnson to be the US Consul in Leith, Scotland.

While abroad, John was involved in the scandal concerning Ernest Boulton and Frederick William Park, who were two Victorian cross-dressers and suspected homosexuals. They appeared as defendants in a celebrated trial in London in 1871, charged "with conspiring and inciting persons to commit an unnatural offence." After the prosecution failed to establish that they had anal sex (which was then a crime), or that wearing women's clothing was in any sense a crime, both men were acquitted.

John met and had an affair with Ernest in the mid-1800s. John wrote many love letters to Ernest; John's love letters were discovered during a raid on Ernest's residence. John was implicated in the scandal of conspiracy to commit buggery. He was arrested and charged and acquitted. He decided to resign as US consul to avoid the involvement of his country in the scandal, even as he continued to maintain that he was innocent.

After the humiliation of the trial, John went to Düsseldorf, Germany. He lived a quiet life painting for about one year. He then briefly moved back to the U.S. But after three years, he moved outside of Paris (where he lived "with an English friend). After a couple of years, Constantinople was his next stop. But finally after several years he moved to Italy. John bought a villa in Alassio—Villa Fiske—and settled in Alassio until his death in 1907.

Since he had no heirs, his estate went to the state and was bought by the Vatican and converted into a school and convent. The nuns lived and taught in the building until it was sold in 2002 to a development group from Milan. The renovation to high-end flats was remarkable, as the church did some really hideous things to the inside of the building; the entire building was retrofitted with hideous brass windows from the 1980s venom-green-colored terrazzo floors. But the developers had a vision, and the villa blossomed into the beautiful edifice it had once been. John Fiske had been very interested in botany, and the grounds surrounding the villa were still breathtaking; the gardens in front and in back were returned to their former glory and the mature trees John had planted were a stunning monument to his passion.

CHAPTER 9

Love Is Supposed to Be a Many Splendored Thing

I talians tend to put their modern mark on most things old and beautiful. In general, they are not fans of old buildings, and will likely outfit a beautiful stone masterpiece with retrofitted modern design touches. It's what makes finding a property in Italy so difficult. With Villa Fiske, it was hard to look past the brass window moldings with locks, the worn and not-so-pretty terrazzo floors. Mind you, I am a huge fan of terrazzo, so finding that ugly ones do exist was news to me. But, mostly, the glorious design possibilities staring Rupert and me in the face were super exciting.

The flat was small, so it would have to be functional. Lucky for us, it's what Italians do best: form and function. So we set to work on the floor plan. We had purchased 1500 square feet—about 150 square meters. I would have to start thinking in centimeters and meters while designing this space. It would take me a while to figure out the dimensions of things in terms of the metric system. But I am always up for learning something new; it's what makes life exciting, as far as I am concerned. We had two huge windows in what would become the kitchen and master bedroom, and a big long *loggia* that would serve as the main sitting area as well as double as an extra sleeping space for three people.

We had another smaller window in what would become the proper guest room. Rupert and I planned all the walls and divided the space into rooms, placing the walls on the hand-drawn plan in pencil. After many weeks of back and forth, we came up with what we thought was a great floor plan: two bedrooms, open kitchen, and two bathrooms cleverly placed in the small space. It was the perfect seaside flat—smallish rooms, but the high ceilings would visually make up for the lack of space and make the flat seem more expansive. We handed the plan to our architect Carlo, who was heading up the project, and hoped he would sign off so we could get started.

One thing that was a big surprise to us was that Italian law states that if the Vatican had owned the property previously (and they had, since it was a nunnery and then a Catholic School), the Vatican had twenty-one days to decide if they wanted the property back. It means that they could buy back our flat at a reduced rate. Oh, Italy, just another thing that is hard to explain, but makes perfect sense to Italians. Frank almost flipped when he heard this from our *compremesso*, which was tediously being translated for three hours at our first closing. But as one does in Italy, we just went with it. As luck would have it, the Vatican declined buying the property back. Whew.

Once we were in the clear with the Holy Father, we started finalizing everything in earnest. Carlo signed off on most of our plan. But since the villa was a historical landmark, we would have to deal with the *Sopraintendenza dei Beni Culturali*, the officials in the historical architecture office in the commune. Basically, you can't do anything to a structure that is listed as an architectural landmark. These officials (the "culture police," as the Italians like to call them) have to sign off on everything. We had to deal with these guys, and let me tell you, what they came back with was a mystery to us. Carlo showed up at one meeting with plans in hand. He rolled out the plan, and pointed to the wall that would divide the *loggia* (the main sitting area that had a bank of windows, like a sunroom), and the guest room. We wanted to put a wall there and a door there, but the culture police wanted a glass wall, not a brick and mortar wall. When Carlo brought this idea to Rupert and me, we were, as they say, gobsmacked. This was an insane suggestion, one that I certainly had never heard of.

"*Perche?* [Why?]" we asked in unison.

Carlo responded matter of factly. "*Perché puoi vedere quei muri dalla passerella sottostante e questo inibisce l'elemento storico di come era una volta la villa.*" ["Because you can see that wall from the walkway below and that inhibits the historical element of how the villa once was."]

"Oh," we both responded in unison once again.

Now before I go on, I must tell you this: Carlo was doing all the design for the villa; he was the main architect. The building was being fully renovated. One would think it would be designed with history in mind. But the thing about all Italians is that they truly love modern things. They have no problem retrofitting a historical building with, let's say, modern windows, or an old building might have a modern structure attached to it willy-nilly. So Carlo telling us with a straight face that a glass wall inside our flat made perfect sense was, well, insane. Not to mention that the entire project had adopted the Italian philosophy of adding modern touches to the "historical" building. For example, Carlo had designed an annex building behind the villa that would have more affordable tiny weekend flats—it was both modern and hideous. All the windows in this villa were modern, brand new, and pretty ugly. So where were the culture police when this project was approved?

After trying to figure all this out, Rupert and Frank and I concluded that it was Carlo—he was the culture police—and since he was a little insulted he was not hired to design our space, his little touch would be this glass wall. He was the *Sopraintendenza*!! Letting Carlo have his way was a *bella figura* (a good move) and was properly Italian, so we just let it lie. I learned that not everything here is by the book; in fact, by the book is the exception in Italy, not the rule.

I bit my tongue and agreed that a glass wall was a great idea, although secretly I thought it was super crazy. I was concerned how this would be put into place—in the US this would be a huge feat, and expensive—not to mention how in the world were we going to put a door in the glass wall like we had planned?

Rupert assured me it would all work out. But I still was not too sure.

The nice thing about designing a space in a residential development is that the material choices were readily available, and buying the basics like sinks and toilets and choosing paint and finishes and floors were easy. The sales office had so many choices that Rupert and I breezed through selections for the flat.

Buyers Tip: One thing I do advise is if you are a first time buyer in Italy, a set-up like this is ideal; no need to run all over the country to find resources.

Of course, since Rupert and I both had design backgrounds, there were going to be some custom touches. We were excited to plot the custom kitchen when I returned in a few months. In Italy, kitchens are treated like furniture; in other words, you can take them with you when you move from one residence to another. Italian kitchen stores are dreamy, and it's so easy to design a super custom kitchen.

My best friend Oma decided to come with me to Italy on my next trip. Oma is the executive editor of *Better Homes and Gardens* magazine, so she obviously has a great understanding of interiors. I thought it would be a great idea to have her along as a sounding board for our kitchen design. We flew from Atlanta on a Friday and landed in Alassio on a Saturday. Oma and I checked into the hotel and promptly were out the door and up the hill to check out the flat at Villa Fiske. She loved it, loved the floor plan, the view, and how central it was for walking into town and to the beach.

Rupert met us on the boardwalk for a late lunch. Alassio has an amazing boardwalk, directly on the beach, and it has many great restaurants and bars. One of my favorite things to this day is having seafood at one of the many restaurants, with everything so fresh and delicious.

Alassio also has my favorite *focacceria* in all of Italy, and we had a fantastic and filling lunch of *focaccia di Recco*, fried calamari, and a giant salad *mista*, washed down with a crisp white wine. Oma and I headed back to the hotel for a nap, and Rupert and I made a date to meet at the kitchen store in Genova the next day. Only an hour drive from Alassio, Genova was the closest big city and the best place to find everything we needed. Most importantly, it boasted the nearest IKEA, which is something no one in Italy can go without—it's their version of Target. We go there monthly for everything we may need for the home.

Oma and I slept right through dinner and woke up at 7:00 a.m. the next morning. After two espressos, we were ready to hit the *autostrada* and drive to Genova. With *pausa* taking out half of what Americans would consider the workday, shopping had to be done early morning or late afternoon. Being on the road at 8:00 a.m. was jarring to Oma, but the only way we would power through designing an entire kitchen in one sitting was to leave early.

Rupert was waiting for us at the kitchen store, looking bright and perky. Oma and I were sort of perky, but bright, not so much— even though we had stopped for one more bulletproof espresso at the Autogrill on the *autostrada* (my favorite place in Italy to drink espresso.) A word about the Autogrill on the *autostradas*: If you've been to Italy, most likely you've driven past one. For those of you that have stopped to check it out, you know it is amazing. AMAZING. It is a gas station with full amenities; in most cases it has a restaurant, and for sure it has an espresso bar and toilets and a fully stocked store—everything from gummy bears to local wine, water, parmesan cheese, and salami, and phone chargers, books, and sandwiches! All things at the Autogrill are magical; the brioche and the sandwiches are delicious. Since Italians have a low tolerance for bad food, the Autogrill is a direct reflection of that. Did I mention the espresso? It's delicious. I always take any visiting friend to the Autogrill to have this quintessential Italian experience. It's simply the best. One of the things in Italy I most enjoy.

Back to Genova: at the kitchen store we were greeted by a well-dressed woman who walked us through the design process. She escorted us around the showroom, which was a bit overwhelming for me. There were so many choices and everything was beautiful. How would we choose? As you may already know, I am a food stylist and a passionate entertainer, so it was very important to have the right kitchen configuration to maximize the small space.

Although we all fantasize about the BIG Italian farm kitchen where we all gather around the table, the reality is that most Italian kitchens are tiny. Spaces are a much smaller scale in general here; Frank always says Italy is built six inches too small. In the US we are used to large kitchens, so with this in mind, you can imagine my small kitchen space in Italy was in actuality a very large kitchen by Italian standards. In fact, most Italians that came to the flat for dinner or a party would comment on how large they thought our kitchen was. They would say, "Are you opening a restaurant? Or is the flat built around the kitchen?" I would laugh and respond, "You know I am American," to which they would nod and laugh.

After our kitchen store tour, Rupert and I were ready to start making decisions. Our saleswomen powered up the computer and scaled our space, and we started plunking in our components: a dishwasher, hidden fridge, washer/dryer, and a huge center island that would be the epicenter of the kitchen space. I was thrilled that Carrara marble was so inexpensive, so we decided on a huge slab—so big that it took a crane and eleven people to put it into place when it arrived! Even Oma piped in—without understanding Italian, she still spoke the international language of design—and made a few suggestions that ended up in the final design. Kitchen finished, we headed to a local fish spot for a workers' lunch.

A workers' lunch (*pranzo di lavoro*), is a cheap meal with several courses obviously geared towards laborers and office workers, but everyone can, and often should, partake. It's a fixed menu, although most of the time there are a couple choices for *primi* and *secondi*. (A first course is usually pasta and a second course is some sort of protein, fish, or meat.) Usually for around ten euros, your meal includes wine, water, *primi* and *secondi*, espresso, and dessert. A real bargain. An easy and delicious bargain. In Genova there are some great lunch places to choose from, and since Rupert lives in Genova he knows all of them. We headed back to Alassio after lunch, said goodbye to Rupert, and felt extremely happy at what we had accomplished for the day. As one of our friends who had lived in Rome for a while said, when he found out we were planning to spend part of the year living in Italy, "If you get one thing, one errand, done a day in Italy, you have had a good day."

So according to this statement, Oma, Rupert, and I designing a whole kitchen in one morning made a spectacular day by his standards. I will say that I think about this statement all the time living here, but I think even Italy has "moderned up" a bit since he lived here. Now I manage to get at least two things done per day.

Our to-do list of what to get for the flat was getting longer by the minute, so I decided that when I got back to the US I would fill a container with dishes and pots and pans, flatware and linens, bed linens and decorative objects for the shelves, and coffee tables and send that container to Italy instead of spending all my time in Italy buying essentials for the flat. At the time, online shopping in Italy was not a thing. You literally had to go from town to town and store to store to get everything you needed. As our son Levi says, the US is built for convenience, but Italy is not. Truer words were never spoken. If you're thinking of moving here, put convenience on the back burner and relax.

Being the multitasker that I am, and putting my logistics talents to use, I crafted a plan to shop for a year. Full disclosure: I shop for a living, so it was not hard to collect everything I would need to furnish and style the flat in one year while the space was being renovated. I would shop for a styling job and see things on sale or special props that would work perfectly in our space, buy them, and pile them in our garage. Luckily, our daughter was at college, so we had a free parking space in our garage—all of my stash went into her parking space. I filled up the garage space about two months before we finished the flat. It was time to figure out how to get it all to Genova.

Since Genova was a main port, it was not too hard to hire a container and send it to Genova, then to meet the container and head into Alassio and move into our flat. The day the container arrived at our house in Atlanta, they loaded our stash and drove off. Next stop, Italy. That was the day it hit me that we would be living in Italy on the Riviera very soon—in fact, in a few short weeks.

The container made its way to Genova, and Rupert was there to greet it. He made plans to lead the driver of the truck to our new place in Alassio. The day I got the phone call that everything had arrived and was all in the flat was one of the most exciting days of my life.

Rupert has always been good at logistics. He had everything arranged. His housekeeper would clean and then unpack every box, and all I would have to do was arrive and place and style everything. Easy! I arrived on a Sunday, in May of 2006. Rupert was waiting—and not quick to leave—when I arrived to officially move in. In fact he would not leave. I think he was nervous to leave me alone. Or perhaps he wanted to make sure he approved of all my styling ideas. Who knows? All I know is that as I arranged everything on shelves, cabinets, and drawers, I had my very own style consultant supporting me every step of the way—whether I wanted it or not. Actually, I thought it was rather sweet and protective that he sat around on the sofa in his boxer shorts judging my every move; it was comforting to me. He did all his criticizing while watching episodes of *Absolutely Fabulous* and sipping chilled white wine.

On the fifth night after my arrival, as we were sitting inside my new flat watching the "Morocco" episode of *Absolutely Fabulous* and eating pasta out of my new pasta bowls, we looked at each other and both decided this was getting weird; we were like an old married couple, him in his boxers, me in my PJs.

Rupert departed for Genova the next morning. After a lovely farewell, thank yous, etc., he sped off in his vintage convertible Fiat Spider. I was ready for my first morning run on the boardwalk, as a new resident of Villa Fiske. I headed out of the gardens through the giant wrought-iron gate to the sea about three blocks from our flat. I had a great run along the boardwalk all the way down to the next town, about four kilometers away. I bought an icy *shakerato* espresso and headed back to our new home by the sea. I was so happy. Unfortunately, that happiness was short-lived when I realized that my key did not fit the door. Rupert had driven off with my new set of keys.

I thought, "What to do?? What to do?" I quickly decided to run to the hotel we had frequently stayed at while we were under construction. They would know me and let me use their phone (since I left my phone in the flat—of course). On the way down the stairs I ran into one of the developers on his way up to his own flat. I was a bit embarrassed because I was a sweaty mess, and he looked like Italian fashion perfection. He smiled and said *ciao* to me on my way down. Since it is all about politeness in Italy, instead of a quick wave I had to stop and say hello. He asked me how everything was, as I wiped my sweaty brow. "*Bene*," I said. "Super *bene*." I smiled and apologized for my state, "*Fatto footing* [I am running]," I said. "*Mi dispiace sembro un disastro!*" I said in my infantile Italian ("Sorry I look like a disaster). He smiled and said *ciao*, and I was off like a shot to the hotel to retrieve my keys.

On the way, it occurred to me that I did not know Rupert's number by heart—of course I didn't, with my phone there was never a need to memorize numbers (the downfall of society, in my opinion). I did know Frank's number by heart, so that was something. I blew into the reception lobby of the hotel like a crazy person. Once my breathing slowed, I managed to tell them my situation. Of course they remembered me—one thing about Italians is they never ever forget a good customer. Never. I am always shocked to this day when I walk into a store I patronized two years ago and they remember everything. It's an amazing Italian talent.

I picked up the phone and dialed Frank.

"Hello, what's the matter…what time is it?" croaked Frank.

"Hi, it's me," I said. "I need you to call Rupert. I was out running and I realized he drove off with my keys. I can't get into the flat and he's the only person with a set."

"Really?" said Frank.

"Really!" I said.

"Hold on let me check if I have his number, wait a sec—Jesus! It's three in the morning. God…hold on," said Frank.

"What else have I got to do? I am holding on," I said.

"Yes, yes I have it. I will call him and call you back," said my savior, Frank.

"Great. Super. Let me give you the number here," I said.

"Where are you?"

"The Grand Spiaggia. They remembered me and let me use their phone."

"No kidding they remember you, Annette. You lived there for two years!" he said with a chuckle.

"Okay, here's the number. You're pretty awake with the snide remarks at three a.m.," I shot back.

The truth is that Frank is a doctor, a surgeon, a person that can wake up from a deep sleep in a matter of seconds—years of training—hence the quick wit at 3:00 a.m. Frank called Rupert, who was speeding towards Genova; he turned around and met me in the garden of Villa Fiske. I was very happy to see him. We decided I should hide a key in the garden behind a rock on the expansive stone retaining wall. To this day it's probably still there, hidden; I never had to use it and forgot all about it until the day I moved out of Villa Fiske and decided to leave it there, a treasure for someone to find hundreds of years from now.

CHAPTER 10

The Honeymoon Stage

Here I was, in this beautiful flat—Frank was not due to arrive for another month—and I was in Italy all alone. I did not know a single soul (well, except Rupert, who lived in Genova and had his own life). I knew one English-speaking person who had worked on our house, although he was much younger than me, in his twenties when we met: Leonardo Apruzzi. He was sweet, kind, and my lifesaver—he was one of the foremen on our job, so I saw him daily during the renovation. My Italian was terrible and I used it sparingly because I was really quite timid, which for me was a very new and uncomfortable feeling.

I still had a few things to finish up on the flat, so I hired Leo to help me and we became fast friends. I had no idea where anything was in town so he helped somewhat with that, too, although at age twenty-four most young men are not tuned in to where to find the dry cleaners or the grocery store. Mainly, I made it my job to walk all over town, go into every store, and take a mental inventory of what was for sale or for hire. As a stylist, one learns to be dropped into a new city and work it out. Thank God for my years of training; I managed to walk into every place in town, have espresso at every café, and try all the *gelato* in Alassio. I quickly started learning all the best places in town and would visit them a few times per week. I loved researching all the food vendors in town; it became my obsession.

For example, if you're looking for bread—*focaccia*, for example— you would go to a *focacceria*; if you want meat, you go to the butcher; the fruit and vegetable vendor for those items—you get the idea. Most grocery stores have all these things, so it depends on the quality of these items you want to consume. The separate vendors have the freshest food.

I experienced a learning curve for grocery shopping in Italy. Italians all have their favorite places to shop—for anything from pastries to meat. They will not disclose this information to a stranger. Maybe you can catch where they think the best meat is sold, if you overhear a heated discussion at dinner. For two years I ate the most fantastic roast beef at a friend's home. She swore by a particular butcher in town, but was very vague about his whereabouts. I was desperate to find out who this butcher was and where his shop was located. One day we were walking back from her beach club, where I had been her guest for the day, and she said, "I need to stop and pick up some roast beef." I swear I heard angels sing—finally the mystery would be solved. We walked right into a butcher shop that I had walked by a million times. Amazed, I asked her, "This is your butcher?" She replied *"Si, si."* I laughed, "For two years I wondered where you bought your meat, and you would never tell me!" She responded, "Well, now you know." This is a typical Italian response by the way. With Italians you must be in the fold, and then the Italian secrets will be revealed—a lesson I would have to learn repeatedly in the coming years.

We lived about ten blocks from a pretty decent grocery store, but I had to plan what I needed and figure out how I was going to haul it back ten blocks to our flat, since we had no car. So I would make a list, starting with the lightest things I urgently needed. Then I would go back the next day for laundry detergent and diet coke—the heavy items. Of course, Italians do not drink water from the tap. For a long time I thought you couldn't, but it turns out you can, the water quality is fine. I have come to find out the populous has problems with drinking tap water for two distinct reasons:

1. They think water flowing through the bad pipes is bad for you.
2. They hate the water company and refuse to pay for tap water (which is insane, because rumor has it the bottled water they buy comes from the tap, and doubly insane because, if true, they schlep about a hundred of pounds of bottled tap water to their homes every month). After about three years of carrying my weight in water bottles ten blocks, then up our hill, then up the stairs every week, I bought a Brita and called it a look.

I am here to tell you, Italians have crazy habits—water-buying being just one of them. For daily chores like banking, Italians do their banking in person. You have a banker and they have a personal relationship with you. When we first set up an Italian bank account, we were lucky to find a lovely young woman—the sexiest banker we had ever seen, Simona—who took immaculate care of us. Guiding us through the endless reams of paperwork, auto-billing, taxes, and bank fees. In a bank, you can experience another thing about Italians: THEY LOVE PAPERWORK. I have never seen so much paperwork in my life. Italians love a paper trail. Emails not so much. They use texts like emails—it's weird. But Simona did all the endless paperwork with a big smile on her extremely tanned face with happy eyes behind her sparkly purple glasses.

With the flat and all our banking in order, it was time to pick a beach club. This was a decision that carried much weight for the family. I tried a few clubs on the boardwalk, but, in truth, they just did not have what I was looking for. While I had visited many beach clubs over many years while "dating" Italy, I'd never actually committed to one. And now that I was committed to the country, I figured I might as well commit to a beach club too.

I did not know enough about Alassio to know the "good" beaches, so, much like our house-hunting experience, finding a beach club was like searching for a needle in the haystack. There was no guidebook to the best beaches in Alassio, I had no friends in Alassio to ask, and Rupert and his partner Reynaldo were of no help. I later found out that Rupert and Reynaldo did in fact know all the best beaches, but I guess I did not warrant the information. In Italy, unless you are deemed "worthy" (like the roast beef from the best butcher) no information is coming your way, period. So it was up to Frank and I to somehow figure out the best beach for us.

Frank arrived soon after I had launched my beach search. He was a good sport and window-shopped beach clubs with me; he's a trooper. Frank loved taking his bicycle for a spin every morning. It was the perfect way to investigate and explore our new surroundings. I ran every morning while he was out, and then we had lunch together overlooking the sea. It was a pretty good routine. One day after a long bike ride, Frank came home and announced he had found our beach club. It was about a five-minute drive to the other side of a peninsula couple towns over, which was also the location of a charming working lighthouse. Two towns over to the west, in the seaside town of Andora, the club was close enough to easily navigate but far enough away to have the perfect spacious beach we were looking for. We agreed to head over the next morning and check it out. I was so grateful that Frank thought to check out beaches other than the sardine packed beaches of Alassio. It proved to be a great find for our family.

The next morning, as planned, we headed to Rocce di Pinamare, the beach club Frank had discovered on his daily bike excursion. We loaded the car with beach essentials and drove the winding road five minutes from Villa Fiske. When we arrived, we found a large, well-appointed parking lot, which is quite a hot commodity on the Riviera. We parked and headed down the steep stone steps which plunged down, down, down, through a wild tropical jungle with the loudest choir of cicadas I had ever heard. When we finally reached the bottom, we found a cute retro bar and restaurant, and further down another set of steps we found an expansive beach—soft sand that snaked around a deep blue sea—with a flotilla of cobalt blue lounge chairs and fluttering blue umbrellas imprinted with the beach's logo. Beach chairs are called *lettini*, and we intended on reserving two for the day. It was all very visually appealing and done in the style of the 1970s—very retro Riviera. It looked like a beach club stuck in time and we loved it.

Like most beach clubs, it was run by the senior lifeguard, Sergio, who would become my friend over the next ten years. Since this was our first visit, we were regarded as tourists. Once you join the club, you're treated differently in Italian culture; you have to earn your place, your beach chair location, your friendships, and your rank at the beach club—this is a pretty universal rule about many things in Italy. There is always a special price if they know you—a discount (*sconto* in Italian)—but you have to earn it. Since we were tourists, we did not get the good seats; we were all the way in the back as far from the sea as you could possibly be—right up against the cabanas and basically lying on the major walkway of the major traffic artery to the beach club. It was relatively unpleasant that first day. But I knew that once we joined and showed up summer after summer, we would warrant the good seats and be treated like locals and get the locals' pricing and position.

Needless to say, we joined the beach club, Sergio and I became buddies, and I spent every summer thereafter in the best seat on the beach, and it only took us two years to get there. The third summer we showed up at Pinamare, we were greeted like old friends. Before that time, Sergio barely noticed us, but on the third summer his greeting was so warm that I literally looked behind us to make sure he was indeed talking to us and not another family.

Sergio gave us a big smile, and said, "Welcome back, so nice to see you. This is going to be a great summer." Totally stunned, I just managed to say, "Thanks, Sergio, nice to see you, too." I followed him to our usual chairs and I realized our real friendship had just started, only two years after we met—it was just so Italian. That first summer, when we told Rupert and his boyfriend that we joined the beach club Pinamare in Andora, they matter-of-factly said, "Oh, yes, that is a beautiful club, one of our favorites."…REALLY? I thought, really??? Rupert was sometimes my caretaker, doing it beautifully, and sometimes he was a withholding Italian—

Once we had the beach club sussed out, we were pretty much set for summer activities since all people on the Riviera do is go to the beach club daily. Of course, since we are not Italian, we wanted to explore our surroundings beyond Alassio and Andora. We'd been in Alassio for a year and we had seen Monaco, Menton, Genova, and Portofino. Another thing about Italians is they never disclose places they like to go. I had asked a lot of people, including Rupert, where some of his favorite unknown spots were on the Riviera and, of course…he had none. I find this so odd about Italians, and I still have a hard time with it to this day. You have to discover special places yourself, something about earning the right to know the secret places. I literally lived in Alassio for ten years before our banker shared that her favorite nearby magical beach was Varigotti beach, about a half-hour drive from Alassio. I had never heard of it. At *aperitivo* that night I asked our friend Leo if he knew Varigotti beach and he said, "Oh my God, it's just gorgeous. We love going there." *What the heck?* I thought. *Were they kidding me?* Never had he ever mentioned this beach to me, and we saw each other every day? Italians are so withholding, just like a really bad boyfriend.

CHAPTER 11

Will You Stay Forever?

rank always says, "Everyone wants to visit, and that's to be expected when you have a house in Italy." When you have a house in Italy, people positively come out of the woodwork. Frank said it would happen, and he was 100 percent right, as he is with most things.

The first year we had our new flat I had fifteen requests from friends to visit. Of course, I considered all the requests and since there are only sixteen weeks in summer including September (the perfect month in Italy), when you do the math it's not possible to have everyone visit. So we did sort of a first-come first-serve thing and agreed to the first five requests.

The truth is that I love hosting guests. But like with everything in life, there is a give and take. My experiences have led me to this conclusion: we all have expectations. As a guest, there is the expectation that the host will be taking good care of basic needs and offer travel tips and support. As a host, one expects guests to say thank you and be a little self-sufficient as well, so the burden of showing them a good time does not become overwhelming. I pride myself in making sure guests feel comfortable, but over the years my giving personality has been tried time and time again. The result of many years of hosting is that I can manage to maneuver any guest crisis or sticky situation. My attitude is that at the end of the day, it is their vacation and they deserve a good time.

Since we had rented homes in Italy previously, we were pretty clued in to the guest game. Some guests are self-sufficient and some are not. It's hard to tell who's who until they arrive. We have even witnessed a few nervous breakdowns over the years. Yes, it's true, you can have a nervous breakdown while on vacation in Italy—who knew? One of my first guests was a photographer friend. She and I worked together quite regularly. She was a very nice, straight-forward sort of gal. A business-minded person, nothing kooky about her. Which is why I was surprised when she arrived a bit unraveled.

I picked her up at the Nice airport, and she just seemed tired—which is perfectly normal for a long flight. Not particularly chatty. She had arrived late morning, and when we arrived at the flat about an hour later, she wanted to go straight to the beach instead of napping. Again, not an unusual request; some guests want to go right into the day to avoid jet lag and a sleepless night. So we packed up our beach gear and headed to Pinamare, our beach club. We had a lovely lunch at the club, and the photographer friend commented on how yummy it all was.

After lunch we went to our sunbeds and I decided, like every other Italian on the beach, to take a nap after lunch. The beach is quiet from around 2:00 until 4:30, with everyone snoozing or reading, reclined and silent.

I was abruptly awoken by my guest screaming on her phone, apparently at her husband. I wasn't sure, because I was in such a deep drooling sleep that I had no idea where the hell I was or why I was hearing someone screaming in English. I think I had forgotten the she was with me for a minute. When I finally came to I said, "You're going to need to quiet down, please. You have woken everyone up at the beach, like an ugly American. I am so embarrassed."

She looked at me like I had four eyes and quickly screamed goodbye and hung up. I swear, if she could have slammed the phone she would have. But with a mobile phone all you can do is hang up and throw it into the sea, which I wish she had done, since this behavior would be ongoing during her stay.

"What the hell is going on?" I asked. She responded by telling me she was having marital problems. "I sensed that," I said. "Yes, it's pretty serious," she replied, "but I don't want to talk about it." "Okay," I said. "I am so sorry." Sorry for so many reasons! I surmised that this was going to be a challenging trip, but I was ready to help, listen, give her space, and be her friend.

Late afternoon we headed back to the flat, and I made an *aperitivo* and we talked about dinner plans. We decided on a simple pizza and a walk through town. At dinner we ordered two pizzas at my favorite pizza place on the boardwalk (the owners finally sort of knew who I was and no longer gave me the worst table near the bathrooms, so that was good). We sat and talked and finally she told me what was going on with her. She wanted a divorce—was no longer in love or attracted to her husband; she just wanted out, and he did not. We left it at that; I just listened and offered support. I wanted to keep it as light as possible since she seemed very agitated. We walked down the boardwalk and did a little window shopping.

After a good night's sleep, I hoped she would feel a little better and we could have a nice, relaxing day of shopping, lunching, and touring Alassio. All went well, and I was convinced all was well and wrote off the drama as the result of jet lag and a long flight. That night I planned a lovely evening with some friends, Leo included, and we ate at one of the most beautiful restaurants above Alassio, with the best view in town. All went well until one of Leo's friends, a nice but serious young man, decided to have a deep conversation with my friend; he spoke amazing English and was enjoying using it. The mood at the table shifted and somehow the conversation turned into an argument. The argument was silly; if I remember correctly, they were talking about taxes in Italy versus America, nothing to get upset about, but everything was setting her off, even taxes. I was unsure of what to do. Since we had a great day, I thought the black cloud over my friend's head had disappeared, but it had not, and now she was engaged in a full-blown argument. With Leo trying to calm the situation down, my friend stepped outside and I followed.

"What's going on?" I said. "I have no idea but I am just angry and having the worst time and that guy is a jerk," she said. "Well, I am sorry, but it's such a gorgeous location and such a beautiful night—can't you focus on that? And he's not a jerk, he's just trying to have an intelligent discussion about taxes," I said. I wanted to say, "Jesus, lady, you're in Italy on vacation in the most beautiful place, and this is where you decide to have a meltdown?" But of course I didn't. I paid the bill and we decided to head to a nightclub on the beach that was one of our favorites—it always offered a good time.

Then came the dilemma of whether she should join us or not. After twenty minutes of debate in the parking lot of the restaurant, I finally convinced her to come—that it would be fun, that the spot was pretty and she would love it. I have noticed that when some people travel abroad, everything that was bothering them at home seems magnified. This would not be my first or last experience of this kind as a host.

We entered the club, were shown to a lovely table with an ocean view, and ordered cocktails for everyone. We were all having a great time when one of our friends noticed on a stroll back from the restroom that my distressed friend was sitting at the ocean perched on a rock, crying her eyes out.

Oh, God, was my first reaction, and then I made the decision not to go to her and just let her work it out. After all, I wasn't sure there was anything I could do. So that night, I danced and she cried. We gathered everyone and headed home around 2:00 a.m. I was happy and she was depressed.

We had planned to go to Forte dei Marmi for the fabulous outdoor market the next day. Forte is about a three-hour drive and it closed at

1:00 p.m., which meant we had to get up early, around 7:00 a.m., to make sure we saw all of the market. Sleepy-headed, we got in the car and I drove. After stopping at the Autogrill for some jet fuel espresso, we felt alive again. My friend seemed pensive and silent, which was fine because I was driving like a bat out of hell and needed to concentrate. We arrived at the market around 10:00 a.m., bolted into a bar for one more espresso, and headed into the market crowd. I sensed that she was getting anxious again; she had been on the phone the night before.

"Are you okay?" I asked.

"Yes I am, but I just don't like it here," she answered. I was perplexed, but robotically nodded my head up and down like I totally understood (which I did not). We had been at the market all of fifteen minutes. "Maybe something to eat might make you feel better."

"No, I am fine. This is just not my thing. I am not a shopper," she replied.

Needless to say, the next hour and a half was painful, but I drowned my sorrows by buying well-priced cashmere shawls for holiday gifts and an embroidered swimsuit cover-up, all the while dragging a mopey friend by my side.

"I'm hungry," she finally said, after hours of silence.

"Okay," I responded. "Let's stop at this bar and have a Coke and talk about where we would like to eat lunch." We ordered Cokes and sat staring at each other and sipping our drinks.

"No, I am super hungry. We have to eat here in town," she decided. "Okay, let's look for something; what are you in the mood for?" I asked. "I don't know," she replied. I could not figure out if this was a passive-aggressive reply or if she was just depressed and really could not decide. This was where it gets tricky with guests; when things are not going well, how does one right the situation? I said, "How about you walk around the corner and check out that cute restaurant we passed, and I will meet you there after I pay the check." She looked at me and screamed, "I DON'T WANT TO!" Everyone at the bar turned around and stared at us. "Calm down," I whispered. She promptly stood up and stormed off. I have two kids and I would never let them behave this way. Friend or not, I decided I was going to have to deal with this as I would one of my kids. I paid the check, and as I was paying I saw her come around the corner.

"Let's go," I said. "We are going to head home." We drove home for the next three hours in silence; finally, she dozed off and I could gather my thoughts. When we arrived back in Alassio, she went into her room, closed the door, and did not come out for several hours. In the meantime, I called a friend and asked for advice. I was desperate to solve this situation and salvage what we had left of the week. We had four days left, and I was determined that I would show this girl a good time. It's my nature to make sure guests enjoy what Italy has to offer; after all, it was my happy place....but not so much this week.

I decided to prepare a few snacks. I knew she was probably starving, and I nibbled as I put together a charcuterie tray. Olives, cheese, and crackers could solve any problem, right? Finally around 6:00 p.m. she emerged and informed me she had changed her flight and she would be flying home the next day. I said, "Are you sure?" Full disclosure, I felt this was the kindest thing she could do for both of us; she was not enjoying her time in Italy and she was, well, torturing me.

"Yes, I am sure," she replied. "I made some snacks. I know you must be starving," I offered. "I'm not hungry," she replied. So I made some cocktails and we sat down and sipped in silence. I decided to make us dinner; even though she had said she was not hungry, I was. I made a light lemon pasta with a mixed salad, and served it with some leftover focaccia and glasses of white wine. I sipped mine while I set the table; she just sat and watched me. She devoured dinner like it was her last meal. In a manner of speaking, it was. After packing, she announced that she wanted to go into town to buy some gifts for her family and friends. It was 10:30 p.m. and I was exhausted after driving six hours, being yelled at, and then given the silent treatment. I was frazzled and wiped out. But, still trying to save her experience in Italy, I agreed to walk into town with her. Lucky for us, in the summertime in Italian vacation towns the stores are open until midnight. She manically ran up and down the pedestrian shopping street buying anything she could get her hands on. I sat in the square eating a *gelato* and watching this shopping marathon unfold. I could not help but think about earlier in the day when I had driven us to the best shopping in Italy, and she had told me that she's not a shopper. Shaking my head to myself, I decided to move past it and enjoy my *gelato*. Around midnight we trekked up the hill to the flat, and I went to bed.

The next morning we got into the car and headed to Nice airport. During the hour drive I could sense she was thinking, thinking hard, and she was anxious for what lay ahead in the US. She had a lot on her plate, and coming to Italy was not the reprieve she was looking for. As we rolled into the airport departures drop-off line, I felt a huge sense of relief and gratefulness that I was about to say goodbye and put this awful guest experience behind me. She jumped out of the car and grabbed her bag; I gave her a hug and said good luck and good-bye. She headed toward the entrance, then stopped quickly, turned around, and headed to the driver's side window to tell me something. I rolled the window down and—expecting an apology—I smiled and said, "What's up?"

"YOU COULD TELL ME WHERE I GO IN," she screamed. I literally jumped with fright; I thought she was going to punch me, she was so angry. "Right through that door," I pointed in the direction of the door that said DEPARTURES. She nodded and slammed her hand on the windshield and she was off. I was really shaken for the first fifteen minutes of the return drive. As I headed towards Alassio, slowly my nerves calmed, and I started to feel better.

I did not hear a word from her for a year. I found out through mutual friends that she had gotten divorced, that she was better and felt bad about how she acted during her visit. I arranged to meet with her in the US in the fall, a year and half after her visit, to tell her not to worry about it, we all have bad spells. It was unfortunate that it happened to be when she was on vacation in beautiful Italy. It was the first time I found out that guests can be very challenging, but the most challenging was yet to come.

By the following year, year two at our flat in Alassio, I felt like I had the guest thing down pat. We had fewer guests, and Levi, now thirteen, was planning on spending more than a month with me. He planned to fly over with our guests, a couple from Florida. They were old friends; well, truth was we knew the man better than we knew his wife. He had been staying with us for years when he was in Atlanta on business. He was a sweet soul, kind and caring, and a great guest in Atlanta. Obviously, we were expecting to have a great time with them since he knew all the ins and outs of our Italian adventures, and he was dying to come visit.

They flew into the Nice airport and I was thrilled to see Levi again. It was a gorgeous hour-and-fifteen-minute ride up the coast of the Riviera to our flat. Our guests seemed exhausted from their trip when we piled into the car, while Levi was his usual, chatty self. He told me all about his trip as we drove; they remained silent in the back of the car. As soon as we arrived they went to bed. Levi and I hung out, read books, and did some chores until around dinner time, with no word from our guests.

We decided to make a little supper, then watch a movie, and I made enough food in case they woke up hungry. We heard nothing, no movement, no sound from their room. Levi and I watched a movie and then went to bed.

The next morning, I woke up around eight o'clock. Levi rallied and we went out to get some breakfast. As you know by now, our breakfast consists of a brioche washed down with a strong espresso. We picked up a couple of brioche and a few pastries and headed back to the flat to greet our guests. Much to our surprise, they were still asleep.

I thought we would hang around and wait for them to awake, but after three hours, we decided that we would head to the beach club and return around 4:00. We left a note to that effect, and we were off. As you know, all over Italy *pausa* is from noon to 4:30. Stores close, the banks close, everything but the restaurants close. So having our guests sleep through the afternoon was no biggie, since they could not do anything anyway. We returned home as planned at 4:00 to find our house guests awake and getting dressed.

"Wow," I said to them with a chuckle. "I thought you were dead."

He laughed and admitted, "We took some melatonin and we had our ear plugs in, so we were out of it."

"Are you hungry?" I asked.

"Nope, we ate the pastries and made ourselves some tea."

His wife was a tall drink of water, with short, cropped blonde hair, and the remnants of what was once great beauty. She looked and dressed like an all-American, middle-aged lady. Her husband was handsome, dashing, and charming. He was the star of the show in so many ways.

The evening of day two we decided to go out; stretching their legs seemed like a good idea. We stopped for an *aperitivo* on the boardwalk. Since they did not have a credit card (which seemed very strange to me), they could not hit the ATM for cash, and the bank was closed for the day to exchange money. I paid the bill for both *aperitivo* and dinner. I had made plans to meet a bunch of people for pizza that night and they came along. He was very social and engaging; she was brooding and quiet all evening. I thought to myself: *This is going to be interesting.*

Levi and I awoke the next morning and made some breakfast, American-style. Toast, eggs, and bacon. Surely the aroma would wake them up, I thought. But like the day before, they were dead to the world.

We waited until 10:30 a.m. and decided to head to the beach and return for a late lunch with our guests. We walked into the flat around two o'clock and...nothing. How could this be? Again they were fast asleep, snoozing their vacation away. We cobbled together some Italian sandwiches with leftover *focaccia*, some tomato and prosciutto, and a smattering of fresh mozzarella cheese. While eating, we decided that evening we would venture to a favorite restaurant on the other side of the bay—a seaside place, with hip décor and a seafood menu. Levi and I decided to take a nap, and, like our guests, we were fast asleep in no time. When we woke, we heard rustling in the kitchen. I looked at my watch and it was 4:30. *Wow, what a nap*, I thought; we had slept for about an hour and a half.

"*Ciao*," I said when I went to the kitchen. "Great nap."

"Oh, I know. We did the melatonin thing again," he answered.

"No, I meant us—Levi and I fell fast asleep this afternoon."

He smiled and took a bite of what looked like the identical sandwich we had made for lunch.

"Hey," I said. "That's what we had for lunch, too."

"Great minds." He smiled and carried the sandwich into the guest room, closed the door, and disappeared for an hour.

Meanwhile, Levi and I grabbed our books and hung out for a few hours reading and sipping Cokes while we waited for their next move. They both rallied around seven in the evening. After showering and dressing, we piled into the car and I drove them up the coast. Barely a word was exchanged. I realized my friend was much more guarded around his wife; maybe it's why he took a week away from her every month. We had not spent any time around her, so this was all new to me. I causally mentioned that they had been with us three days now and still had no euros on them.

"Maybe you guys can set an alarm and head into town in the morning for some cash," I suggested.

"Yes, yes," he said. "We will pay you back for the dinners."

"That's not necessary," I replied. "It's just that the banks open around 8:30 in the morning and then close for the afternoon; by the time you wake up they are closed again. Since you don't have an ATM card this is the only way for you to exchange dollars."

"Yes, that's true," he agreed. "We'll definitely wake up and head to the bank in the morning."

We made a plan to walk to breakfast and then I would take him to my sweet banker and friend, Simona—she would get them all fixed up. The next morning I was happily surprised that they were up and dressed when I came into the kitchen.

"Ready to go?" he asked with a big smile on his face.

"Yes, just let me grab my bag." And we were off, just he and I, heading to the bank.

The city was bustling with activity, as it was every morning.

We grabbed a quick espresso and headed to the bank. Simona was waiting for us. Since she was in the customer service department, she sat behind a standard issue desk in a glass cubicle. She wore a crop-top in pink with black skinny jeans. Silver mules were the finishing touch to her office outfit. She always looked like she was going to the club instead of working in a bank, but this was one of the many things I loved about Italy. She was a hoot, and competent to boot.

"*Ciao*, Simo," I said, and in the middle of the bank she gave me a kiss on each cheek and said, "*Ciao cara*, Annette." Simona's English was perfect, which was a perk in a small Italian town. Of course, she dealt with all the international clients, so it made perfect sense. She was a delight to work with, and I loved having her take care of us over the years. We sat down opposite her and got down to business right away.

"My friend does not have a credit card or ATM, so we need to exchange some money," I explained.

"No problem," she said. He then moved forward in his chair as if to share a secret. I was a little perplexed by his body language and wondered what he was about to do. Simona and I both leaned forward in our chairs as well, staring at him intently.

He wiped his brow, as he was sweating a little. Then he grabbed his shirt and hiked it up to reveal what looked like a stuffed fanny pack. Simona and I looked at each other. We were both wondering what was going on? He unclipped the bag and said, "I want to exchange five thousand dollars."

Simona and I looked at each other and I am sure we were thinking the exact same thing: *What the heck?* I was not sure what to say. Was my insane guest karma going to embroil me in some crazy money laundering plot this morning? I had thought he was going to exchange a few hundred dollars, that it would take no time, and that that would be it.

Thank God Simona chimed in before I did. Simona simply said, "We cannot exchange this amount."

"Um, right," I said—the only words I managed to muster. *What is going on here*, I thought. *Who travels with this much money wrapped around their belly?*

"Only one thousand dollars—that is our limit," Simona explained. "And that will have to be run through Annette's account, since we really only allow an exchange of five hundred for non-clients. If we exchange more it will get flagged. This is international law. But since you know Annette, I will allow one thousand, we will deposit into her account, and then she can withdraw it and give you the cash." I was pretty shaken up, and certain my friend and his wife were international money launderers. I let my thoughts get a little carried away, yes. What I really wanted to ask him was why the hell he was carrying all that cash out of the US, but I checked myself and didn't say a thing. Although to this day I do wonder what was going on.

As we stepped out of the bank, Levi and the wife were waiting outside. Levi had a big smile on his face because he was headed to the bike store, his favorite place in town. We all began to walk the two blocks to the bike store, when the wife decided she really needed to see a travel agent to book tickets for a ferry ride to Ponza.

"Ponza." I said. "Where is that?" I was not at all familiar with this island. Later I discovered it is off the coast of Italy, in the region of Lazio, about two miles south of Cape Circeo. It's since become a tourist destination, but this was about eleven years ago and no one was talking about this remote island.

I agreed to walk the two blocks to a travel agent with her—one that might know about the ferry schedule and how to book a ticket. The office was brightly colored with many travel posters and brochures. The agent was cheerful, in a floral dress and bright, beaded necklace. She had long back curls that framed her face, and liberally applied eye makeup. With a big smile, she greeted us in Italian, "*Buon giorno.*"

"*Buon giorno,*" I replied. "*Parla Inglese?*"

"Of course," she replied. "How can I help you?"

We pointed to the map behind her and said we wanted to go here, indicating the remote island of Ponza.

"Ah, Ponza. It is not easy to get to. There is one ferry per day, and only one train per day to take you close to the port where you meet the ferry. Once you depart the train, you must take a bus to the port. So timing is important," she explained.

"This seems complicated," I noted. Levi and her husband walked through the door of the travel agent as I made this comment.

"What seems complicated?" he asked. His wife shot daggers with her eyes at me and snapped, "It's not that complicated. Annette's just being negative."

"I'm not being negative. It just seems that you need to time everything perfectly and there is no room for error. With the Italian train system, you're taking a chance you'll be late and miss the ferry, that's all," I explained. "Maybe renting a car might be a better idea?"

"Don't get involved, Mom," Levi chimed in.

"Yeah, don't get involved!" the wife agreed.

Wow, I had been put in my place. I mumbled apologies that I was only trying to help, then stepped out of the office, grabbed a seat at the bar next door, and ordered my third espresso of the morning. I would stay out of it. I just sipped and waited. About thirty minutes later they emerged, Levi in tow, with tickets for the train and the ferry—they would have to buy the bus fare on the bus. They were set. I was still not sure this was all going to go as smoothly as planned, but I kept my mouth shut. I did!

I got up and took not more than three steps, when the wife began yelling at me that I thought I knew it all, and that they knew what they were doing. Frankly I did not care what they did, as long as they were gone by the next day. I hated to feel this way, I was so fond of him, but she made me feel awful. I looked at this as a learning opportunity and decided to make their last day as pleasant as possible. I hoped her mood would improve, fingers crossed. That day I realized that sometimes travel did not bring out the best in people and I made a mental note.

Unfortunately, the beach didn't improve her mood; in fact, most of the day she was pretty sober. Only when the African woman selling beach coverups showed up did she smile. We endured a fashion show, as she tried on every piece of clothing the vendor had to offer. We complimented her with every wardrobe change. It was nauseating, honestly. She bought two rather age-inappropriate dresses, too short and too tight, something a seventeen-year-old might choose. All I knew was that she was in a good mood for an hour, so that was fine by me.

The African woman departed and we all decided that maybe a swim might be nice. She suggested to her husband that they snorkel, and Levi joined them as they ran off, snorkel in hand. It was a childish move on her part to leave me out, but I welcomed the quiet and was fine with not being included.

They left the next day. I drove them to the train early in the morning. "Goodbye and good luck," were my parting words. When I walked back into the flat, Levi met me with a laugh. "Mom, you deserve a pajama day. Those two were rough." Levi was completely right. Later that day he filled me in on his travels to Italy with those two. He told me that when they landed in Paris to change flights to Nice, the two of them never waited for him as he made his way through passport control and to the gate alone. Levi was thirteen, but still, they did not wait? It said a lot about these "friends." Needless to say, we never spoke again. I did eventually find out that they missed the bus, the ferry, and barely made their second train, plus they lost their phone, so it sounds like they had a challenging travel day. Trains in Italy are challenging, and some guests are even more challenging than the trains.

The last really, truly, awful guests I welcomed were a very "famous" blogger from England and his long-suffering boyfriend. The blogger had reached out to me on social media a couple years earlier, complimenting me on my blog and asking me for styling advice. We became social media pen pals. Although I was much older and had an established career, he regularly wrote me very charming emails, and I viewed him as someone I was mentoring. He was new to styling and interior design, his projects were very budget-minded, and his color palette was childish and colorful. Not really my wheelhouse, but when you're young, bright colors and wild patterns are an easy look to make a big impact. He was very passionate about design and eager to learn. He seemed super sweet and innocent. Since he lived in England with his boyfriend, we made a plan for them to come visit me in Italy.

I met them at the Nice airport and we drove to Alassio. It all started well, as it does before it goes south. The blogger was charming and excited and chatted away on the ride home. I distinctly remember that first conversation with him—something about a book deal advance that he was negotiating. He asked me all sorts of direct questions, which I found very bold. It seemed strange talking money with someone I barely knew. He was all business and very intense for someone on vacation. His partner was very quiet; it was obvious to me who was the star of this show. It was starting to become clear that with every visit involving a couple, one was clearly the decider, the star, or the boss.

When we entered the flat, they were quite sweet and handed me a housewarming gift made out of wood, and it was missing pieces. I surmised it was a re-gift, but of course kept that thought to myself; nothing wrong with a re-gift, although usually it wouldn't be missing pieces. They were cute and oh-so-young and trying hard to be grown-up and sophisticated. We had a rest and then headed to *aperitivo* and dinner at the seaside. They were both very conversational and loved everything.

The next day we headed to the beach club. That afternoon after lunch I noticed that the blogger had become rather grumpy, not enjoying the club or the food and being really mean to his partner. I was shocked at the bossy way he treated his boyfriend. He just seemed very unhappy. I tried talking about work, but that didn't please him that day. He accused me of trying to get information out of him that he was not willing to share. Well, this was not my first time dealing with grumpy guests. I read my book, took a nap, and swam in the ocean. I let him work it out.

Over the next day, Mr. Picky became even more insufferable, behaving very unpleasantly to his boyfriend, who took it like an abused puppy. Since I did not know them that well, I decided to stay out of it and spend my time waiting for their stay to end. I could hardly wait. I tried very hard to be a good hostess. One night I made dinner at home. I had invited a girlfriend to act as a buffer. Carla was a lovely girl, a beautiful, bright, and very mature young woman from Milan. They were all about the same age, so I thought it would be good for them to be around someone Italian and younger. She spoke perfect English as well, so that was a big plus. I placed everyone's dish in front of them, and Mr. Picky announced that his meat was too raw; he could not and would not eat it. He practically threw it at me. Carla was appalled. He was like a child throwing a tantrum—unfortunately it would not be the only tantrum of his visit. His partner sat silently, eating. I quietly stood up, put his meat in the oven and sat back down. "It will be about five minutes," I announced, and continued eating. After five minutes I returned his portion, cooked very well done; it resembled a piece of rubber, and probably tasted like it as well. But he liked it and that's all that mattered.

The next day one of my sweet friends visited, a photographer from California. He had come to shoot a mini-video of *aperitivo*. Since we had visitors, we thought why not have them help and appear in the video? Mr. Picky loved the idea—no surprise, he loved being the center of attention. Since he was a blogger, he could help in the production as well.

The day of the shoot, we all pitched in. I asked Mr. Picky to help plate food and arrange flowers. He answered, "I can't help. I have to get dressed for the video shoot."

"We all do, and we all need to help load the car and bring the props. All hands on deck." With that said, he agreed to help plate a pretty platter of nibbles to take along. As I was showing him how to do this, he sniffed, "I can't do this," and promptly burst into tears, crying so hard that his partner had to walk him around the grounds to calm down. *What the what*, I thought.

Thank goodness, Leo and his girlfriend Elisabeth were there, as well as the photographer and his assistant. We all plated and packed everything and headed off to the venue. The location was the Hambry Tennis Club, a beautiful, retro-designed spot. The Englishmen caught up later, after we had unpacked everything and set up the shoot. Like nothing ever happened, they were all smiles and animated during the shoot; Mr. Picky was indeed the star of this show, in his mind anyway.

Leo and I had planned a fun evening after the shoot. One of our favorite bands was playing at our beach club; Leo bought tickets and made reservations at the restaurant on the beach. It would be a beautiful night, so we thought.

The Englishmen sat across from Leo and I, and Elisabeth joined us later. We ordered wine and lovely entrees. It was a gorgeous location, and we were all having a great time. It was a blast, two thousand people on the beach, yachts docked to enjoy the music, and everyone was having a great time…except one sour Englishman. I think his poor partner was trying hard to enjoy himself, despite his miserable boyfriend.

During the dinner Mr. Picky began insulting me, telling me how he loved old ladies, and naming some of my older social media friends as well. Age shaming me while I was trying to enjoy my evening was not cool. I felt he was being ungrateful and mean. I could tell that Leo was becoming really angry. We couldn't blame it on his drinking too much because he didn't drink. He was just a nasty guy. He was really miserable all night, hating everything about the event, and he let us know how much he hated being there, but we did not let him ruin our night. Sometimes just ignoring bad behavior is the best plan. Naïvely I had thought Mr. Picky would be as he portrayed himself on social media and in his emails—friendly and fun. It's true that when you meet someone on social media they can pose as anything or anyone. Most folks I meet on social media are what they represent, but this imposter was the exception. This was a big lesson for me on so many levels.

The next morning they departed. I truly have never been happier to say goodbye to anyone. I genuinely think that Mr. Picky's partner felt bad, and I whispered to him, "Hey man, you're really the star of this show." I felt a huge weight lift as they drove away. The worst guests? Perhaps not. But the most unpleasant ones, for sure.

CHAPTER 12

The Users

B y now I really thought I could spot them: the users—people who discover you have a house in Italy and want to come visit, not because they love your company but because they see a free holiday. People you barely know, like the English blogger. I was disappointed in myself for not understanding that many people would see me mainly as a concierge during their stay—ready to fulfill their every wish. And I filled that service again and again, hoping they would enjoy Italy as much as I did!

I was determined not to let these vitriolic visits lessen my love for my second home, so I decided to invite *only* close friends in the future. One Christmas in Atlanta we thought we met the perfect couple to be fellow Italophiles and friends. If only.

We met them at a fabulous holiday party held in a photographer's studio. It was wildly fun, with three bars and a DJ spinning loud dance music. Everyone in the styling and photography, advertising, and magazine industry was there, people I had not seen in years. The décor was amazing: hanging lanterns, lights, thousands of hand-cut snowflakes, flowers, and the most beautiful food spread I had ever seen—it made us regret eating dinner before we came.

As we were approached by one of the hosts, I realized I vaguely knew her; she owned an ad agency that had rented our house many years before for a photo shoot. She was married to the photographer who owned the studio and shared the space with the photographer that had invited us to the party. She offered us a shot of Jägermeister from the holster of a belt she wore around her waist. Her party look reminded me of Morticia from the Addams family—rather Goth, with black boots, a black mini with black tights, and a shiny purple top. Her hair was long and very dark, and the sharp features of her face were emphasized with bold cat-eye makeup. Odd, but interesting.

Frank and I politely refused the shots, we exchanged smiles, and she swept off to tempt the next party-goer. Her husband was a stylish guy, with long hair and a big smile that was the first thing you saw as he approached. Kind of like an older rock star. He had a look. We exchanged pleasantries before he moved on to his other guests.

Frank and I decided this was a great party and we were happy we had come. As the party ebbed, the photographer and his wife came over and we chatted genially about a lot of things. Then he said this: "You guys live in Italy part of the time, don't you?" It was obvious that his studio mate, whom I worked with, had shared this piece of information about me.

"Yes." I admitted, "Well, I live there in the summer and Frank comes back and forth when he can." Talking about Italy is my favorite subject, so they did not have to prompt me to enthusiastically describe our house there and the area. I did this all the time, and it did not serve me well. This was a bad habit and I knew I had to stop it. As a result, we had already hosted a bunch of visitors we barely knew. However, the conversation flowed that evening, and I felt like we had found our new best friends. The photographer and his wife seemed enthralled. I have since learned that users make you feel like you're the most interesting person in the room and everything you say matters; they know this speaks to the most vulnerable part of your ego. I am embarrassed to say I was not immune.

"Very cool," they both kept saying, as I talked on. They seemed so nice, so cool, and so interested! Then I said those famous words: "Next time you're in Italy let us know." Full disclosure: I have stopped saying those words to strangers over the years. Full of holiday euphoria, we said our goodbyes and headed out the door.

Before summer began, we made a point to become fast friends with this couple. We had lots of dinners and drinks. They arrived the summer after our first meeting in December. Of course I offered to pick them up at the airport. We got them set up in the guestroom. They were not jet lagged since they had stopped and stayed in a friend's flat in Paris, so they were ready to go. For the next ten days, I drove them all over Italy, so many kilometers and so many stops, schlepping them from activity to activity. I have found that with most timid travelers, they expect you to show them everything without a moment's hesitation. Now mind you, not all guests are like this. But the users want ultra schlepping. They want first class service. They are entitled and unapologetic with their demands, like rock stars. Even if they just look like they are with the band.

Over the years I have perfected the art of identifying who the users are, and who are the timid travelers, and who are the seasoned travelers; there are big differences.

- **The seasoned traveler** is the self-sufficient guest who has been abroad many times, comes to visit for only a few days (three or four), is helpful, and most definitely comes with their own car—and never asks you for anything other than your address.
- **The timid traveler** has not traveled abroad much if at all and asks you for everything. They never rent a car because they are too timid to drive. If they drive, then they require lots of instructions involving lots of back and forth. They expect the host to arrange everything.

- **The users** are seasoned travelers who have figured out how to travel by staying with friends and having those friends take them everywhere.

This particular user couple visited us year after year. By the fifth year they felt so comfortable with us that they started telling us where to take them and even how to get there. The straw that broke the camel's back for me was a trip we took to Milan. It takes a solid two and a half hours to get to Alassio from Milan. The husband sat in the passenger seat, the wife was in the back; I, of course, drove.

Truth be told, I hate driving in Milan; in fact, most Italians hate driving in Milan. It's really difficult, with lots of one-way streets, some that are forbidden to drive on, parking restrictions, crazy traffic—you get the picture. So my anxiety levels were high that day. Adding to my high stress was that he was yelling instructions about how to get to the parking garage, and his wife was grumbling in the back seat that she was carsick. I was so frustrated that I pulled over, got out of the car, took a breath and counted to a hundred. It was either that or I was going to pop him in the lip. As you know by now, I am not a violent person, and I have driven in Europe my whole life, so the fact I needed a break gives you a good idea of how awful the drive was. After I counted to one hundred, I got back in the car and somehow—without the help of anyone—managed to make my way to the hotel.

They had invited me to join them in Milan because they had set up a fashion photo shoot. I had helped them find a photo assistant and had driven them there. When it was time for the photo shoot, they were busy working and I wasn't even invited to watch the production! It was clear they considered me their driver and personal tour guide and arranger, but not the stylist. To add insult to injury, I was an unpaid employee. They paid for everything related to the shoot except me and my hotel room.

After this Milanese adventure, my view of these two "friends" changed. When they booked their trip for next year, I said okay, but told them that this time they needed to rent a car. I also limited their time with us to four days rather than their usual ten days. They agreed to this. We had some fun plans lined up, and the best part was that they would be the drivers and Frank and I would be the passengers.

Our first day trip down the coast was to Forte dei Marmi market, quite a few hours away, which meant a 7:00 a.m. departure. While he drove, Frank and I slept in the back. We spent a few hours at the market, then turned around and drove back stopping in Portofino for our usual *aperitivo*, arriving back at the flat around 11:00 p.m. As we were walking into the flat, he said, "Wow, that was exhausting." Realizing he had never even thought of the hardship they had put us through all their previous visits, I smiled to myself and thought, *Yeah, man. And I did that for five years—ten days every visit—without any thanks.* But what I said to him was, "Thank you for driving us."

The truth is that sometimes you wind up in friendships and have no idea why you're there. This couple only saw us ten days in Italy every year. We barely saw them back home, and when we did it was lunch with their parents, with Frank and me as a buffer to whatever family drama was going on. Social media has really impacted how one perceives people, and it took a while to realize that every photo they posted online with their "real" friends never included us. Their posts with friends in the States having "the best time ever" got old, and it showed their true colors.

In the end, one day I woke up and said to myself *enough*. I just ended it; it was that simple. It was a short email, not mean, just explaining that we really had nothing in common. I didn't get much of a response, which we expected. It was a good lesson for me, and I have those two to thank for it.

CHAPTER 13

Lovers and Friends

Although it was wonderful to have lots of friends from the US visit every year, it was very important to establish real friendships in Italy since I spent a lot of time alone. So after five years in Alassio, I turned my attention to making friends in my town. Italy was my love, after all, so it was time to give it a little needed attention in that department.

After we completed the flat, my relationship with Rupert began to fade away. I saw him less and less and once the flat was completed, we saw each other once or twice. I was frankly—and a bit selfishly—freaked out that my rock would be gone. One day he simply said he was not interested in a friendship and that we needed a break. So we took one.

Life without Rupert made me explore my new surroundings, and develop new friends and habits. Making friends in a seaside town can be difficult. It's a transient place and people are only there for a couple of weeks or months.

Rupert had always said, "Annette, you'll have a hard time making any Italian friends and if you do it will take seven years." I didn't understand and this made me mad; after all, what did he know? I had always made friends easily. But he was right, it took me seven years to make my first real Italian girlfriend Monica and she was a doozy.

Our next-door neighbor was a nice Italian housewife from Turin and the mother of two small children. Her husband was always away working, so we found ourselves in the same boat: new house in a new place. Our initial conversations in the hallway were about where to get groceries, the best pizza, and beach clubs. She spoke great English because they had lived in London a few years. I wasn't concerned that she barely spoke to me after our initial conversations, because her little ones kept her super busy; we barely saw each other that summer. Later I would find that people from Turin are very guarded, which means that they are not the friendliest—not like Americans. Northern Italians are more reserved. I hate to group people, but over the years I've found most of these stereotypes to be true. Italians in general keep to themselves and trust no one. They come by it honestly, having been occupied over the years and not being united until 150 years ago.

Over the years we summered at Villa Fiske, I watched their children grow up to be young adults, but we never had more than a cordial "hallway" relationship. For twelve years we just waved and said hello in passing, which is why it struck me as very odd that when I told them we had sold the flat and were moving to the Lunigiana, they were very upset, hugged me, said they would miss me, and seemed genuinely sad. I was taken aback by this reaction. But, again, it's very Italian.

One person that paved the way for me to meet people was Leo. From our work relationship, we formed a lovely friendship. I was like his aunt; he was like my nephew. We would meet for *aperitivo*, and he would introduce me to his friends. The neat thing is that he had friends of all ages, which is a very Italian thing (actually in the EU I have found this to be true in most cases). Age is really just a number in Europe, and not that all important to most. Again, I hate to generalize, but this has been my experience.

We started going out to the local club late at night, which was always super entertaining for the people-watching. It was an interesting cross-section of locals, people of all ages from all walks of life. The club was a heart-pumping, gyrating experience, even more enhanced by loud electronic music and the throngs of people dancing in every corner of the space. There were people dancing on the tables, on the beach, and on the bar.

The club was located in Albenga, which was a town about four miles down the road from Alassio. It had a Moroccan theme, with a tented ceiling and Moroccan furniture strewn about, tons of Moroccan rugs and textiles draped about, and hundreds of Moroccan lanterns hanging from the tented ceiling. During the day it was a beach club, and at night it morphed into a dance club. We always had a private VIP table, because Leo knew everyone in town since he had grown up there. We were popping bottles stuffed in giant ice buckets that were loaded with fireworks that were set on fire as they came to our table—bottles of champagne, vodka, and tons of lemon soda as mixers. It was pretty over the top and appropriately decadent for our rowdy crowd—the perfect late-night summer activity. Leo was my conduit to ingratiating myself to my neighbors in Alassio and he did a great job at it. He probably has no idea how important he was to me in those early days. I am truly forever grateful for his generosity.

Once I had been in Alassio for a couple years, I felt much more comfortable and started making friends on my own (although I would continue to find that befriending non-Italians was much easier). I met one such friend at our beach club. One mid-summer day I was approached by a cute little blonde girl about eight years old, who asked if I was an American. She spoke perfect English, so I was intrigued about how she got here; how had she landed on this perfectly Italian beach? We rarely saw other Americans.

Following behind this beautiful child was her beautiful mother. "Hello," she said in what sounded like a British accent, so I was a little confused. "Are you American?"

"Yes I am—and you?" I said.

"Norwegian, but we live in Switzerland, and my husband is from England. I am Inga."

"Ah, that explains my confusion. Since your daughter speaks with an American accent, I was not sure."

"Her English teacher at school is from America; that's why she speaks English like she does. This is Flossy, and my other daughter is Stella." Stella looked to be around four years old. She had very white blonde hair and was tanned and really pretty.

"They are lovely girls!" I said. "I'm Annette and I live in Alassio in the summer. Are you here visiting?"

Inga shook her head and smiled, "I have been coming to this beach club since I was her age. Actually, I got married here; met my husband right here on the sand."

From that day forward, we spent every day at the beach club together. Inga's parents had been members for thirty years. It is through them I met the Norwegian beach club owners—hard to imagine non-Italians owning a Riviera Beach Club! Beach clubs are usually owned by Italian families, so here they were an anomaly of the Italian Riviera. It explained why there were lots of Swedes and Norwegians at the club.

That summer Inga and her family and I had dinners and *aperitivi* quite frequently. They were all friendly and very inclusive. Since Inga was on her own with the kids, she loved planning all sorts of shopping trips, and loved clubbing when she had the chance with all of us at the Moroccan dance club. Later that summer I finally met her husband, Stan, who was a rather subdued Englishman—exactly what I had envisioned. He was very entertaining in a pulled back sort of way, and was great with his girls. A nice guy all around.

Speaking of marriage, one thing I had noticed over the years at the beach club is that all the women/moms were on their own at the beach during the week, and most of the weekends they were on their own, too. Their husbands worked in the city (mostly Milan) the entire summer and only came to spend time with their families about once or twice during the summer months. When Frank and I first visited the Italian beaches with our small children, this was not as noticeable. Living there all summer, it was a phenomenon that became evident to me, and it was mainly mothers with teenage children. Most of the ladies with toddlers and babies had their hubbies by their side. It took a while to clue in to what the story was, and poking around led me to this conclusion: the husbands were "working" in Milan. But the truth is that Italian men have mistresses, and the perfect time to gallivant around (another) town with their mistresses was during the summer months when the family was enjoying a vacation at the beach. The Italians all knew and no one seemed to care. It had been this way for generations, I was told. It was as deeply ingrained in the fabric of Italian family life as the tomato sauce recipe that your *nonna* makes. I wasn't shocked or surprised, I was just mystified that everyone just accepted it and never complained. Every year I ran into the same women, gossiping and buying beach coverups from the same African lady from their reserved beach loungers. Every year I watched the children get older. Every year I said hello, smiled, and wondered when their husbands would make the obligatory beach weekend appearance. These summer ladies were impeccably dressed, beautiful, tanned, and fashionable—well-kept, as they say—and alone. Many had grown up at the same beach clubs from babies to teens to sexy young women…to mothers. Just waiting to be a devoted *nonna* to their beloved grandchildren.

That's the thing about Italian families: they are very provincial, they always vacation the same place every year. Same beach club, same people, same food, over and over again, year after year—which I find fascinating. They will venture out for a week or two to a foreign country, one week in the summer and one week in the winter. But it's always summer at the beach club, and winter at the chalet in the mountains. There always seems to be a family house in the mountains. This is a fact: Italians have loads of houses. Family houses that they never tell you about, ever. Unlike Americans that tell everyone everything…you will never hear an Italian tell you about their house in the mountains, at the beach, or in the city or the countryside. They may have houses in all these locations. No matter what the economic situation, they have loads of houses. It's an insider secret and now you know.

Three true facts I learned during my summers in Italy are that Italians don't make new friends, Italians have lots of homes, and Italian men take lovers. I guess in a way, I did have a deep understanding. After all, Italy had been my summer lover for so many years.

CHAPTER 14

The Seven-Year Itch

e'd been at our flat on the sea for about seven years. Just as Rupert had predicted, we had made very few friends. Although people were friendly, they never quite got to the point of inviting us over for dinner. For example, we had become quite friendly with our upstairs neighbor, the developers of our complex who lived in the penthouse. I had been to their home for the occasional *aperitivo*, or casual supper but mostly with their young daughter, Carla, who would eat out with me, and I occasionally partied with her group. The truth is that her mother and father were more my age, but they seemed hardly interested in striking up a friendship with an American. They were always warm and friendly—to an extent—but never made any move toward a friendship. Carla was sweet and warm and funny and lots of fun. She spoke perfect English, and I kind of think she was friendly in order to practice her English with me. She even came to the US once to visit us for ten days. I treated her like a daughter and she had a great time in the US shopping, although the food was not to her liking. One day my assistant and I took her to one of our favorite Mexican restaurants and she hated it, hated everything. We were truly perplexed by this. But the Milanese eat very bland food, with no garlic or onion (which they consider beneath them and only for the southern Italians—no. I am not making this up). So I chalked everything to the fact that she was from Milan.

It was very funny to watch her try American-style food; when she hated it she would make a face and say in her Italian accent, "I don't like." It actually became a thing in our family to say "I don't like." For some reason Italians leave off the "it," but I never corrected her because I thought she was so cute.

Carla and I were friends for years, but one thing that became a huge milestone in our friendship was when she invited me to her beach club. It was in the chic part of our town, very exclusive, with club members that had been going there for generations. It was a big deal. When she invited me I felt so special, and thought perhaps I had finally broken that Italian friendship barrier. But when I got there I realized she had only invited me for lunch, and there was no lounger available for me on the sand. I had been invited for one hour and then she said goodbye. I was not sure how I felt about that. It was a bit of a punch in the gut, but not as bad as it would have been four years before, because I had come to understand how Italians view outsiders and friendships. I regarded it as progress. Even though she had stayed at my house in the US for ten days, this was all she could offer. It was most definitely a cultural difference I understood…for the most part.

Leo was always my real friend. He included me in everything. Probably because his mother was British and his father was Italian, and he understood what it was like to be an outsider. He was so kind and I really did regard him as one of my kids after seven years of friendship.

The seventh year after we met him, Leo started a new job working for a very well-known designer on the Italian Riviera. New jobs in Italy are hard to come by, but he was recommended by a vendor that knew about the job opening and thought Leo would be perfect. I learned that Italian law says employers cannot fire employees that have signed a contract. The employee can leave, but the employer cannot fire anyone once they are hired. This is why so many people there work for the same employer all their life, or work in the family business. That's why getting this new job was huge for Leo. The new employer had to really make sure that Leo was the right fit, and Leo had to make sure she really was the employer he wanted to commit to. It's a whole different decision-making process than it is in the US.

Monica Damonte was a force of nature. She owned a home furnishings store by the name of Odulia and was an interior designer. I had shopped at her store quite a bit and I loved her taste. But in all the years living in Alassio I had never met her. Monica was very connected, according to Leo. He said she knew everyone and worked all over the EU, not only in Italy. She was very chic, a jetsetter with all the right friends and all the important clients. She sounded amazing.

I had to take everything Leo said about Monica with a grain of salt, however, as Italians are known for being extremely good at marketing themselves. Having a habit of using words like…"most important person in Italy"—or in town, or in the region—you get the picture. The best example is when my Italian friends introduce me they say that I am "very famous in in America." Which is totally untrue. I used to correct them, but after a while I stopped when I realized this is how they introduce people they admire. I now find it quite charming. The idea in Italy is "fake it until you make it," a marketing tool that is quite successful. Good for them for figuring that out. Love the confidence. Needless to say, Leo got the job with Monica, and I was really excited to meet her.

Monica and I met for the first time in Milan in April, during the furniture show at the Salon del Mobile Milano. I went with my friend Kelly, an architectural designer from Austin, Texas, who was shopping for a giant project she was working on. She asked if I wanted to tag along, and of course I said yes. Leo and his new boss, Monica, would be at the show, and Leo thought it would be great timing for Monica and I to finally meet. He described her as a larger than life character, full of energy, and unbelievably talented. I had all sorts of wild expectations, and when I finally met Monica, she did not disappoint. She reminded me of one of my favorite characters, Edina Monsoon, the outrageous London-based interior designer from *Absolutely Fabulous*. The sort of person that is not necessarily lovable, but endlessly fascinating. Usually not my type of girlfriend, but I was open to something new.

We all planned to meet for lunch at the convention center. Mind you, this trade show is enormous, miles and miles long, and very confusing. Kelly and I arrived early and headed to our appointments. I started texting Leo, "We are here. Where shall we meet and what time?" I received nothing. I waited another hour and texted again. Beep. A text from Leo said, "No idea what time. Monica will not give me an answer...be back soon." It was around 11:30 a.m., so there was plenty of time to set a place and a time.

My friend and I continued on with our appointments where we were treated like VIPs. Since her project was a 50,000-square-foot house for a billionaire, we were literally treated like royalty. Everywhere we went we were hauled up stairs, into the back room for coffee, pastries, lunch, champagne, anything we desired. It was quite fancy and we were loving it. Finally the text arrived from Leo saying where and what time to meet. I must admit, I was very excited to meet Monica after all the build-up from Leo.

We met at what appeared to be a food court in the middle of the convention center. Picture a big outdoor walkway in the middle of two gigantic buildings. We met them in the foyer of the restaurant, and it was probably the worst meeting place ever. It was filled to the max with people and so loud you couldn't hear anything over the blasting music and a thousand people in a spaceship-sized cafeteria. It was pure chaos and impossible to find a table, much less food or drinks. The only way to sit would be to join another table of twenty, which we did. We somehow braved the crowd to choose and pay for our food—for me, a very sad-looking Caprese salad and a sparkling water. We elbowed our way to a table, squeezing our way in with coats, computer bags, handbags...and finally we sat down. Then we said hello. She was dressed in all black, carrying the biggest Hermes bag one could buy. She had perfectly cut curly locks that fell all over the place but still managed to look totally chic in a way only Italian women can pull off. She wore large round sunglasses, even though we were indoors. She talked nonstop in her broken English peppered with lots of Italian about the things she had seen, and what we needed to see. I could not follow a single word of her quick staccato sentences over the loud drone of the crowded dining room. I just nodded my head up and down at every word she spoke and drank my water and ate what I could of my mediocre lunch.

Monica talked and talked all through lunch. She stopped abruptly and stood up and walked out the door. We all grabbed our things and barreled through the throngs to follow her outside. She casually lit a cigarette, offered me one, and then told us we were going to all the most important and exclusive vendor parties that night as her guests. Stops would include Hermes and all the other most important vendors in Milan. We would all meet at the Armani hotel for *aperitivo* at 7:00, and we would go from there. Mind you, most of this was in Italian. At the time my Italian was, well, really bad. So I barely understood a word other than "party" and "Hermes." But Leo was our translator, so I got most of the information afterward. Kelly and I were so excited. We would be partying like rock stars, according to our new friend.

When seven o'clock rolled around, we were seated in the spectacular bar of the Armani Hotel overlooking the roof tops of Milan. With a fancy cocktail in hand, we were feeling quite excited. Monica blazed into the bar as if her hair was on fire, her daughter Vicki (who was studying interior design at the art school in Milan) trailing behind her. She was a beautiful young lady around twenty years old, with the same good looks as her mother—long dark hair, sunglasses although it was not sunny outside, carrying a giant Chanel bag. But no Leo. I said, "*Ciao, dov'é* Leo?"

"Leo is not coming," she said. "He is on the way back to Alassio. We have much work there." *Oh, oh!* I thought to myself. *How the hell are we going to communicate?* "*Ciao*," said her daughter Vicki, "So nice to finally meet you." There you go, I thought, Vicki speaks perfect English.

I breathed a sigh of relief. We were all going to be able to chat after all. Vicki was a wonderful translator as we talked and drank and nibbled and laughed for about an hour, and then it was off to the first showroom party. The showroom was in walking distance, so we all headed down the street like ducklings behind our fearless leader, Monica. Her couture outfit bellowed behind her, and she looked the true diva—the first real diva I had ever met! She was an intergalactic planet and I was in her gravitational pull. We all were. And I loved her for it.

The first showroom was rather boring, but she said we had to make an appearance. "Don't worry, we will go to much better places," she reassured me. Her English cracked me up; like her Italian, her English was gunfire-quick, but with lots of misfires. I could not help but smile.

"This showrooms is horrible," she announced rather loudly. "We go." We all followed her to a parking deck and piled into her daughter's Fiat 500. Now the Fiat 500, called a *Cinque Cento*, is quite small; it's a miniscule two-door capsule of a car. Kelly and I looked at each other and had the same thought: How many people could we cram into a *Cinque Cento*? Kelly piled into the back with Vicki, and Monica would drive with me sitting shotgun. We pulled out of the parking lot at light speed. It was not surprising that Monica drove like she did everything else—fast and furious, while smoking a cigarette, continually shifting, and talking non-stop. Vicki directed her mother how to get to the next party. Of course, as soon as we pulled out of the parking deck, it started pouring rain. At a roundabout, Monica was screaming at Vicki and Vicki was screaming back at Monica, while smoking and sliding around the traffic at ninety miles an hour in the rain. It was like being in a Fellini movie, and I knew we were going to die. I looked back at Kelly who gave me this look that basically said "What the hell have you gotten me into?" That look made me start laughing. The what-the-hell kind of laughter one has when faced with something so insane that the only way to deal with it is hysteria.

After getting lost several times—and after lots more yelling and smoking—we made it to our destination. Monica parked the car in the middle of the street. Not exaggerating, it was the middle of a street. We had unsuccessfully looked for a parking space for about an hour, and I think Monica just could not take it and just stopped the car. The streets were quiet—it was about 10:30 at night—so she felt confident this parking spot was a good choice. As she walked briskly into the showroom, she laughed and said "I park like I am from Napoli." This is the moment I thought, "This lady is funny and fun—and crazy!"

As we entered the Baxter furniture showroom in the outskirts of Milan, everyone was all crammed into the first floor dancing, talking, laughing loudly, and jumping up and down. Kelly smiled at me, and at that moment one of the guys dancing nearby grabbed her and danced her into the middle of the crowd. All I could see was her face with the "What did you get me into" look. Then she was swallowed by the dancing crush of revelers. Monica set out to find the bar, and we wound our way down the staircase in the middle of the showroom to the ground floor of the building. The showroom was full of gorgeous rooms perfectly furnished. We agreed on that as we grabbed a drink. Monica started a deep conversation with someone at the bar which gave me the chance to retrace our steps to go to find Kelly. She probably needed a drink. I found her desperately trying to remove herself from the whirling dervish that had pulled her on to the dance floor; I could tell by the look on her face that she needed rescuing. We wound our way back to the bar, where Kelly ordered a stiff drink. "What the hell?" she laughed. "This has been beyond crazy! Monica is a kook."

I said, "I kind of love that about her. I'm starving; let's find the food."

We headed to what looked like a food table, and stood there stuffing our faces and observing the bedlam that was all around us. After about an hour Monica and Vicki reappeared.

"You had fun?" Vicki asked. "Oh yes lots." I said. "And you, Kelly? Dancing fun, yes?" said Monica. "Oh yes!" replied Kelly, so convincingly even I believed her. Vicki was hungry and wanted to go eat. We had just eaten a lot off the buffet table, but we were along for the ride, so why not? It was 11:30 and I asked, "Is anything open?"

"Of course," chimed in Monica, "it is Milano, a big city, everything is open, let's go."

And like that, we were back in the 500 that sat in the same spot in the middle of the street—no ticket, nothing. Monica lit a cigarette and again proceeded to shift and talk and smoke while getting directions from Vicki from the back seat. I would have been fine going back to the hotel, but Monica insisted that she was taking us to the best restaurant in Milano. One thing I learned that night is that she was not someone you said no to, not ever. With that in mind, I released myself to the universe and was open to anything.

Monica instructed Vicki to call the restaurant to let them know we were on our way. "Tell them we are with Dolce and Gabbana, and will be arriving in ten minutes."

Vicki said she would do no such thing, "Are you crazy? They will know we are not with Dolce and Gabbana. No way I am saying that."

"Say it say it say it!" Monica yelled. I was sitting beside Monica and laughing so hard I was crying. Monica said to me, "I know Dolce and Gabbana, it is their favorite place." This was so outrageous and she had such commitment to her crazy plan that I knew we had to be friends. She had the best fake-it-til-you-make-it attitude of anyone I had ever met, and I had to love her chutzpah even though she was clearly over the top at all times.

The night ended after three failed attempts to get a reservation under the Dolce and Gabbana name—which still to this day cracks me up. We parked and ducked into a classic *trattoria*, and I had the best risotto I can remember ever eating. There was no one in the place except us, and we were all pretty worn out. But what a night. What a first encounter with the infamous Monica Damonte!

CHAPTER 15

Adventures with Monica

onica was having us to her house for a big party of a group of friends. Nothing special and very casual, she said. Leo and his girlfriend would be there, so that was good, since I was not sure how much Italian would be spoken. The party was on a Tuesday, midweek, but since it was May, the season had not begun and everyone was still in the lull before the summer rush. Alassio was a seasonal town, so in the winter and spring it was rather sleepy and those were great times to gather friends. Frank was in town then, so we were both thrilled to have an invitation to someone's home. It was like pulling the golden ticket, and we were excited.

Monica's home was in a tiny village about twenty minutes from Alassio's city center. It was at the end of a short road off the main road and very easy to find. We pulled down the drive and parked near a beautifully handmade iron gate. I was a bit nervous since I did not know many people, plus Leo had texted me as we were driving up that he was unable to make it. So we were on our own. I am a brave person, unaffected by fear in social environments. But that night, I must admit, I felt a little out of my element. Frank and I walked through the gate into a breathtakingly beautiful garden enclosed by a stone fence and with a river running along one side. A small seating area was set up near the river, with a wrap-around banquette made of stone, layered with monogrammed terracotta-colored cushions. There was an incredible round stone table and stone chairs resembling toadstools. It was all quite welcoming and chic. As we headed on through the garden, we spotted an enormous olive tree shading a small pool. We rounded a corner and walked down steps to a large dining area, completely furnished as an outdoor living space. A built-in banquette with navy blue cushions, trimmed in white cord, was loaded with pillows. Adirondack chairs faced the banquette, and nearby was a large dining table with seating for twelve people.

We hadn't seen a front door, but we spotted a door on this level that led in to the kitchen. The house was filled with people. Monica spotted us and ran to give us a kiss on both cheeks. "*Brava*, Annette," she exclaimed, "You come to my party. I am so happy." Her English was much cuter than my Italian, I imagined. "Come, come, *vai, vai*, we have a drink and some food, you eat, yes?" Monica said. We walked into a living space filled to the brim with people, some of whom I recognized, some of whom I did not. Right away I spied the fancy hairdresser from town, Gianni di Muro—he was someone I wanted to meet as he was a most fashionable person. His salon was known throughout Italy, and, to be honest I was a bit intimidated to go into it. I was so excited to finally have a chance to make his acquaintance.

Of course he spoke no English. As we were introduced, Monica translated that he had wanted to meet me and was hoping that I would come to the salon, but I never did.

"Oh, I definitely want to come see you. I will!" He nodded his head and said in Italian "*Prossima settimana* [next week]?" "Oh sure. Sure," I said, "*certo, certo*." Monica went on to tell me that he was "the best, very famous, and amazing." I would find that this was a reoccurring review of most people she introduced me to, and of most places we visited. I loved her enthusiasm and devotion to her crowd. I soon became someone she introduced to everyone as "very famous, and the best." Which I loved.

The house itself was a beautifully renovated old mill that Monica did her design number on. Everything was custom and lovingly done—from the arched doorways to the incredible domed ceiling in the entry which also served as a dining room. The bathrooms were modern and flawless, and her master bedroom had a rain shower that poured into a gigantic stone bathtub that had once been a vessel used in the original mill. It was perfection and I decided that Monica was a design genius! Not only was the house a dream, but the food was gorgeous. I had never seen a bigger charcuterie board in my life—it was a series of three large boards, about thirty inches by thirty inches each, laid out on a giant ottoman that served as a coffee table in the living room. It was loaded with every type of cheese, meat, *crostini,* and roasted vegetables, crackers, breads, spreads, fruit, and twelve kinds of olives. Frank's eyes got very big when he saw it. "Wow. It's like a giant raft of meat and cheese." We both laughed and dug in.

We had a great time; even with the language barrier, we managed to have fun. There were plenty of people to watch, and things to see, and certainly plenty to eat and drink, loud music and lots of laughter. We stayed very late—so late that the party turned into a dance party, with people even dancing in the kitchen. We didn't want to leave. Finally, around one in the morning, we headed home. When Frank and I got into the car, we both had a smile on our faces and the exact same thought: *We made it. We are in!!! We have real Italian friends.* Frank and I had waited so many years to be part of it all. Finally we could say that we were.

After that night, my friendship with Monica was solid. She called me every morning, and invited me for *aperitivo* at least twice a week. I stopped by the store once a week and we would duck out for a quick lunch—pizza, a sandwich, or sometimes a hamburger, her favorite. There's a saying I learned: In Italy, you're mostly out, but when you're in you can't get out. Plainly said, Italians are very co-dependent. Not in a bad way. It is a behavior I grew to love. The idea that a person has to have you by their side is very flattering. Monica was great for the ego, not only because she was the perfect partner in crime, but also because she was my number one supporter. Monica was the tonic I needed.

In the first years after meeting Monica, there was never a dull moment. She would take me on endless adventures, showing me things in our area I would not have otherwise seen. She was the keeper and the sharer of many secrets. She came up with harebrained schemes. One year she decided she wanted to buy another house, one closer in Alassio so her kids could walk into town in the evening. She would plot and dream up the most insane scenarios of how to buy a property she wanted.

As you know by now, buying property in Italy is a challenge. One night she decided we should all buy an abandoned castle nearby. One of my girlfriends, Sharon, was visiting from the US. We were having dinner, and Monica started telling us about a castle up the road. "We should buy it and have grand parties and weddings there," she said. My girlfriend was a party planner, and I surmised that Monica came up with this plan on the fly as she listened to Sharon talk about weddings she planned and the parties she created. Sharon, who's a little kooky, was all in on the idea and swore she wanted to move to Italy. I rolled my eyes and kept my mouth shut because it was fun to see these two nuts interact. So I went along, nodding my head and smiling. We wrapped up dinner early and hopped in Monica's very fancy, very large SUV and headed up the hill to this supposed castle.

Now, when in Italy and given an offer to see a castle, my advice is to always say yes. I promise you it will be a highlight event. Monica drove us up the mountain in the pitch dark at breakneck speed. It got to be a bumpy ride and I got a little worried, but I trusted Monica and was anxious to see what she was so excited to show us. After about ten minutes driving straight up a steep hill, we arrived at a small village with a lovely little chapel brightly lit by the government-issued utility lighting. It seems that all churches have this horrible harsh lighting—a not-very-pretty utility lamp mounted on the side of a wall with a 1000-watt bulb illuminating the façade. Not a great effect. But it did make for a spooky atmosphere. Further up the hill we found the castle and got out of the car to scout the private driveway leading to the front of the building.

I said to Monica, "I think it's too narrow to drive up there with your big car."

"No, it's okay," she said without hesitation in her heavy accent. "*Si si*, get in the car," she said. I managed to take a few photos of the pretty little chapel, as I headed to the car, thinking that these might be the last photos I ever take in my life. I crossed myself (even though I'm Jewish it can't hurt, right?). Monica headed up the hill with Sharon and me holding on for dear life, branches and brush cracking and scraping against the truck as we bolted up the narrow pass.

"Slow down!!" I finally shouted.

"We are here," Monica stated, and she put the emergency brake on and shut off the motor. What we saw in front of us was like something out of a horror film—a medieval gate with spikes on top. Behind the gate we could make out the outline of a giant building that appeared to be teetering on the edge of a great mountainside. The "castle," as Monica referred to it, was nothing but a shell of what it once was. If it were human it would have been screaming for mercy. It was certainly not something I would want to buy. Monica started to laugh, I started to laugh, Sharon started to laugh, and as we looked up at the collapsing structure and back down the mountain, we all had the same thought. We realized that we had nowhere to turn the car around. We had come up the narrow drive so quickly that we were more fearful of dying than worrying about how to get back down.

"Monica," I said as seriously as I could, having just laughed my ass off for ten minutes, and just about peeing my pants. "Monica," I repeated, using my serious and deeper voice, "How are we going to turn around?" It was obvious to me that the castle drive was built to enter the gate, where one would have ample room to turn around and come out. *Shit, shit, shit*, I thought. It was about a two-mile walk to the bottom of the drive, into the little village we had come from. The woods were probably full of wild boars and who knew what other critters, including undesirable people lurking about. The people part probably was not true, but my imagination was running wild.

"Oh God," said Sharon in her Philly accent, punctuated by a long pause and then another, "oh God."

Monica jumped back in the car and turned on the headlights to see better what our options might be. "*Cazzo Cazzo (fuck fuck),*" she groaned. "This is a mess," she said in Italian. I understood it all, unfortunately. Ultimately, Monica told us to get in the car and she proceeded to back down the narrow driveway, dense brush on one side and a hundred-foot drop on the other. I closed my eyes and said a little prayer, and, for what seemed like the longest time, we rolled down the hill and finally arrived at the bottom of the drive. I must say I was relieved and impressed.

Smiling, she headed down the road to the main drag. We passed by a handful of villagers chatting on the street corner and Monica stopped the truck to talk to them. Sharon and I looked at each other, puzzled. We both got out of the car and walked over to the corner, only to hear her ask, "Who owns that castle?" One of the men said, "It is owned by an old family from Milano, and they never come to the castle. It has been in the family forever. They want to sell it. Do you want to buy it?"

"Yes, yes I want to buy it. Who are they?" asked Monica.

The man looked surprised at Monica's response and shrugged his shoulders. "I don't know their name," he said. "Yes, you do," responded Monica. The man smiled and shook his head. "Here is my phone number; I will call him and if he lets me I will tell you his name and give you his number." Then he wrote his name and number on a small piece of paper with a pencil he had in his pocket and handed it to Monica. "*Buonanotte,*" he said.

This is how it starts, business in Italy. We said goodnight and headed back to the car.

"Are we buying it?" I asked. Monica laughed and said, "I don't know." "We should buy it!" Sharon chimed in. " I want to live in Italy." We never spoke of the castle again, but this would be the start of many nighttime adventures with my new partner in crime, the *very famous and very talented* Monica Damonte.

CHAPTER 16

Parties in Penthouses

I really felt a part of Italian life with Monica as my friend. She invited me to her home for dinner about once a week, where I met her other daughter Genevra, "Genny" as they called her, a teenager with more angst than any teen I had ever met. She was flat out grumpy 24/7.

When I first me Genny, I said "*piacere*" (nice to meet you), but she just stared at me. I asked if she spoke English...more staring. So I said, "Okay, that's enough of the niceties," and I walked away. Genny was the brooding sister, and the younger of Monica's two daughters, Vicki being the older and the more social one. Genny was almost a decade younger than Vicki and had a different dad. Monica had been married twice, and divorced twice, from what I could surmise. She never talked about the dads, or husbands, much—not in the time I knew her. She did share her house with husband number two, Nino, and they had an interesting relationship.

The thing that I find interesting about Italians is their style of communication. Everything is on a need-to-know basis. The phrase "time will tell" was invented here. Italy is very much like an onion—so many layers that it truly takes years to feel like you know anything about the country or even about your Italian best friend.

Monica was quick to tell everyone that you were A) Very famous or B) Very talented or C) Simply the best or D) all of the above; but she never mentioned why you were famous, or what you were the best at. This is Italian. Here in the US we might introduce someone like this: "This is my friend Monica, she is a very talented interior designer in Italy and also owns two home furnishing stores—one on the Italian Riviera and one in Saint-Tropez." Very specific, right? Same introduction in Italy goes like this: "This is my friend Annette, she is very talented and super famous in America." That's it. An Italian will leave it at that. They never, ever, introduce someone by explaining what you do for a living. It took me ages to get used to this.

Italians do not talk business in a social setting, but they will always talk socially in a business setting. Introducing someone by naming their profession will get you some strange looks; believe me, I have experiences that make me recoil with embarrassment, having violated an unwritten code.

So the idea that Monica would divulge her innermost secrets to me after just meeting was absurd. She barely shared she had another daughter after we'd known each other for a few months. Later, I had a much better grasp of the family dynamics, but it took about two years. I met Genny's father a year after meeting Genny. Monica never spoke of him so I knew not to ask. The rule I have hit upon is don't ask, just wait to be told; in my fifteen years in Italy this philosophy has served me well. I am sure there are folks who would challenge this—expats who have had a very different experience—but I think most would agree that it's best to listen and not ask too many questions, especially about family dynamics and exes and business.

One evening, Monica and I were going to a dinner party down the coast. The plan was we would meet at her store and drive together to the party. We met at around 7:00 and headed to her house for her to change into her little black dress. As she headed inside, I made my way to the banquette near the river to wait. I heard the sound of water, and realized it was not the river—it was the sound of water gushing from a hose at the end of the garden. I just figured it was the gardener watering and did not give it a second thought. All of a sudden I saw Monica running outside and yelling a name, "NINO, NINO, *NUDO!*" and then some words I did not understand—all sounding very urgent. I jumped up and followed the half-dressed Monica, only to round the corner upon a man an older man, maybe around seventy, nude and watering the plants. He turned around slowly, unconcernedly, with a lit cigarette hanging on the end of his grinning lips.

"*C I A O*," he said slowly. "*Come stai?* Who is this?"

"Oh, Nino, you are crazy and nude" said Monica. "This is Annette."

"Oh, *piacere*," he said. I managed to eek out a quiet "*Piacere*." I was so surprised with this nude man standing in front of me, I honestly can't remember what I said. Monica quickly ordered him up the stairs at the rear of the house. Nino dropped the hose, turned off the spigot, and casually headed up the stairs, nude as the day he was born. Monica turned to me and said, "That is Nino. Genny's papa. He lives in the apartment upstairs."

"Funny guy" was all I could manage. We both broke out laughing.

"Nino *nudo*," she muttered, laughing and shaking her head. "Come. We will be late." I zipped her dress as we walked quickly out the gate, jumped into her car, and headed down the coast. That's how I met Nino, Monica's second husband. Monica went on to explain to me in the car that Nino was once a very rich and important man. He had a huge construction company in Monaco. How he lost his fortune and came to live in the apartment above her house were not mentioned. This was many of the family secrets my friend would keep. Very Italian.

Over the summer, Monica and I had many dinners together and I got to know lots of her friends. One special friend, Carlo, was a dentist—he was something between a boyfriend, a companion, and a self-proclaimed business advisor, though his advice was never very welcomed by Monica. I was a little unsure if he actually worked since he would mostly go to cosmetic dental conferences all over the world when he wasn't hanging out at Monica's store, annoying my friend Leo.

Carlo was definitely an interesting character; he spoke perfect English, was a bit of a charmer and a great cook and, of course, had very nice teeth. He won me over the night he made a delicious plate of saffron risotto—a Milanese specialty—in Monica's kitchen. Food has always been a surefire way to my heart. When he wasn't hanging around Monica, he lived in Bergamo. He was considered stylish, but I thought he tried too hard to dress hip. He wore a lot of ascots and designer sunglasses inside the house. He took loads of selfies of his "jet set" life and posted them on Facebook; he was what Italians call a "dude." I found this to be both endearing and entertaining. One thing that really amused me to no end was that he had loads of opinions about Americans. He was particularly interested in racism in America, a subject he brought up time and time again—a subject I did not want to touch with a tenfoot pole at a dinner party. Funny that Italians will not talk about their personal life or work with you, but they will talk about weighty subjects like racism, politics, and religion at social gatherings like dinners. It's the total opposite of Americans. It was a bit upside down from my perspective, the subjects that were socially correct and those that were not in Italy. For a long time this made me gun-shy about what was considered appropriate conversation at the dinner table. I tended to listen more than talk in Italian company.

Carlo loved baiting me at the dinner table, but I always smiled at him and said "I don't know" (*non lo so*). He was a bit of a troublemaker, and maybe that's why Monica was attracted to him. I mostly think she liked having someone on her arm at special occasions, like fancy charity events in Monaco. They first met through mutual friends at just such an event in Monaco—an eccentric pair that touted themselves as part of the jet set on both the French and Italian Rivieras.

I met the eccentric couple that introduced Monica and Carlo at Monica's store one summer afternoon. I had stopped by to grab an espresso with her, as we often did. When I walked in, Monica was having a serious discussion with what looked like a ship's admiral and a supermodel. He was a big man and wore enormous Gucci sunglasses and a white suit with epaulets, and had thick black hair and dark tanned skin. The model towered over him—she was very beautiful and thin, with light brown skin and her hair tightly pulled into a ponytail. She dressed impeccably in a floral sundress, Prada sandals, and a bright pink Birkin bag the size of a small Italian car. She wore Gucci sunglasses, too. They were like something out of a movie. He had an ominous aura I could only describe as creepy. Monica introduced us with the usual fanfare, glossing over the important information, like who these people were. I smiled and nodded and shook hands with both of them. The supermodel turned to me and said, "We've heard so much about you."

"You have?" I responded. I wanted to say, *I have not heard one word about you*, but of course I kept my thoughts to myself. The admiral said nothing, just stared at me silently—which creeped me out even more. Perhaps he was a diplomat or ambassador or something official like that? He was wearing epaulets, for God's sake!

I hung around and chatted with the supermodel wife long enough to find out that they had a summer place in town, they had two sons, and were all international jet setters, with one son dating a middle eastern prince's daughter. When I felt I'd learned enough, I said my goodbyes and headed out the door, wondering when I would run into these two again, and why was Monica so impressed with them?

The invitation arrived the next week, through a text. I guessed Monica had given them my number. I accepted their invitation to dinner in their home by the sea because Monica begged me to come. "They are wonderful people," she said. "You will love them. So nice." I was skeptical and curious at the same time, so, what the heck.

Dinner was at seven in the evening. I got directions from Leo; Monica was so scattered that there was no way she would give me the right instructions. I soon learned that Leo did everything for her and she was very scattered most of the time. I had never had a friend like this, but she was entertaining most of the time so I put up with it.

They lived in a penthouse overlooking the Ligurian sea. I arrived and headed up an elevator that opened onto the top floor. The door to the flat was wide open, so I made my way in. My first impression was that the décor was excessive. There were huge pieces of hand-carved French furniture, and everything was painted with gold leaf or was over-stuffed or marble. There were about a thousand candlesticks lit all over. A petite woman dressed in uniform who was clearly part of the staff asked if she could take my wrap, and pointed me to the narrow terrace with the sea view for *aperitivo*. I headed to the balcony, taking in the millions of vases, picture frames, candles, and tchotchkes along the route. It was hardly a terrace—merely a sliver of a balcony with way too much furniture on it. I reached over an armchair in my path and said hellos, kissed and shook hands, and was promptly handed a drink by the uniform lady who appeared out of nowhere.

"Hello and welcome," the supermodel greeted me in perfect English, because she was originally from New York. "So happy you could make it." She was wearing a floaty silk caftan, hand painted in bright flowers; it was simply perfection. Her skin was sun-kissed and aglow, her makeup flawlessly applied, and her hair styled in loose ringlets that fell all around her face. She was really beautiful. Months later I found out her full story. The story goes, she had met the diplomat (as the admiral turned out to be) in New York when she was a young up-and-coming model, and she was swept away by his charms. She dropped everything to be with him, they married, and the rest, as they say, was history. I looked up at her and I smiled and said, "Hello." I was still trying to get my eyes focused; there was a lot to take in. The oddness of it all, this gorgeous woman living in this penthouse with this troll of a man dressed like a cartoon sea captain…it is as if I landed on some weird reality show and was surrounded by the strangest group of people I had ever met. My only comfort was that Monica was standing right next to me, smiling and smoking a cigarette. We did small talk while the staff readied our dinner in the miniscule kitchen.

I will never forget the first course. It was probably one of the most disgusting things I had ever put in my mouth. It was supposed to be grouper carpaccio, but it was room temperature and the consistency of dried Elmer's glue. I could not choke it down, so I very stealthily spit it into my napkin and put my fork down. *This is going to be a long night*, I thought, and I was right. I managed to endure the most absurd conversation with the diplomat who shared he had "Jewish blood"—and that's a direct quote. Obviously this was an effort to bond with me, since Monica must have told them I was Jewish. Sharing this must have been an attempt to connect with me, but for me it had the opposite effect. I could hardly wait to get out of this Riviera version of the cult movie *Blue Velvet*. I was miscast in this scenario. As the night was ending, I rose from the table and headed straight to the door. I said "thank you" and "goodbye" and bolted towards to the stairs, not even waiting for the elevator. I was out of there as fast as my feet could carry me. Monica followed my lead and we were both standing on the boardwalk below their terrace in no time. As we walked to the car, all I could politely muster was, "Interesting night." Monica smiled and said, "I will tell you all about them sometime." But for now I was calmed by the fact I would be in my bed in about ten minutes and this would all be a distant memory in no time.

Over the summer months, I loved having everyone to our place. I would arrange *aperitvi* and we would sit by the large window in the kitchen to look out at the sea. I loved cooking for people and entertaining Riviera style. Leo and Elisabeth would bring pizzas after work and we would all drink and talk into the night. Sometimes Monica would stop over for a drink; it was all lovely. We laughed a lot, and our friendships grew. It was a great time in my Italian life.

When I returned the following year, Leo said to me, "Annette, I think you should make an American dinner for all of us. What do you think?"

"I think that is a great idea!! What shall I make?"

"Whatever you make is great, as long as we have margaritas," Leo said.

"Done and done," I said. I had to think about the menu for a minute. American food? I could not make BBQ or fried Oreos; maybe apple pie, could I? So I made a plan to do Mexican. Most of the ingredients were available in Italian grocery stores. *Everyone likes Mexican*, I thought, so it made perfect sense to go with a Cinco de Mayo theme. I built the menu around the cocktails, a perfect plan. Or so I thought.

The evening of the dinner everyone arrived at eight o'clock. I had prepared margaritas, fajitas, and guacamole, salsa, and chips. I had amended the margarita recipe by adding *limoncello* to the mix. The cocktails were delicious and packed a punch. The guest list consisted of Leo and his girlfriend Elisabeth, Monica and her boyfriend Carlo, and Carlo's brother Alex from Sicily, so with me it made six of us. Alex arrived a little later from Sicily, coming from the airport in Nice. He brought Sicilian pizza with him. A lovely gesture, but honestly I think he was worried about the Mexican food. Italians are very provincial and prefer to eat Italian food whenever possible. It is true that over the years they have become more adventurous in the food department, but Alex was an older generation and more timid when it came to food experimentation, so he brought his own pizza just in case. I placed it in the oven to revive it from its trip, and in the meantime handed Alex a margarita and told him to try the guacamole. I had the Mexican playlist on full blast, and everyone was enjoying margaritas while I plated all the dinner fixings and headed to the table.

What made me think that chilled shots of Tequila with salt and lime would be a great idea escapes me. In retrospect, it was a pretty bad idea. But we all did shots, and I poured another round of margaritas as we began to assemble our tacos. Leo had asked me to make chili, even though it was not a Mexican dish—somehow that did not matter. We ate chili and chips and kept drinking. One thing I had forgotten was that Italians were not big drinkers. Sure, they enjoy their *aperitivo*, but unlike in the US, getting drunk was not a big thing.

By the middle of dinner, though, this party was getting out of hand. The music got louder, and a few people including myself were dancing at the table. As we danced the night away I noticed that Alex had left the table. He was nowhere to be found…until we heard the sound of puking in the bathroom. Leo offered to check on him, but about that time Carlo started looking a little green as well. Leo then offered to take Carlo outside for some fresh air. There's nothing like fresh air— and a little vomiting into the neighbor's bushes. I remember thinking our Mexican fiesta seemed more like *Animal House*, Italian style. But I remember very little after that, as I had my share of tequila as well. All I remember is waking up fully clothed, shoes and all, in my bed. It felt like there was a hole in my stomach. I managed to make some scrambled eggs to fill the hole and then returned to bed. I did take a moment to survey the damage. The flat looked like a tornado had come through. Needless to say, I slept until three in the afternoon, and then showered and started the process of reassembling our home. The bathroom looked and smelled like the bathroom at a frat house. What a night. Everyone was suffering the next day, except for Monica, who felt fine.

Which made me think she might not be a real Italian after all.

CHAPTER 17

Love Is a Six-Hour Drive Away

Around midsummer I had fallen in love with a neighborhood dog whose name was Marshall. Italians love their dogs more than anything. Most likely, if there was an Italian love scale, it would go like this:

1. Babies
2. Dogs
3. *Nonni* (grandmas and grandpas)
4. People and everything else

Dogs can go anywhere in Italy and they are treated like rock stars. They are brought water at restaurants and boutiques, and they are fawned over and exalted, like nothing I had seen before. So I decided I wanted a dog like the neighborhood dog I had fallen in love with. Marshall was a shop dog. His owner, my friend, owned a bathroom accessories store in the middle of the main walking street in Alassio. Marshall hung out at the store every day and was so sweet and passive. Marshall is called a *Bassotto* in Italian, in English a *Wirehaired Dachshund*, and I was deeply in love. I asked my friend where Marshall had come from and was there a breeder nearby? She told me when I was ready she would introduce me to the breeder. Fortunately for me—not so much for him—Frank was arriving the next week, and that would present the perfect opportunity to meet the breeder and talk about getting a mini-Marshall of our own.

Poor Frank had been in Italy for only forty-eight hours when I dragged him to my friend's store. When we rang the doorbell, Marshall waddled out to greet us. Frank was not sure why we were in the store to begin with. I guess he assumed we were buying something for the house. He certainly never thought we were here to buy a dog. My friend popped her head out of the back room to see who'd come in.

"*Ciao*," I said. "I brought Frank to meet Marshall."

"Oh, wonderful," she replied. "*Ciao*, Frank." She pulled back the linen drape covering the entrance to the stock room and headed toward us. Frank had a puzzled look on his face like he'd missed something.

"Frank," I explained, "I am thinking I would like a dog to keep me company here in Italy. A dog I can take everywhere, a great companion."

"What?" Frank said, obviously baffled by the thought. "Are you kidding me?"

Before we could finish the conversation, my friend was on the phone with the breeder. She and I had decided that a standard Dachshund was too large to travel with, so we would get a mini Dachshund, which the breeder also offered. Before Frank could say another word, my friend had located a female at the breeder and had told the breeder we would be there the next afternoon to see her. She went on to explain that the breeder was in Bergamo, forty-five minutes from Milan—or about three hours from Alassio.

"It is a quaint town in northern Italy, Frank. It would be a great day trip to go meet this dog," I said. "The dog that might be our dog…in Bergamo," I added, not sure where I stood at this point with Frank. I ushered him quickly towards the door, and thanked her as she slipped me the address, phone number, and name of the signora who was the breeder. She wished us luck and we were out the door.

I am pretty sure Frank felt like he'd been hijacked into buying a dog by two crazy women; his instincts have always been good, because we had done just that.

We woke up the next day and I was super excited to meet our new little addition. In my mind she was already ours. But for the sake of a peaceful ride I decided to keep that to myself. The reality was too much for Frank, who does not have an impulsive bone in his body (that's why he has me!). Driving to Bergamo was no problem; we had driven to Milan a million times and Bergamo was just outside Milan—what could go wrong, right? But once we drove to the outskirts of Milan, the GPS lady went haywire. We drove right into the middle of town and to the address we'd been given. Like many Italian streets, some had the same name, and it turned out that this was the case in Bergamo. We pulled the car over once the GPS lady told us "you have arrived at the destination," but it was clearly not our destination. Frank was so mad he jumped out and walked up the street just to cool off. Truth is that there is nothing worse than being in a foreign country, terribly lost and terribly late for an appointment. It will bring out the worst in people every time.

I jumped into the driver's seat and re-entered the address, this time with a different county, and then told Frank I would drive for a while. GPS told us that our destination was thirty minutes away. There was no time to lose. Frank buckled in, still steaming mad. About fifteen minutes into the ride, we found ourselves on a large-ish road, like a small highway. The area seemed very industrial and very rural at the same time. If you've ever driven off the beaten path in Italy you know what I mean. The outskirts of cities are sometimes the ugliest parts. In fact, so ugly that you can't believe you're in the same country. This was one of those areas. As we drove down the road, we spotted a chair with a very young, scantily-clad woman sitting on it. She appeared to be wearing evening attire. It was such an odd site. She was wearing a very, *very* short cocktail dress, with fishnet stockings and platform shoes, and she wore lots of makeup and was smoking a cigarette and talking on the phone. It took us a couple of seconds to realize she was a prostitute, a common site on the trucking routes in Italy. We both looked at each other and chuckled; we had both come to the same realization at the same time. "Oh, Italy, you're so beautiful," I said. Nothing like a roadside hooker to lighten the mood when you're lost. Now we were confident that we were most likely on the right road. Not because of the hooker, but because we both had a feeling.

After another thirty-five minutes, the GPS lady lost the plot. Once again we were unsure if we were going the right way. The constant construction on the roads in Italy messes up the navigation systems, it seems. Finally I pulled into a hotel in the middle of nowhere. I could only surmise who stayed here, but there was someone at the front desk and I figured they would be helpful. The hotel looked brand new; it was big and had a huge, garish lobby, with lots of windows and a hideously modern desk and a modern chandelier that occupied the entire ceiling. The woman behind the desk immediately asked how she could help me, of course in Italian. When I asked if she spoke English, she ran down the hallway and disappeared into a doorway. *Okay*, I thought, *that went well.* I turned to see Frank sitting in the car; our eyes met and I shrugged my shoulders.

The desk clerk returned with a young man in tow. "He is speaking English," she said. "Perfect," I responded and smiled at the boy. "We are looking for this address." I showed him the crumpled paper with all the information on it. "Oh, you are very cloze," he said. *Thank God*, I whispered to myself. "Yes, yes, come-a with me I show you outside," he said, and motioned me to follow him. We stepped outside, and Frank rolled down his window to hear the directions. "Okay lady," said the boy, "You make a the right-a on the road-a, see-a the garden houze?"

"Garden houze?" I replied.

"Yes-a the garden houze," he said again. He looked at me, probably to make sure I was listening, because at this point I was talking to Frank as well. "What the hell is a garden house, Frank?" I implored. Frank didn't know. I could tell he was annoyed. I tried to take in all the information this sweet fellow was trying to share. "Make a right there, is that a road?" I asked. "Yes-a, Madame that is a street-a," he replied. "Okay then, I think I have it." I thanked him and hopped back into the driver's side. "Okay, Frankie, I think I have this," and we roared off, the cute boy in the rearview waving like a maniac and giving me the thumbs up.

We made a left back on to the main road, and then a right at the "garden house," which was actually a nursery full of plants. "Oh," said Frank. "A nursery, a garden house, ahhh that's funny." I made the right and we were on a dirt road; on either side there was running water so that if we made one wrong move we were stuck. *Are you kidding me*, I thought. *This is insane.* (Much later we found out that there is a word for when things are questionable; Italians will shrug and simply say "*normale*," it's normal.) I very carefully navigated us down the narrow dirt road. We both knew at any minute things could go to shit. When we finally came to the end of the dirt road, there was a gravel road, and that road wound around what looked like a compound. I don't know about you, but when I arrive at a new destination, sometimes I am overwhelmed and miss the most basic things. This is what happened to me when we started on the gravel road—I headed around the compound and completely missed the iron gate embellished with little iron wiener dogs. Once we realized that the compound was abandoned except for the first house, we backtracked and it was then we saw the embellished gate with the wiener dogs on it.

"This is it," Frank said, looking at the house number. "We have arrived, no thanks to the GPS lady, I might add."

We rang the bell and were greeted by ten large barking mountain dogs—not sure what breed they were, but they were enormous. The signora made her way to the gate. We greeted each other and I said, "We are here for the dog."

"*Si, si* come inside," she said.

Frank looked at me in horror. "'We are here for the dog'? Don't you mean we are here to look at the dog?"

"Yes, of course, but it is easier for her to understand," I said.

"As long as you understand, Annette, that we are looking at the dog. That is it," he said.

"Calm down, I get it. Now come on." I led him, following the signora down the path. The big dogs followed us to the back of the house.

Once we were in the backyard, I saw the kennels and all the pretty dachshunds. In the center of the courtyard was a small fenced-in area filled with puppies. If you've ever seen a dachshund puppy, you'll know there is nothing cuter—nothing. Really. And there she was—our girl. Very tiny but not timid, she came right up to the fence and smiled at us. Her furry little beard was adorable; everything about her was perfection. She stood right there—not barking, just smiling.

"This is the female," the signora finally said. It seemed like time had altered and we had been staring at each other for an eternity. This is what love was. "Frank, is she not the cutest?" I said. "Look how perfect she is."

"She's pretty cute," he admitted. I was a bit surprised by his answer, given I had to drag him up here kicking and screaming. The signora picked her up and handed me the furry little bundle. The puppy squirmed and finally settled into my arms. She was really a cute little wiener. She licked my face and my hands, while staring into my eyes. "Here, you want to hold her?" I asked.

Frank just looked at me and said, "No, that's okay, I'm good."

I gave him a look and he said, "Okay, okay, give her to me." As I passed the furry little ball to Frank I could see a tiny glimmer of love in his eyes. She was now ours, there was no denying it. Her fate was sealed. I took out my phone to document the day with our new little girl, and they both smiled for the camera. As we left the kennel that day, we both smiled and even giggled that we had been so swept away.

I came up with her name in about four seconds. Frank and I collect black and white photography, and most recently we had a attended a show that had touched us very much. The photographer was Vivian Maier. Vivian was a bit of a rebel and a super talented street photographer. She had captured us, just like our puppy. Vivian was the name I chose and Frank agreed wholeheartedly. Vivian could not be brought home until she had all her shots and papers in order. The signora told me to come back in six weeks. Of course it seemed like an eternity, but I went home to the States and planned to return just in time to pick up our new baby.

Somehow I roped Leo into joining me on my journey back to pick up Vivian. I arrived a couple days before we were scheduled to go, and Leo was excited as he loves puppies, dogs, cats, and kids. He's a great guy. The morning we left, I packed the car with puppy treats, a crate, and the GPS. We headed out around 6:00 a.m., which would put us at the kennel around 9:30-ish. We headed to Milano on the *autostrada* and were almost to Milan when we had to make a pit stop at my favorite Autogrill to down a *doppio* (a double espresso) and a brioche (Italian for a croissant). I was energized to once again find this mysterious place in the countryside and the signora and our Vivi. We plugged in the GPS lady and listened to her every word. After driving for about an hour, Leo asked me, "How the hell did you find this place?"

"Well, we haven't found it yet," I said, and we both laughed. We were still laughing when we noticed three women on the road, one of them leaning into a car while the others smoked and looked off into the distance. They were again dressed in evening attire. Leo realized what they were doing and I interrupted him before he started to explain. "We saw another lovely creature sitting on a chair on the side of the road last time we drove up here. This must be a regular spot. The good news is that at least I know we are in the right place." We both laughed again and sped on down the road with confidence. Finally we rolled past the new hotel where the sweet boy had come out to the parking lot to point to the dirt road, and I knew we were almost there.

Again Leo asked, "How the hell did you find this place?"

"Honestly Leo," I said. "I think this place found us."

I carefully glided the car down the narrow dirt road and parked right in front of the iron gate, and as I rang the bell the big mountain dogs once again greeted us with their loud barking and out came the signora. After introductions, she asked Leo, "*Tu Italiano?*"

"*Sì,*" he replied, "I am Italian. Annette tells me you speak very good English," he added. Leo and I smiled and followed her to the backyard. Before I turned the corner, I could see Vivi bounding her way to me, running like a crazy person. She was so cute. I was definitely in deep love. She ran right up to me; I picked her up and she showered me with sloppy licks and kisses. It was magic.

What followed next was the inevitable paperwork. For about an hour, Leo read over everything and I signed things. Thank God I had brought him along—it was much more complicated than I had envisioned. In retrospect, I can't imagine why I thought it would be a quick visit; after all, Italians love their paperwork. I held Vivi while Leo read, Leo held Vivi while I signed and handed over the remainder of the cash. At one point I put Vivi on the floor, where she promptly peed. I instantly apologized to the signora. She laughed, mopped it up, and said "They all pee-a in the house. Not a problem-a." But this actually *was* a problem for me. I thought that this might result in tough house training. But we would tackle that problem later; for now I just wanted to finish up and head home with Vivi.

We said our goodbyes and headed down the dirt road towards home.

Vivi, who was so outgoing and vivacious at the kennel, suddenly went limp when we put her in her new crate. She was comatose. I had no idea what to do. When we stopped for all of us to pee, she simply lay on the grass motionless. It was all very dramatic. This behavior went on for about two months. It was how she apparently adjusted, but for me it was puzzling. She flew home with me to the US with her brand new *passaporto*. All dogs in the EU have them for travel—it makes so much sense, since it has all of their updated vaccines in this little booklet. I was thrilled that it was so easy to travel with her. She was a perfect angel on the plane, but to be honest, she was still in her comatose stage. She just slept the entire flight.

In Atlanta, she behaved fine with me one-on-one, but in her new surroundings she would go limp, like a noodle. She adjusted slowly to her new family. She was very shy and only wanted to be with me, attached to my person like a baby kangaroo. It took about three months for her true outgoing personality to come through. But when it finally did, there was no stopping our little Italian wiener dog.

Strange Bedfellows, or Screaming Italian-Style

The summer routine was pretty locked in after years of spending the season in Alassio. I went to the beach club, entertained guests and friends.

My friend Monica decided she wanted to open another home furnishings boutique in Saint-Tropez, France. Her daughter was about to graduate from interior design school in Milan, and, like all Italian mothers, she wanted her daughter to take over the family business. What better way to teach her about the business than having her help open a branch of her interior design business in France?

Monica had already been doing business on the French Riviera. The invasion of wealthy Russians had hit the coast hard and they were buying up properties as fast as they could. Of course, this meant that Monica and her assistant, my good friend Leo, spent lots of time schmoozing Russians—which to me sounded pretty awful. I had noticed an influx of Russian families at our own beach club. The Russians at our beach club tended to be loud and flashy and overbearing. My impression was not a good one. Monica, on the other hand, who gets along with everyone, found herself spending lots of time with her Russian clients. In fact, they monopolized her time.

One day, Monica thought it would be a great idea to take me to her Russian client's project in Nice and show me around. We would then head to Saint-Tropez and spend the weekend. It sounded like a wonderful plan, and I was very curious about what she was doing at the project. So as I always did, I said yes. Her plan was to pick me up in the morning and we would drive to Nice and then Saint-Tropez. Sounded easy enough. I was waiting in front of our flat at 9:00 a.m. when she roared up. I noticed that she was not driving; she was seated in the back of her black Jeep SUV, which the Italians pronounce "soov." Her driver was none other than the infamous ex-husband Nino. *Nudo* Nino would be driving us, but at least he was dressed today. I thought to myself, *This should be interesting.*

I hopped in and Monica yelled "*Andiamo*" and we sped off, bound for Nice. The music was blaring some euro techno as Monica explained the "project" to me in Italian. I gleaned 80 percent of what she said—enough to understand that is was a big project, hung off a cliff, and that money was no object.

"It sounds like a dream job," I said.

"Well, not really," she replied. "They are very difficult. They don't pay me now. They pay me in the beginning, but now, no. I am not sure what to do. it is just difficult. You understand?"

"I think I understand, although he seems like a guy you would not want to piss off," I said. I had met the man and his wife at a dinner party Monica threw a few weeks before, and had been very unimpressed with them. He seemed more like a thug than a businessman. Monica laughed, lit a cigarette, and told Nino to drive faster, "*Cazzo cazzo* [fuck fuck]. Nino, *vai vai* [go go]." We drove, music blaring, for about an hour at breakneck speed, Monica working on emails on her iPad in the back seat. When we arrived at the Nice exit, I saw that Nino looked incredibly stressed. Then the car started making weird noises—it was a little hard to tell what was making the clunking noise because Monica began yelling "*Avanti, avanti* [forward forward]" so loud it made me flinch. Most of the time Monica had no filter. Maybe this was an effort to complete her endless to-do list. Whatever it was, she sometimes came off as thoughtless, and then would flip and be the most thoughtful person ever.

"Stop!" Nino shouted at Monica. "We are having some trouble up here. The red engine light has been on the entire trip! *Basta!* [Enough!]"

At that point, we all realized the car was dead and barely rolling off the exit ramp to Nice, so we all started silently praying. The car behind us noticed that our Jeep was rolling without a sound and he kindly gave us a little nudge so that the car rolled a bit faster down the incline.

With Monica in full bedlam mode, Nino—cool as a cucumber— steered the car into a Ford dealership parking lot right off the exit. Turns out that was where all the dealerships were in Nice. How lucky could we get?

Once we safely parked the car, Monica called her project manager at the Russian's home in Nice to come get us and take us to the Jeep dealership down the road. The call was then followed by a screaming match between Nino and Monica that loosely had something to do with who was going to drop the car, who was going to wait for the car, what would happen if the car could not be fixed right away, contingency plans, and calling each other every dirty name in the book. "*Stupido*" was a word I did understand. It was a scene right out of an Italian sitcom.

Finally the project manager showed up to break up the fight and get everyone to their various destinations. Nino to the dealership and Monica and I to the Russian design project. "*Ciao* Nino," I said. "See you soon." Nino replied with a lit cigarette in his mouth, and a grumble and nod and a very weak wave. We sped away in the project manager's giant truck, Monica all the while talking non-stop.

We arrived at a huge gate and were whisked down a steep drive to a parking pad that was cantilevered high above the ocean, to finally glimpse a modern house literally hanging off the edge of a cliff. The design was a series of ultra-modern boxes stacked in a very pleasing manner over the ledge. It was huge, quite a sight to see.

"Annette come and see, you will love it, et is incredible." I followed her to a small hole in which was perched a very wobbly looking ladder. She scurried down it like a tiny Italian mouse and yelled up to me, "Es a stable, come on, you are a cheecken." I set one foot on the ladder and she started to jiggle it, laughing. I wiggled down the wobbly ladder, all the while hoping not to slip and kill myself. It was worth it; the lower level contained the living room and kitchen, and the views were breathtaking. Wall-to-wall windows looked straight down to the sea. The construction site was still in shambles, but I could tell it was going to be incredible. Monica has an incredible eye for design and a fantastic sense of compositional balance. This kitchen was one of three in the house. The Russians planned to have a modernistic palace—a dark, luxurious place filled with fine art and custom finishes. Monica told me she was going through a dark design period. "The colors of the sea and the sand are always expected in Nice, but I am going to shake things up and make everything in the house deep and lush like the bottom of the ocean." I loved how her mind worked. She was crazy, sure, but a crazy genius, one of the things I loved about her.

We toured the house for about an hour, then she looked at her phone and said "NINO…okay we go." I figured that we were going back to get the car and drive off to our next stop, Saint-Tropez. The one thing about Monica is that you never really knew what was going on, or what was going to happen next. It was fun, but I was always a little anxious and on edge with her, a little bit how I felt about Italy in general, really. We hopped into the giant truck and went to meet Nino at the Jeep dealership. I hoped for the best.

When we arrived at the dealership, Nino was munching on a bag of peanuts in the waiting area. "*Tutto apposto*, Nino? [Everything okay?]" asked Monica, this time as sweet and docile as a new bride.

"*Si, si cara* [Yes love]. I am waiting for pay the bill and then we go," he said.

Nino pulled the car around to pick us up. Turns out the problem was nothing major and we were good to go—or at least that is what I gleaned from their conversation. We headed to the gas station to fill up and Monica got out to shop. Turns out you can buy the perfect French picnic in a service station in France—candies, pastries, cheese, bread, foie gras, and wine—who knew? Monica did.

Of course we got hopelessly lost in Nice trying to find the road to Saint-Tropez. We stopped to ask a group of teenagers by the road the way to Saint-Tropez, and they looked at us like we were aliens, speechless. They didn't know either! We laughed all the way to the *autostrada*, punchy from the morning adventures. Finally on the road, we elatedly nibbled bread, cheese, and foie gras, and drank wine while Nino chauffeured us to our final destination.

Monica's Saint-Tropez house was on the outskirts of town high on a hill overlooking the city and the sea. It was part of a village, and the houses were as close as they could be without being connected. As Monica and I stood on the terrace and enjoyed the view, Nino yelled from the front of the house for Monica to come upstairs. What followed was the equivalent of World War III. I could not quite make out what was being screamed, but it was not good. The tile guy who was working on the terrace looked at me, and I gave him a what-the-heck grimace? Without missing a beat, he nodded and smiled and said, "*normale*" and we both laughed. Turned out the tile work wasn't finished, so that weekend we stayed in a pretty hotel not far from the house.

The next morning we headed to breakfast by the pool. Nino was grumpy as he sipped his cappuccino. Monica and I had an espresso and decided that we would drive to the antique stalls in L'Isle-sur-la-Sorgue about two-and-a-half hours away—one of my favorite places to *brocante* (flea market). What I did not realize, which was typical, was that Monica had planned to bring her friend Elena. Normally I am like, the more the merrier, but in this case I was not thrilled with our special guest. Monica's friend, who was her lawyer, also had a house in Saint-Tropez and lived a few miles away. She was someone I had spent very little time with, but in the time I had spent with her I found her to be very spoiled and a show-off, always dressed head-to-toe in designer clothes, which I knew because she always told me the price of everything she was wearing. "Chanel bag, darling, it was ten thousand euros," she would say.

Monica said we would pick her up on the way out of town. We had had lunch together a few months back and it was clear she did not care for me. I surmised she was jealous of me; perhaps she felt I was Monica's new obsession. With Monica's manic tendencies, I knew she had a habit of becoming smitten by someone and focusing entirely on that person. At the moment I had her admiration and devotion, but I knew it would wear off—I am a realist—but I would enjoy it while I was number one on her hit parade. But Elena was unhappy about our blossoming friendship. When she opened the door to get in, she was surprised to see me sitting in the passenger seat. Elena promptly insisted I move to the back seat, which I was fine with, it to be honest. Less pressure to be witty, and I could just lay down and take a nap.

The two of them chattered away while I snoozed. Once we arrived, I woke to the sound of Monica shouting out the window at the parking attendant that she was "a very important client; therefore, she could park here in the reserved spot!" I sat up to see Monica parking, the whole while the attendant kept saying, "No, no, Madame," but she pulled into the parking spot anyway without a second thought. You got to hand it to her—she makes things happen. The poor attendant did not stand a chance. Lucky for him she handed him a twenty euro bill and a sweet smile and gave him the keys. He smiled and waved and said see you later.

Monica was on a mission and there was no stopping her.

We walked all over the market. There were many incredible vendors and Monica knew all of them and joked with them, and asked about their families; the vendors loved her—she is the ultimate networker, very natural and so good at it. I met about a million people that day, all to whom I was introduced as a "very famous American designer," which of course could not have been further from the truth. But the real truth is as a stylist this place was my Mecca; it was a place that I had always loved, even when I had come with my family so many years before. Shopping with Monica honed my eye and made me see things in a different way. As a stylist, this is of great benefit and a way to stay fresh creatively. It was great to have another stylist to share this rich landscape with.

Elena was quiet most of the morning. That is to say, she did not say one word to me. Around noon we decided a little lunch would be wonderful. I had scouted out a fresh market that served lunch; the produce and the cheese looked divine, and what was on the plates around the tiny restaurant looked amazing. I suggested we check it out. It was relatively packed, but we liked this sweet spot and only waited about ten minutes to be seated.

The place started to really fill up since it was around 1:00; we noticed the line was much longer. Monica went off to the ladies room and I sat with Elena, alone and silent. Elena broke the silence by saying, "I don't like this place." I was confused at first because she said it in French (just to mess with me I am sure). I thought she said, "I don't like you." To which I replied, "Well, I don't like you." Her face froze and turned red. She looked like she was going to explode. Monica returned to our table, and Elena, repeated herself to Monica, only this time in Italian, " I don't like this place." I began to laugh and said, "Elena, I am so sorry. I thought you said you did not like ME." At this point I was laughing so hard neither one of them understood me. While I was having my laughing fit, Monica stood up and ushered us out of the restaurant.

"What? Wait, where are we going?" I asked.

"Elena does not like, so we go," Monica said. And just like that, we were standing in a queue across the street four people deep to eat at another location, one that Princess Elena picked out. I was not surprised that when we were finally seated they were out of everything. But in France, instead of being nice and telling us what they were out of, they would wait for us to place our order and say, "No, we are out of that." So, after we all named at least three things they were out of, we finally were able to order salads and *frites* and call it a day. It was mediocre at best, and I was sure that the first place would have been better with local cheeses, meats, and breads, and wines. But *c'est la vie*. We finished up lunch and made the last round through the stalls and decided to call it a day. We had a couple things to pick up that we had bought from the various vendors, so we walked back to the car and wound our way around the narrow streets packed with tents and antiques.

It was amazing how well Monica navigated her Jeep through the tiny roads and alleyways. Once we gathered everything, it was time to decide where we would go next. I loved these adventures with Monica, because A) She was always up for some adventure and B) She knew all the cool places. "Let's go to Baumanière," Monica said. "It is incredible and gorgeous and you will love it; it's amazing." "Okay," I said. Elena froze in her seat. "I promised my husband I would be home for dinner," she said. "Why?" said Monica. "It's only three, so we can make it back later for dinner." "Okay," said Elena, but I will call him and see if he can make it to meet us for dinner." "Why?" said Monica again. "We are about two hours from the hotel. We will have an *aperitivo* and then drive back home." Now even I knew that we were at least a four-hour drive back if we made the trip to see the hotel. But of course, for me, it was not a problem—but it seemed to put Elena into a panic.

We drove off, all the while Elena on her phone trying to reach her husband with no luck. We drove further into Provence, holding Elena hostage, apparently, because she was super unhappy and on the verge of tears. I was in the back seat wondering what the hell was going on and why this woman was unraveling at the prospect of exploring Provence; wouldn't most people kill to be in her place? It was obvious she had some issues at home and some control issues as well, which may have contributed to the issues she had at home. In any case, I was staying out of it and enjoying the view while she had a full-blown meltdown going in the front seat. For the first time I saw Monica quiet and concentrating on the driving rather than on her dear friend. We drove in silence for two hours, which was quite lovely. The views were amazing. About two hours in, I sensed that we might be a little lost. Since Monica was doing this all by memory with no map, it was to be expected. When she looked back at me and said, "Pull out your phone, Annette," I replied, "Okay," and pulled out my phone. I then calmly told her I had no reception. She started to laugh, which for me was a weird reaction. I looked at my phone again and now had reception. I plugged the address in the GPS, which told us that we were thirty minutes away. When we finally pulled up it was 6:00 p.m. "Just in time for *aperitivo*," I said while Monica parked the car.

The hotel was in the mountains, a breathtakingly beautiful, remote, and private location. The styling and appointments were a designer's dream. Monica ran up the stone staircase, turned around, and announced, "Beautiful, right? I was right." I smiled and Elena burst into tears, loud hysterical sobs, like a child. I walked up the stairs to get away from her and passed Monica as she went down to console her. As I walked toward the gift shop, Elena's sobs lessened and so did my stress levels. Nothing a little retail therapy could not fix.

As I wandered around the grounds of the hotel I found the most beautiful stone outbuilding, which turned out to be French cookery heaven—a beautiful boutique filled with treasures. I wandered around, taking in all the wares: cookbooks, aprons, linens, copper pots, wooden spoons, and cutting boards. Jars of canard paté and olives. I picked out a few things, paid, and headed to the car to stash my goodies. When I arrived at the car, Monica and Elena were hugging each other and Monica rolled her eyes when she saw me. I put my shopping bags in the trunk. I looked at them both and announced, "I'm heading to the bar."

I sat at a poolside table and ordered a Negroni, determined to be alone, and enjoyed the view.

Ten minutes later, they joined me. Everything was fine now. They ordered drinks that came with some tiny nibbles, French style. In Italy the *aperitivo* treats were substantial, but there in France they served minuscule canapés—three for each of us.

"I don't know about you, but I am starving," I said, grabbing a tiny appetizer that looked like a bug. I popped it into my mouth. "Delicious! Try one." Elena looked at me like I was insane to suggest such a thing. "I wait for my husband," she said, folding her arms on top of her handbag and sitting straight up.

We sat in silence finishing off our nibbles and Elena's nibbles and our cocktails. Then I said to Monica, "What's the plan?"

"I think we go home," said Monica. The truth was I was so wrung out from Elena that driving three hours back seemed worth it just to be done with her insanity. The ride home was long, but Elena managed to be quiet most of the ride. Around 8:30 we pleaded with her to stop for dinner because we had at least another hour and a half to go. "No, no, no," is all she would say; Elena was a terrorist, in my opinion. We finally hit the outskirts of Saint-Tropez after a long, arduous drive on the curvy back roads. Driving to Saint-Tropez is daunting since it's on a peninsula; there is only one road and it's not a highway. But finally we stopped in front of Elena's place and she jumped out. I climbed into the front seat, grunted a goodbye, and Monica drove off at breakneck speed. We looked at each other and laughed and agreed it was a ridiculous day.

"You hungry?" she said. "I am beyond starving," I replied. "Let's go into town and find food," she said. "Great plan." I said. "YES!" we both yelled. We drove to the center of town—surely there would be something open at 10:30. I surveyed the town square and all I saw open was a Middle Eastern food truck, "I will take it," I said as I pointed to the lit truck. We parked and walked into the town square. It smelled divine. "We will take two lamb sandwiches and two *frites*," said Monica in French, "and two beers." We paid and walked to a bench in the middle of the square, deserted except for a homeless guy sleeping at the far end and a couple of teenagers making out on the bench behind us. We devoured our sandwiches and downed the beer. Finally happy, we smiled at each other and then started to laugh simultaneously. "You look like shit," she said. "You look like hell yourself," I said. "We look just like VIPs, right? No one would believe we are scarfing down street food at eleven at night. So chic, right?" Monica teased. We'd been through a war together, and it was forever bonding. We threw out our trash, walked back to the car, and drove happily off into the night.

Just when I thought we'd had enough for one day she drove us to a hotel. Not the one we were staying in, but another. "Where are we?" I asked. I was delirious and thought I was imagining that we had driven to the wrong hotel. "Oh, I forgot to tell you, we cannot stay at the other hotel. No room. So we are booked into this hotel for tonight. Nino brought over all of our stuff this afternoon," she said. Nino, her long-suffering ex-husband, did all sorts of things for Monica. The truth was that they really had a nice friendship and co-parented and served a purpose in each other's lives. He was her rock and she was his best friend.

"What?" I said, rubbing my eyes and trying to focus. This hotel was clearly a step down from the last one. It was stuck in the 1980s and not in the good way. We checked in and were punchy and started a critique of the décor. Monica did a brilliant commentary of the décor. I almost peed my pants laughing. "No, Annette, come on, this is super trendy now," she said, pointing to the fraying carpet in the hallway. When we got to the room, the designer tour continued. "This color is so chic," she said as she pointed to the hospital green worn walls of the entire room. The bathroom was horrifyingly stuck in time. I was so exhausted that I couldn't have cared less, as long as I had a bed to sleep in.

It was midnight when I brushed my teeth and washed my face, which was covered in flea market dust. "Where's my bed?" I asked Monica. "Oh, we sleep together," she said. "Oh, Jesus, why don't you sleep with Nino," I begged. "Nino," she replied. "Oh Annette, *cazzo cazzo.*" That was the last thing I heard before my head hit the pillow; I was sound asleep.

The next morning we woke up and headed to the breakfast room, a gigantic restaurant with about fifty tables and a long buffet that snaked up the middle of the room. We sat down, ordered espressos, and walked to the buffet. It was a depressing selection, so we sat back down and drank our espressos. Nino read the paper and sipped on orange juice.

Monica looked from her cup at Nino, and said, "Eat something." Nino shook his head, "No, there is nothing." We all looked around at the sad hotel with its cheap yet cheerful floral tablecloths and plastic flowers and decided we should head into the town square.

The town square in Saint-Tropez was a remarkable place, and on this day, Saturday, there was a market filled with amazing food products: baked goods, cheeses and wines, jarred confections, and some vintage items like Hermes bags, art, and clothing and some home goods—so a little of everything. It's one of my favorite markets in Europe, and I love going. We all drove into town, then parked and walked to a beautiful bakery for croissants and coffee.

The market in the town square was filled with people and amazing wares, as always, and we lingered and bought our lunch there and had a picnic in the square. Later that afternoon, I was sitting by the pool of our original hotel (Nino had moved us back), when Monica walked up and said, "We are going to dinner at Elena's tonight."

"Are you kidding me?" I asked. "Okay if I skip it?"

"Of course," she said. "I understand. She is a bit much."

We both laughed. Because once you've committed to a person like Monica—or a country like Italy—it can still surprise you and wear you out and make you laugh till you pee your pants.

CHAPTER 19

A Turning Point

My ninth season in Alassio was a very exciting turning point in my life there and in my career as well. I started to style less in the US, mainly because I was spending three months in Italy every summer. It was harder to schedule my work. I loved what I did, but every season has its time, and my time was evolving. Workshops were becoming popular as young creatives were seeking training in my line of work. One of my friends, Cassandra, asked if I wanted to teach a styling and photography workshop in Seattle. She said she could fill it—no problem—so I said why not? From that moment on, my career focus shifted. I had always mentored young stylists, but this was a way to teach and mentor at the same time. The Seattle workshop was great, and I was hooked. As with all things concerning my career, a path had presented itself to me, and, as always, I embraced the challenge.

This first workshop in Seattle led to my staging a couple of styling and photography workshops in Atlanta; they were always full. I did a workshop in Marrakech because I had a friend that owned a B&B there, and she encouraged me to bring a group, so I did. It was an amazing and challenging workshop, and I found that I loved the logistics involved.

So I planned to hold my first styling and photography workshop in Italy. I could use my friends' B&B located down the road in a neighboring city called Garlenda to hold the workshop.

Garlenda is a beautiful town about five minutes inland from Alassio. The first workshop in Garlenda was amazing; we had a wonderful time with our attendees. Deborah Whitlaw Llewellyn was our first photographer/instructor to travel to Alassio to teach with me. I brought an assistant, Kayla, and her friend Hannah and our videographer Megan. Megan had been with me at my Marrakech styling and photography workshop, and she shot all the behind-the-scenes video for my new workshop website. We photographed and prepared local foods, then styled the food for the camera. We visited all sorts of local artisans and purveyors, shot editorial imagery, had a cooking lesson, and photographed that—all the while enjoying local foods. Because I had worked in photo styling for so many years, I had an amazing roster of photographers that could come teach photography with me while I taught styling. It was the start of a new phase of my business. One that had been inspired by my time in Italy and, unbeknownst to me at the time, would inspire some even bigger decisions down the road.

It was also around this same time that I started working on my second book, *Cocktail Italiano*, planned as a travelogue, a cocktail book, and an ode to my adopted region of Italy: Liguria and the Italian Riviera. I had been enjoying *aperitivo* culture for many years and I wanted to share it with the world. It was an amazing experience, recreating recipes from the region and sharing Italian cocktails from the beautiful seaside towns I loved so much. Shooting from Bordighera to Portovenere, the locations made for gorgeous images of the seaside lifestyle. I had made friends with many of the bar owners and bartenders over the years, so getting their special recipes was exciting.

Since we were conducting a workshop at the time of shooting, I had lots of eager help. I enlisted my assistants to stay and help finish up the book photography, and Megan shot the book trailer. It was a blast shooting up and down the Italian Riviera. We would roll into town, hit three to four bars around *aperitivo* time, and order drinks to photograph before the crew would drink them. We could only hit a couple towns a night doing this, but of course I was the designated driver with a very happy crew.

With all this new creative energy coming my way, I had an idea that maybe I was ready for a bigger challenge. I began to dream of a house in the country. I talked to Frank about maybe finding a house with a few out-buildings so we could turn it into a creative compound with workshops, artist residencies, and more guest rooms for the kids and their spouses and friends.

I could see that this was something that I would enjoy, and it was a new way to share creativity in a place that so inspired me. Even though it would involve selling our flat and moving, I thought I was ready for the change. Frank and I wanted to stay in the area, so we agreed to put things in motion slowly, Italian style. As with everything, I like to talk to friends and family about how to go about a major transition. I talked to Leo about selling the flat; he knew some real estate people in town and made a bunch of appointments for them to come view it. We slowly began the process of finding our new right place.

To say that real estate people in Italy are weird is an understatement; I have never understood them. Buying real estate in Italy is daunting, but selling seemed impossible. All the realtors loved the flat and agreed to list it; in Italy, you can have many real estate agents, and unlike in the US, they do *not* work together, for the most part. The all agreed to give us an idea of price and put it on their website. They collected all the photos, data, paperwork...and then we never heard from them again! Not one person walked through our flat to view it that summer—not one. My real estate friends in the US didn't have a clue about how to help me. Finally, Frank and I decided to carry on and start the search for our next place in Italy. We had no idea what we were looking for, but we were excited to begin.

About the same time we decided to sell our flat, Rupert resurfaced after years of silence. It was on the occasion of my friend Oma's arrival;

she had emailed Rupert, letting him know she would be visiting, and he casually texted me out of the blue, asking how I was. I did not know that Oma had contacted him about her visit. Truth is, he so abruptly and unceremoniously left my life that I had not really mourned our breakup. In fact, it was a pattern of our friendship; intense togetherness and then nothing, no communication. So Oma had no idea that we had not seen each other in many years! Bless her, she just wanted to have dinner; she did not mean to open a can of worms.

I responded to the text like it had not been seven years. "*Ciao,* Rupert. What's up?" I wrote. He wrote back right away, saying he would love to come have dinner in Alassio with me and Oma, as she had written him that she thought it would be nice to see everyone.

"Sounds good," I texted back. And that was that, like nothing had transpired. To this day I have no idea what our estrangement was all about. Like any good WASP, Rupert was a champion at sweeping things under the carpet. And for me this was just fine. We all met for dinner, he and his prince boyfriend, completely overdressed for the occasion—as always. We ate and chatted and laughed and reminisced. Rupert met Vivi for the first time and loved her, and Reynaldo sat and observed, as always barely saying a word.

I am not sure if it was at this meeting or the next that I mentioned that we might be interested in house hunting. I knew that house hunting was something that Rupert adored and it was an avid hobby for him and has partner as much as flea marketing was. Rupert was chomping at the bit for a new project, as his country house was complete. He jumped at the idea of helping us find the perfect spot. I informed him we would need to sell our place first and it would be great if he could offer any help with that. Unfortunately, neither he nor Reynaldo were much help in that department, but boy, did they have lots of ideas of where we should buy a house. Our friendship slowly rekindled. I have always thought the timing was interesting. Exactly at the moment we decided to look at new property, Rupert popped up. Was it serendipity, fate, or something else?

In the meantime I was trying to think of ways to sell the flat. I spoke to everyone, including the original developer, thinking that he may want to buy it for his kids. He said he would think about it. I put ads in America magazines and online papers. But no one came to see it for two years. At one point a real estate agent we had enlisted called me and wanted to come see me. I was excited because I thought maybe he had come up with a great strategy. He showed up at our flat with a gift box, which he proceeded to unpack. It was an espresso machine. *That's weird*, I thought. "This is a machine from my family," he explained.

"Oh," I replied, with no idea why he had brought this to me.

"I bring this for you to blog about in America; you try it and tell everyone in your blog to try it. You are famous in America and you can sell these for my family," he said.

I was really perplexed that he had taken the time to bring me his family's machine and said not a word about selling my house. It was like I was taking crazy pills. "Okay," I finally said, after a moment of thinking *What the hell?* He offered to make me an espresso with his machine. "That's okay, I just had one, I am good," I said. "Just leave it here and I will work on it later."

"Wonderful, and thank you. Have a good day." And with that he was out the door. I took the machine to the storage unit in the garage and never thought about it again. Six months later he called me wanting to pick up the machine, which surprised me since I thought he had given it to me. I arranged for him to pick it up at Monica's store and left it in there with Leo. I was afraid of what I might say to him if I had to see him.

This is an example of what the real estate business is like in Italy. Neither he nor any of the other real estate agents Leo and I met with ever contacted us again. Never asked if we had sold the flat, if it was still on the market, nothing.

While I was on the hunt for a house, one summer day Monica called me and said, "I find your house. It is the house of the man that owns my building of my store. It is amazing." I was just beginning to get the big picture about how one finds a house for sale: through friends and family, not through real estate agents. She said we could see it tomorrow, that she knew the people, that we could meet at her store and go from there. Leo texted that he would go with us.

The next day I walked to the store, where a couple were waiting on the sidewalk. She looked familiar; I had definitely seen her in town, but I had never seen him. Leo came out kissed me on both cheeks and introduced me to the couple. They owned the home and were interested in selling. Monica ran out of the store and we headed to the cars parked in the alleyway. Monica, Leo, and I jumped into Monica's car, the sellers jumped into their own giant Audi, and we followed them up a winding hill to a house perched on a hilltop about one mile from town. Most of the seaside towns on the Riviera are perched on the cliffs, and many people owned homes on the mountainside behind the city with a beautiful view of the sea and a quiet, residential feel. The winding road led us to a gorgeous home; I had no idea these beautiful places existed right above town. The house looked like it had been built at the turn of the twentieth century, very much like a mini-castle. It had a scalloped roofline and was painted with a *trompe l'oeil* border in soft brown.

The front garden held a terraced olive grove. It had a terrace in front of the house that was in disrepair; in fact, as we got closer, it seemed the whole property could use some TLC. Elisabeth, Leo's girlfriend, pulled up on her scooter to join us and we walked the entire length of the front of the house with the owners. To the right of the house was a pergola, ramshackle and run down, but it would be a great place to have breakfast, lunch, or *aperitivo*. To the left of the house was a private chapel. Well, you know how I feel about private chapels so it was instant love there. I was a sucker for this house; it had me before I even entered it.

The owner went to unlock the door, but his key was not working. Leo ran around to try the key on other doors. This was strange, I thought. Luckily, before the man was about to make the call for his son to bring another key, we heard Leo say, "This key works on the back door." We all piled through the back door; it was musty and hadn't been opened up in a while. I could see that the interior had potential, and the original checkerboard floors were very captivating, Ligurian in style. The house had been the summer house to a Genovese duke, they told us, built by the Duke's family in 1899. The owner went on the tell us that their family had acquired it in the 1960s. "It is owned by my wife's family," he went on the say. *Ah*, I thought, *the plot thickens*. I was not an Italian real estate virgin, and I remembered the complicated relationships associated with family-owned property. So some red flags came up right away; they didn't own this property. I held my tongue and looked across the room at Leo, who nodded at me and gave me a smirk.

Monica was already redecorating the spaces and talking about how wonderful the kitchen was. It was, but I was leery about this place and just nodded. When we completed the tour, I ended up driving back to town with the owners, who wanted to talk to me. I asked how much they wanted for the house. This is where everything went a little sideways. It was the first time the wife perked up and said, "It is my family house, my brother is the owner, so I must ask him."

"Oh, okay," I said, and that was all I said for the rest of the drive. We arrived at Monica's store and I said goodbye, and they agreed they would be in touch after talking to the brother. We parted ways and I went into the store to talk to Monica and Leo. I had a feeling about this, that something was not quite right. But in Italy I have learned you have to go with it, because there are so many variables, and who knows what the outcome will be? So we chatted about the house and Monica said she would contact them in a couple days to see about price and what the scoop was, for real.

Monica called me a week later; she had heard from the sellers about the castle house and wanted me to stop by the store so she could fill me in. We grabbed an espresso and listened intently to what she was saying. "The house is for sale. It is one million euros and they are happy to discuss it with you and Frank."

"That's a lot of money for a run-down house, Monica," I replied. "Do you think we can give them a lower offer?"

"Yes, that is fair," she said. But you have a few people in the family to deal with."

More red flags popped up. "I have to think about it," I said.

"Okay, darling. I tell him you are thinking."

With that I headed home and weighed my options. I loved the house, but from the looks of it we would be investing a great deal to bring the house up to speed. Frank and I had a discussion about the price of the house and we both agreed that it was priced very high, and that if they did not come down, most likely we would pass. But at least we felt good about starting the search. And this was a good start.

A couple days after our discussion with Frank, I got another call from Monica, who said the sellers wanted to meet us at their flat to discuss the price. Monica apparently told them that I thought one million euros was out of our price range.

I met Monica and Leo at the store and we walked over to the sellers' flat together. Monica lit a cigarette and talked to me very seriously about listening and not saying anything. She was very protective; I could sense she was not fond of these people and she did not trust them. This was the first I sensed that she was not a fan; she was a little nervous and wanted me to be on my guard. Again, I did not have a good feeling about this, but in Italy you just never know whether to trust your feelings—or even have feelings, for that matter. The best way to buy real estate in Italy was not to fall in love. That was tough for me. This house was very special—very unique—but I could not let on how much I loved it.

When we arrived we were greeted by the entire family. Later I realized that it was normal for the whole family to be there while you walked through their house, but I found this quite odd and unnerving. The son and the daughter both spoke English and were in their early twenties and quite fashionable. They led us out to a rooftop terrace with a beautiful view of the sea on one side and the hills on the other side. We all settled in on sofas around a coffee table that held all sorts of *aperitivo* nibbles and cocktails, pre-made for us. It was all very proper and very nice.

After about an hour of small talk, Monica and Leo and I all had confused looks on our faces. Was this a form of torture? Were they trying to wear us down? I felt like this evening would never end. We all knew why we were here. In Italy, business is not ever first on the agenda for the most part—always small talk first—then eventually it becomes business. But this was becoming ridiculous. Finally Monica said, "Are we going to talk about the house for sale?" *God bless her*, I thought.

He looked at Monica and said, "Yes, of course." Very passive-aggressive. I was starting to really feel uncomfortable. "What is your price?" I blurted out. Blunt, I thought, and very American of me; it was either going to fly or not.

"Monica says you are willing to pay seven hundred fifty thousand, no more." I thought to myself, that Monica, she's a clever one, she had given them a lower price. I had to love her for that.

I looked him straight in the eye and said, "Yes, that is the most we would consider paying for that house. It needs a lot of work."

"Okay, you have a deal. I will draw up the papers." I was shocked, I was shaking, and I was excited and freaked out all at the same time. He was a lawyer in Milan; I assumed he knew my *notaio*—who would be looking everything over—and he did, of course. He smiled and said he would email me later next week.

"Okay," I said. "Talk soon." And with that, we gratefully departed after two hours on the rooftop.

You know that feeling when you think you have not got a chance of dating this person you have a big crush on and he stops you in the hallway one day and says, "You want to grab drinks?" Well, that's the feeling I had—surprise and elation at the same time. I was giddy, Monica was laughing, and Leo just stood there on the street with his mouth open. "What just happened?" he asked.

"We bought the house," cheered Monica. "Now let's go get a drink to celebrate."

CHAPTER 20

Looking for Love in All the Wrong Places

I asked myself, was this it? Had I found the one? It had been two weeks since we had met with the sellers of the little castle, and we had not heard a word. Monica tried calling them, but with no success. After another week the sellers finally showed up at Monica's store. Later, at *aperitivo*, Monica told me the sellers had a contact ready and wanted to go over it with me. In the meantime I had let our *notaio* know that he should be expecting to hear from the sellers and he could suss it all out. Our *notaio* was a wonderful man, a very dapper, all-knowing type of guy. After he had saved Frank and me from the evil Germans, he held a special place in our hearts. We knew that if he had any qualms about the sellers he would let us know. I was still unsure that these people were for real. I was definitely in love, and even though Frank had not seen it in person—only in pictures—he trusted my judgment. But he could also sense that I was a little tentative because the sellers were, well, odd.

After a couple weeks of phone tag and unanswered emails, we finally connected our *notaio* and the seller. They did know each other through peripheral friends, which was no surprise. But when they finally connected, our *notaio* emailed both me and Rupert (who was now involved in the whole thing) and told us that they had not told the brother-in-law—who was the legal owner of the property—about the sale. So, in fact, the house was not for sale and the "sellers" were trying to pull a fast one on us. They wanted us to put down a deposit and then they would hope that they could talk the brother-in-law into completing the transaction. Because all Italians seem to be connected in some way, our *notaio* made a few phone calls about the property in question and ended up talking to the brother-in-law, who was surprised to hear that his sister and her husband were showing the property to buyers, even though it was not up for sale. Our *notaio* concluded the investigation by calling the "sellers" and informing them that he had talked to the real owner and that the property was not for sale. Needless to say, this discussion did not end on a good note. But lucky for us, we knew to go to the right resources and make sure the house was indeed on the market. I felt like I had dodged a bullet. I always listen to my gut and have learned to take my time when it comes to buying real estate in Italy. Finding love is not easy; I was now open to other possibilities.

Leo and I set out to look at as much property in the area as we could. We would scour the internet and talk to everyone we knew. Amazingly, everyone we talked to had a house for sale! Or an aunt or uncle or mama that had a property for sale! There was no lack of places to see, and I was still sure I would find the one and was eager to start the hunt again.

Rupert took it upon himself to enlist the help of his own real estate agent from the Lunigiana region. This agent was Federico, and he had helped Rupert and the Prince find their own country retreat in Codiponte, a village in the Lunigiana that is located between Emilia and Liguria in northern Tuscany. Their little village was called a *borgo* in Italy—a village with connected homes where essentially everyone lives in very close proximity to each other. Something like our townhomes in America. Rupert and Reynaldo's place consisted of three buildings beautifully appointed and charming as could be. Rupert said he would arrange some viewings with Federico the agent as soon as something interesting had come up. I was not convinced that we would be living in Lunigiana, and I certainly did not want to live in a *borgo*—too much togetherness. So for now I wanted to look around Liguria, but I wanted to look near Alassio at first because I felt at home there. But I did tell Rupert to proceed, because one has to have an open mind when looking for love.

What I did not realize at the time is that Leo was keen on us staying near Alassio so he could oversee the renovation, and Rupert was interested in us buying in Lunigiana, so *he* could oversee the renovation.

Monica was still on the lookout for properties for us to look at as well. One Saturday she called me early in the morning and said that Monday we would look for properties together. She had a friend that she had gone to school with who had some interesting properties to show us. Monday was a sunny day, and she picked me up in the Jeep, sunroof open and euro electronic music blaring on the radio. We drove to one of my favorite villages. Even though I was not keen on living in a *borgo*, this one was really pretty. We parked in the tiny parking lot in front of the agency.

Here's what I cannot figure out: Real estate offices in Italy are very posh. They all seem to have lots of properties for sale, but the agents just never seem to actually do any work. When you pass by an agency you will see all sorts of great properties in the window, nicely presented in frames with descriptions and even pricing in some cases. But the agent sitting at the desk inside is on the computer doing God knows what because they are clearly not working. I have entered the offices to ask about properties on several occasions, only to get a blank stare, and then they stand and come out to look at the photo and usually say yes, I can call you and we can go look. You write down your name and number and never hear from them again. Are these offices a front for something? Do they actually sell properties? I have never had a satisfying interaction with any of these real estate offices, so I didn't have much faith, even if the agent did go to school with Monica.

Her friend Marco was sitting behind the desk on the computer, and looked up and smiled and stood to kiss Monica on both cheeks. "This is my friend, Annette," Monica said in Italian. "*Piacere*," said Marco, as he extended his hand to me. Marco was a small stout man, around forty-five, with a full head of hair that was graying on the sides. He had a pleasant face, dark tan, and was wearing jeans and a t-shirt that said, "Show me the money," and sneakers. Italians are always wearing funny t-shirts with American sayings that sometimes make no sense to me. But this shirt was very spot- on, and I giggled to myself when I read it.

Marco first showed us a stone house near the office that I immediately knew was not at all what I was looking for—it was, frankly, hideous, and too small. Monica and I agreed without saying a word that it was pretty bad. We walked into the village this time, and stopped at a nine-foot-tall door near the middle of the street. We looked up at the large building and smiled, both thinking, now this is more like it! We entered a large foyer with twelve-foot ceilings; the place was in total disrepair, but it had good bones and Monica and I saw a great design potential as we looked past the crumbling walls. Whenever I enter a space, the first thing I always see and feel is the light. The quality of light hits the back of my brain somewhere deep and primal. I can't put my finger on what it is exactly, but it is most likely what makes me good at what I do. And for me, the light in this place was spectacular. It was a deep light, a light that evoked "*chiaroscuro*," which means strong contrasts between light and dark. It is something that Italian artists like Caravaggio are known for, as well as Dutch painters like Vermeer. Simply put, it is the drama of lighting. This place was full of it. If I like a space, I start taking pictures with my iPhone. It's my way of testing the quality of light for photography, and I began snapping photos like mad. The place was enormous, really gigantic. It was clear that this was a building that had housed many people. It had a staircase to the left, and a wide hallway that led to a kitchen in the back that obviously was used to feed a crowd. There was an antique butcher block in the center of the room and a large ceramic sink. Industrial lights hung above the cracked marble counter. There were whitewashed cabinets and shelves that were hung over peeling pale blue paint, which I loved. No appliances—those were long gone. The kitchen had a small room off to the side that most likely served as the pantry, a place to store vegetables, canned goods, jams, and fruits and to hang salami; it would have been what Italians refer to as the *cantina*.

"What was this place?" I asked Marco. He smiled and said it was a hospital. "It's always hard to say, but it was most likely built in the 1600s and renovated at the turn of the twentieth century," he explained. For a hospital is was on the small side, but it had all the right parts since I intended to teach here and live here. The downstairs had a great room, a dining room, and a small room off the great room which we surmised was used for triage and operations on patients, since a few vintage surgical instruments were strewn around the floor. This creeped me out, I have to admit.

We climbed to the second floor (which Italians call the first floor; their first floor is called the ground floor). There were six bedrooms on this floor—lined up as you would expect in a hospital—all off the wide corridor. Two bathrooms were at the end of the hall, one to the right and one to the left. We inspected each room, some of them still with their rudimentary hospital beds that resembled cots on wheels. There were even a few hospital supplies like bedpans and test tubes and red rubber tubing, and a metal pharmacy cabinet with some old medicine bottles still inside. The thing that amazed me was the selection of paint colors they had chosen: warm rich tones like terracotta, blood red, mustard yellow, and deep indigo, pale blue; odd choices for hospital rooms, but who knows what the norm was for institutional spaces at the turn of the twentieth century? The light on these tones was beautiful and saturated in daylight, and very comforting, so on some level these color choices had been made with the patients in mind. Honestly, I questioned the *feng shui* of the place in my mind and was not sure about its emotional energy. When I walk into place, I immediately start thinking about the energy and what went on there in the past. Was it a peaceful place? In this case I was concerned that this was a place of pain.

I think house hunting is a lot like dating; when you meet someone, your initial reaction is to the exterior visual clues. Then you are exposed to the inside of the person. Just as in dating, visiting a house has to be measured by looks first, then emotion, and then potential. It's just like going on a first date for me. This date was going well, but there were a few quirks that had to be sussed out.

We scaled the last set of stairs to find the attic space. The roof was gone and birds had taken over this floor. There were nests everywhere, some abandoned and some with eggs in them. It was clearly a safe place for the birds to live. It was amazing, truly magical. All I remember is the deep whimsical happiness I felt when I saw the light streaming through the openings in the roof with the birds fluttering everywhere. This space had potential.

"This would make a gorgeous master suite, or a studio," I said to Monica. She nodded her head but Marco warned, "Be careful here, the floor is not secure and you could fall through." We would later find looking that safety was always an issue when you are looking at ruins, and you had to really mind yourself. We all carefully walked towards the stairs and headed out of the building.

"Come with me," said Marco, and we followed him to the back of the building where we passed through an iron gate to a courtyard. "This is the place where patients would enjoy the outside, take in the fresh air." It truly was a beautiful courtyard, with the old rose bushes blooming, and the remnants of outdoor furniture from the turn of the century still in place. Although disheveled, the courtyard was inspirational, and I imagined I could sit there all day.

These were the questions I had to ask myself after our tour: Did the room at the top make up for the pain-soaked second floor? Was this space functional? Did I want to live in the center of a village? We headed back to Marco's office to talk money and details. On a scale from one to ten was this date a ten? Marco brought over tiny cups of espresso and sat down at his computer.

"How much?" asked Monica, cigarette dangling from her mouth. "For the hospital."

Marco chuckled, "Oh yes. Fifty thousand euros." Now, I know this does not seem like a lot for an 8,000-square-foot building with a wonderful garden space, but keep in mind that this building was huge and expensive to renovate, and we needed to know a few things about the state of the house. How was it classified to the county—was it residential or commercial? I doubted that it was residential, and re-classifying and getting what they call "permission" to become a residence would cost us who knows what in time and money. Did Marco have the right to sell the property? Always the numero uno question when buying a property in Italy. And the second most important question: Who owns the property? Was it one person, two, three, or the state? With the obvious renovation costs of electrical, plumbing, kitchen, bathrooms, subflooring, flooring, a new roof, and outfitting the attic space, we were talking at least one-half million euros. Having said that, it could be cool if all of our queries had the right answers. But since this was not my first rodeo, I was extremely tuned in, and based 100 percent in reality.

Monica did all the follow up on the old hospital, while I carried on with ways to sell the flat. Leo called me about a property that had come available—a property in the next town over. It was an artist compound, so at once I was very interested. "Tell me more," I said to him as we walked to *aperitivo* one night at our local hang out. Leo said, "I am not sure, but the agent called me because I had put the word out about your house being for sale. She said that she would help sell it, but in the meantime she thought you might want to take a look since it was something special." Sounded about right, an agent wanting to sell me a house, and having a faint interest in selling our flat. "Okay," I said. "Let's go look at it." "Great," said Leo. "Now let's go order some cocktails." "Now that's a great idea," I said.

Leo picked me up the next day in his Smart car. Oddly, the car was tiny on the outside, but had lots of leg and head room on the inside—the perfect town car, but not something for the *Autostrada*. We jumped on the *Autostrada*, and my life instantly flashed before my eyes. Leo drove 120 km per hour and I just prayed and hung on as the entire car felt like there was an earthquake going on inside it. It rattled, shook, and groaned as we careened towards the seaside town of Ceriale, the next tiny town over from Alassio. We met the agent at the toll booth—a very Italian thing to do. It was a great landmark and hard to miss. There she was, in very high heels and a very short skirt, long black hair and glitter make-up. I remember thinking that she looked a bit trashy, but who cared? She smiled and waved and motioned us to come over behind her, then she headed to the driver's window, leaned in, and told Leo in Italian to follow her. We drove to the end of the exit and then made a quick right down a narrow road to what looked like an industrial area. She pulled over and parked, and we parked behind her. My first thought is that I was so happy that I wore sneakers. Leo made the introductions; we both said "*piacere*" at the same time and shook hands. Chiara, as she was called, was quite attractive behind all the glitter makeup; she resembled Penelope Cruz, actually, and seemed quite nice.

Chiara led us to what looked like a cement bunker. Leo and I walked on a narrow walkway, careful not to slip and fall into what was literally a trench. We dared not look up to see where we were headed. We finally came to the cement box that was the house. The *Autostrada* we had come in on was in front of us. Of course we both immediately knew this was a no, but we were curious what could be inside. We all walked down a short flight of stairs to the living area, which was something out of a futuristic retro sci-fi movie—that is the only way to describe it. It was like *Blade Runner*, dark, damp, and horrible. There was a rudimentary kitchen that was in no way artistic. I think that Leo and I saw it at the same time—a tiny opening in the floor with a narrow ladder. I was having flashbacks of Nice with Monica.

"What's this?" said Leo. "This is the bedroom and the bathroom, downstairs." Just when I thought it could not get any worse. I looked down the dark hole, the black hole of Calcutta, and said " Oh, wow." That's all I could manage to say...I was traumatized. This was not a home, this was a Turkish prison. I would even say a Turkish prison might have been better.

I whispered to Leo, "I am not going down there." He offered to go down, so I headed outside, and as I was walking down the sidewalk, I heard them emerge, Leo saying, "That was interesting." Interesting was our code for *Holy shit, no.*

Chiara smiled at me, "Not for you," she said. "No, not for me," I replied. Another strike out. I was getting the feeling that I was always looking for love in all the wrong places. We thanked her and headed back home.

Rupert came back into the picture full force after this. He had some new ideas of where we should look in the Tuscan countryside. I explained that I was going to try to see if I could find something near Alassio, since I loved the Riviera and had good friends in town. He was not convinced I would find what I was looking for, but he was willing to help me look.

One day, Leo said that his friend who was our real estate agent in Alassio had told him about a great property above Garlenda. We had used the B&B there for my workshops, and my Norwegian beach club friend Inga's parents lived there, so I was familiar with the area. So when Leo offered to drive me up to the property I was excited and invited Rupert to come have a look as well. We jumped in my car and headed to the small hamlet above Garlenda.

On the way there Leo told me that the house was in a *borgo*. But the orientation of the house was such that you did not feel you were a part of the connected village. I was not a fan of this type of configuration, but again one must always look, so we did. The road was uphill so we parked carefully. Rupert was already there with his notepad in hand. The house was at the front of the village; as far as we could tell, it was connected to one other house. The house looked like it was in mid-renovation. Leo's friend the real estate agent was there as well. He greeted us with a warm smile and we trekked up the drive.

As opposed to most agents in Italy that stand in the doorway while you show yourself around, he actually had to show us around since it was a big and complicated floor plan. We followed him up a staircase, the entrance to the house. It was quite a charming entrance, with an arch and lovely patina on the walls on either side of the stairs. I kind of loved it. We landed on the first floor, and to the left there was a small dining room. "What was this?" I asked. "A seminary, most likely where the priests stayed. It's long gone, but the building tells the story," said the agent.

"Here, let me show you where we think there might have been a classroom, or a study room," he added. We walked through a narrow hallway through another archway to a large room, maybe forty feet by forty feet. The floorboards were rotten and some were missing. "Be careful signora," said the agent. "Do not go into the room, it is dangerous." "I got that," I said to him. "Thank you." "This is cool," I finally said to Leo. The room had large windows that faced the mountains in Garlenda; it would make the most beautiful kitchen, I thought. The light was extraordinary, and as we walked down the wide hallways, there were three rooms on each side—six rooms total. They were small but manageable. At the end of the hallway was a window looking out to sea; the view was breathtaking. The terrace wrapped around to the study room with a doorway that had been recently put there. It was a nice size terrace with a stone floor. "What's that?" I asked, pointing to a window on the other side of the terrace.

"That is a neighbor," said the agent. "That is the only place that the property is connected." I did not like that idea, plus I thought that it might be a little small, but I kept this to myself. Living in a *borgo* was something I had to think about; they were asking 750,000 euros for the seminary house.

Before we left the *borgo* the agent winked at me and said, "I have something else for you to look at…400,000 euros." So off we went to another house.

We walked through the tiny *borgo* and up two flights of stairs to a connected stone house located at the other end of the village I often wondered what people were thinking, making these homes so difficult to get to. I supposed it was another way to assure safety. Rupert lived in a *borgo*, and from what I could tell he loved it. He had bought three run-down buildings in a relatively historic place at the foothills of a mountain range that ran opposite to the famous Carrara mountains, in a beautiful valley with a rushing river. He had fully renovated the property in four years; the buildings were lovingly decorated with beautiful flea market finds and family heirlooms. There were beautiful guest quarters where I would stay when I came to visit. It was about two hours from the center of Genova, where he and his prince lived. The perfect country house. Rupert was really an expert at reviving old places and making them livable. He breathed life into them and he loved every minute. So there is no way that he was not going to be involved in the process. I was willing to jump into this great adventure with him looking forward and not worrying about the past. Whatever had transpired was nothing that would get in the way of our mutual love of renovation and design.

Once at the top of many stairs, we passed through a tiny entrance-way and entered the main room. It was huge—gigantic—so big, in fact, that there was an old olive press smack dab in the middle of the living room.

"I assume this was the mill for the village," I said, to which Rupert responded, "Great observation, Annette." We all laughed, even the homeowners who were there waiting for us. They were a German couple; our agent did the introductions and we exchanged niceties. Off we went exploring their house, while they sat in the front room waiting for our comments. "Lovely home," we would all say in unison. It had a layout much like the property on the other end of the village. There was an upstairs and a downstairs. It was decorated most likely in the

1970s and nothing had changed. It was great if you liked the '70s, but for me it was just old and musty and everything needed to be thrown out. The house had big rooms and a decent kitchen off the living room. The main decision here was, did one want to live with a ten-foot-round millstone, complete with wooden turnstyle, in the main room? I, quite frankly, did not.

It was a sad house, in a *borgo*, with steep stairs—my complete nightmare. So for me, the mill house was a no. But Rupert liked it; he thought it had "distinct possibilities," something we said over and over again in the course of house hunting. We developed a code that would help us navigate house hunting trips. Rupert would look at me and say, "Do you want to think about it?" It was his way of saying *We can go; I know you don't like it.* I was thankful that we did. It meant that we could say goodbye without insulting the homeowners eager to hear our reaction and maybe get an offer.

We said goodbye to the mill house and walked the long way around the *borgo* to get a sense of the outer perimeter of it. Along the steep road we looked up and admired the stonework and window frames. We came to the backside of the seminary house—the one I thought was too small—and to our surprise, there was another part of the house that was never mentioned. It was a garage of sorts, a storeroom with a glass double door. "This is cool," I said, not knowing that it belonged to the house we had already seen. I asked, "Is this the back part of the house?" The agent said, "Oh, yes. This is the storage room. Good for a garage. You like it? Would you like me to open it?" he asked. I said, "Yes, please," thinking all the while that the next time we did a house tour I would ask if there was anything else attached to the house I needed to know about. One assumed that an agent would show you everything, but not in Italy. Omitted important information about the property was something that we would witness over and over again.

It was a beautiful, light-filled space. It would be a waste to use it as a garage—it would make a beautiful photography studio for Frank and my workshop students.

"I love it," I said to everyone. "I love it." We walked to the cars parked in front, got in, and the agent said there was a less expensive property down the road. "On the way to Alassio, up high, nice land, maybe you are interested? It is not my property, it is my friend's. Maybe I can call him to meet us there in ten minutes? He is a real estate agent as well." Leo said he couldn't but that we should go ahead. Rupert and I agreed to go. You never knew what you would find. I joked with Rupert, "You know what Frank says: as long as there are no goats or barking dogs across the street we are all right." That was his only demand when I told him we were looking at houses to buy. Frank was pretty go with the flow; he trusted my judgment, and quite honestly he just wanted to buy a house without having to do the hunt. He was not a fan of house hunting. Whenever he was in Italy we managed to look at a few houses together, but we would only look at houses that I had vetted.

We followed the agent down the hill, winding our way to the west side of the mountain. Then up, up, up, and finally he stopped and parked on the side of the road. We saw a house at the bottom of a hill and looked at each other. We did not have much faith this would be the one; we didn't have to say anything, we knew. We hopped out of the car, and instantly a dog started to bark across the street in a field filled with goats. We both looked at each other and laughed so hard that it was hard to get hold of ourselves, and of course the poor agent had no idea what was so funny. We decided to have a look anyway and try to keep it together.

When we walked into the tiny house, the other agent was there waiting for us. It was unimpressive from the outside, a small stone square house with few windows. Through the doorway we saw a few pieces of furniture, a sofa, a chair, both of velvet and oddly stylish, thread-worn but of good quality. There were grand, velvet, deep crimson drapes with gold fringe, and an old terrazzo floor throughout. Weirdly, it was not bad, although everything was full of mildew and mold. There was something strangely beautiful about the interior; it may have been the soft and shadowy light. It was most likely a beautiful space in its day.

I thought of a charmingly decrepit jewel box. It had an eerie elegance about it and the light was beautiful. I pulled out my phone to start photographing it, and the images were haunting. This house was an exhibit, a museum, a shrine to what once was. I thought it looked like a set from a Wes Anderson horror flick, if Wes Anderson produced horror films. I looked at Rupert and said, "Let's go." He nodded his head and we were out of there.

Sometimes house hunting in Italy felt like we were exploring the past, sometimes if felt like we were stuck in time, and sometimes it seemed we were unearthing a modern nightmare. But it was always a visual treat, with unexpected twists and turns—and it was never boring. It's probably why I would carry on until I found the perfect one. Much like dating, you had to look for signs, hear the stories, and deal with the emotional baggage along the way, until the right one comes along. The seminary house, the mill house, and the Wes Anderson horror flick house were not on the list. The pain-soaked hospital was amazing, and there was a moment that Monica was considering buying it. But, in the end, none of these made the cut for a second visit. We moved on.

Alassio, 2011

Alassio Flat, 2011

Alassio Flat, 2011

Monica and Leo

Rocce di Pinamare Beach Club, Albenga

Frank with Vivi at the breeder's in Bergamo when we first met

Castle House in the hills of Alassio

Artist's house in town near Alassio, like a Turkish prison

Wes Anderson's horror movie house, Alassio

Vineyard House, Albenga

Fresco House frescoes

Fresco House upper floor

The Summer House

The Summer House

The house with the barn on the flood plain

The Casola House barn

The Casola House kitchen: it was a school and would have been a great choice had the owner not shared the property

Village for sale, entrance

First photo of La Fortezza I ever posted on Instagram

La Fortezza's front façade, pre-renovation

La Fortezza's front façade and part of
the façade during renovation

La Fortezza scaffolding

La Fortezza studio during renovation

Renovated studio

La Fortezza main house living room during renovation

Renovated main house living room

La Fortezza during renovation, with tile laid

La Fortezza terrace, 2017

La Fortezza view after completed renovation

CHAPTER 21

Distinct Possibilities

I was about a year into my newest house-hunting adventure when I decided that I needed to set parameters—some boundaries—because the real estate agents in Italy clearly had none. It took me about a year to realize that Italians in general (and especially real estate agents) would show you anything. It was fun at first, but then it became frustrating. Frank and I really began to talk about what we were looking for and how we wanted to use the space. So we made a list—we are list makers, and why not make a list of all of the things our new home needed to have to make it perfect? Although we were aware that most likely we would not find the perfect place, why not try?

Around that time the real estate agent Marco re-emerged (Monica's friend from the pain-soaked hospital property), emailing me to say a friend had a property we might be interested in and he would love to show it to me. Rupert was coming to Alassio to visit, so I made an appointment for us to look at the property. The agent said it was a vineyard property right outside of town towards Albenga, an industrial town the next town over. It was also located in the foothills of Garlenda, in a valley perfect for growing grapes. I had not been to the area much;

all I knew was that it was beautiful and that the nearest town located on the top of a hill was beautiful. We set a time to meet at ten o'clock the next Saturday morning, and Marco agreed he would bring his associate so we could meet her.

On Saturday we headed to his office and were warmly greeted by Marco, who immediately sent his associate next door to the bar to fetch three espressos. "This is Helene, my associate," he said as she ran out the door. Helene was dressed in a white pantsuit with black pumps and a lot of gold jewelry—I remember this because my first thought was why is she so dressed up to go look at a ruin of a vineyard house? I just assumed that it was a ruin since it was in the countryside and was priced at only 350,000 euros with twenty acres of land. She returned with three espressos in tiny ceramic cups on a tray with sugar packets. We downed our *caffes* and jumped into the car to follow Marco and Helene to the house. We took the roundabout, bypassing the town of Albenga, and were promptly on a country road with vineyards on either side of us. I was always filled with wonder that one could be in a chic town, and ten minutes down the road was a rural area. It was one of the things that made living in Italy so wonderful as far as I was concerned. It was like dating a really chic guy and realizing he looked perfect whether he dressed down or dressed up. That was Italy in a nutshell.

We drove for about ten minutes and made a sharp left turn down a dirt road, past a group of mailboxes to a gated driveway. In front of us was a ruin of a stone house, the Vineyard House, as I came to call it; simply charming, but in dire need of some TLC. Marco explained, "I don't have the key. My friend was supposed to drop it off, but he went off for the weekend and forgot. So we jump the fence." I thought, *Why the hell did I wear tight jeans?* The gate was about five feet tall—almost as tall as me—so I would have to scale it, then throw my leg over and drop to the ground.

Rupert smiled at me. "You ready for this?" he asked, clearly amused to watch me attempt to pole vault this thing.

"Sure," I said. "No problem. Here, hold my purse," and I handed him my bag. I followed Marco, who was already on the other side, and proceeded to scale the fence and drop to the ground without a problem. Rupert looked fairly impressed as he handed me my bag, and in a gentlemanly fashion turned to offer to help Helene scale the gate. "No, no," she said. "I stay here"

We walked around the Vineyard House. It wasn't big. It was laid out in three parts. Standing facing the house, on the left was room one, a storage room, and room two was the middle room, which could be a living room. Then, to the far right, room three could house a kitchen. There was an upper level where the floor had caved in, so you could look up and see the two bedrooms on either side of the collapsed landing in between the rooms, as well as the top of the stairs which were half gone. Rupert and I were already thinking and talking about how to utilize the rooms. I think that Rupert and I instantly loved the place. The setting was magical and the building a stone square house, something that was not typical of the area. It was more Tuscan, or even French, which I kind of loved. It had once been a very pretty farmhouse. The location was perfect: it was secluded, yet accessible to towns in the area. The view was of the vineyards and a forest in the distance. I looked at Rupert and he looked at me and we both thought the same thing—this is it. We were in love. I told Marco, "This is beautiful; it has so much potential."

Mind you, Rupert and I were in love with a house with no roof, crumbling walls, missing or crumbling floors, no actual windows, and two doors. But the doors were magnificent. The problem with seeing things the way that Rupert and I did is that we saw everything finished and would forget that most people just see a pile of rocks—and by most people I mean Frank. Frank was due to visit, and this house would definitely be on the list to show him. We walked around the vineyard, looking back at the stone house saturated with golden sunlight; I imagined the pool and gardens right in front of the house. Just at that moment, a tractor came down the road. The farmer waved, and I was sold. I wanted a vineyard; I wanted this house. After a year of searching I felt we had found it, we found the one. I had butterflies in my stomach and my head was spinning—I was in love.

Rupert and I scaled the gate and headed to the back of the house. A private road flanked the back of the house, which was really charming with ivy growing up the side and had beautiful little windows—well, what would become windows and now were just openings. These windows would probably be in our bedrooms one day, I imagined. We looked to see if we could add on the 30 percent that was allowed, and there was plenty of room on the sides.

Rupert asked Marco, "Annette's husband is coming next week. Can we come again next Saturday to show it to him?" Marco agreed to the same time next week and promised to get the gate key this time. Rupert and I hopped into our car, waved *ciao*, and headed past the back of the house down the private road to see what was in the neighborhood. Above the house to the right of the road was a large vegetable garden and what I could only describe as a wooden hippy house (obviously a weekend house); funny, but it had its charms. As we wound down the bumpy dirt road, we encountered a very long, beautiful, new stone wall. Behind tall gates stood a beautiful stone house, with a vineyard beyond that was visible from what would be our backyard. The vineyard house view included all the neighboring vineyards down the road. *How wonderful*, I thought. As we drove past the wall, we came upon a dead end where there was a charming stone chapel surrounded by wildflowers. Could this be real, I thought, or was this a dream? It was all too perfect.

We headed back to the flat to have lunch and discuss a plan of action. We needed to find out about the owners, and the vineyard. Who worked the vineyard? Rupert suggested having our *notaio* Ilario check it out. Who were the owners? Was it a business? If it was a business, we would need to have the building reclassified and the land as well. What would this take? We had tons of homework ahead of us. We finished lunch, had an espresso, and Rupert headed back to Genova.

I started doing research on the property right away so I would have some information for Frank when he arrived. I began by sending an email to Marco, asking for a plat of the property to further assess the boundaries. I also asked if we could know that name of the vineyard or the business, and who the owners were. I assumed this was privately owned and not a business, but one had to be sure—dead sure. Italians are not about sharing details, or information for that matter, so I had to do all the asking. What I got back was interesting, and oh, so Italian.

Marco sent me the plat and a blueprint design of the house that could be built using the existing rubble of the building. This was something that happened frequently when looking at ruins. The agent would send or show you a construction drawing of what could be—I think this was for people who had no imagination. But we had plenty of imagination. It was an awful design. The building plans were useful in one way; they showed us how much could be added on to the existing footprint, and that information would come in handy since this plan had been approved by the commune. The plat showed the boundaries of the property, which was a piece of the puzzle. We would need to rely on our detective skills to suss out the entire picture. I was in love, but I was not blind. I sent the plat and the drawings to Ilario, and luckily he was the head honcho of the entire region on Liguria and was very familiar with Alassio—it seemed he knew everybody. So he could fill in the blanks… at least, that's what I was hoping. Then we waited.

Frank arrived on Thursday and I could hardly wait to show him the house on Saturday. We did our usual routine of cooking, partaking in *aperitivo* every night, walking to town, and hanging out at the beach club. Frank rode his bike in the morning, and I made a lovely lunch, always followed by a nap at the beach and *aperitivo* at the beach bar. We had our routines down and we loved them.

Saturday morning rolled around, and Rupert said he would meet us at the house at 10:00. We arrived a little early; I was anxious to get Frank's take before Marco and Helene arrived. When we drove up, Frank admitted, "Wow, what a pretty property." I was so pleased, I smiled from ear to ear. Frank was familiar with the area since he had ridden his bike down this road many times up to the village on the hill. "I have always loved this road," he said. "But I had no idea this was here."

Rupert pulled up behind us. He barreled out of his tiny convertible; the proportions of big Rupert in this tiny car always struck me as comical. The one thing about Rupert is that he liked tiny things—tiny chairs and tiny spaces, tiny beds and tiny cars…even his boyfriend was tiny! Frank always said he was Nancy Reagan trapped in a large male body.

Rupert gave Frank a big bear hug. "*Ciao*, Frank. Welcome to Italy. What do you think?" he asked, pointing towards the vineyard house. Frank said, "So far I like it, but Rupert, there's no roof." "Just a minor detail," I said. We all laughed and Marco drove up and walked toward us, dangling the key in front of him. I introduced him to Frank, they shook hands, and we all walked through the gate and into the front where Frank could have a good look. He looked inside the building and took a minute to think about what to say. Finally he said, squinting into the sun, "Are we calling this a house?"

"Yes, we are calling this a house, Frank," I answered.

"Are we?" he said again, with a smile on his face. "A house, not rubble?"

"I get that there's not much here, but this place has a magical spirit that we can rebuild," I said.

"How much is this?" he asked.

Rupert chimed in, "I think that is up for negotiation."

"Who owns this house?" Frank asked.

"I did ask," I said, "but Marco has not told us yet."

One thing about Italians is that if you're a woman, you're not a man. You're the wife, the mama, but you're not on level ground with a man. I was reminded of this daily. If you're asking the butcher about a cut of meat he'll give you a straight answer, but if you're dealing in matters of business, he won't. It may happen eventually, but if you're a man and you ask a man a question, you will most likely get an answer. That's what happened with Marco. Frank asked him, "Marco, who owns this property?" and Marco coughed up all sorts of information I hadn't heard before.

"The property is owned by a man who has a company; he makes the wine and sells it. He is interested in selling the vineyard and the house, or they can be bought separately. You can also buy the whole thing and they will continue to maintain the vineyard if you pay for the help and the supplies needed to maintain it." Marco smiled and added, "You understand, Franco?"

Frank said, "Wow, that was a lot of information. Good information. So how much?"

"Three hundred fifty thousand euro for the whole property, but I will need to ask if it is only the house," said Marco. We continued to walk all over the property—for over an hour. We concluded with Marco and told him we would be in touch with any questions. But for now we felt all right.

Frank and I headed back to our flat, grabbed our beach stuff, and headed to the club for lunch. We decided that we would just wait and see what Ilario had to add to the conversation about the vineyard house. I loved the idea of waiting because, quite honestly, I was exhausted thinking about it. A break was most welcome. We both liked the house and we all agreed it did have distinct possibilities.

Frank stayed for a few more weeks and then headed back to the States. After he left, my sweet friend Kelly came for a visit. She had not been back since we had gone to Milan for the furniture show, so it was great to see her again in Italy. I was dying to show her the Vineyard House, as I had come to call it. Her opinion meant a lot to me since she was an architectural designer. We had not heard a word from Ilario; we had no intel. But this was the way things go in Italy. Everything was slow and patience was something I was getting very good at, an unintentional perk. So, patiently I waited…and I visited the house regularly.

Kelly and I drove to see the house the day after her arrival. She was excited and commented along the way how pretty the road was. We pulled up, and I informed her she would need to jump the gate. She was game, and over we went.

She loved the setting and immediately knew there was going to be a lot of work renovating. "The house is going to be a challenge. It will have to be completely rebuilt, and everything will need to be replaced. You may want to think about tearing it down—saving the good bits and incorporating those bits into the new house," she said. I explained the layout and what Rupert and I thought would be the best use of the space. To my surprise, Kelly agreed with it all. "Sounds like a great plan," she said.

I walked her all over the property and down the road to the chapel. We spent the morning hiking all over the place, then, tired and hungry, we left to spend the rest of the day at the beach. We discussed the Vineyard House all afternoon. I said goodbye to Kelly a few days later.

In the meantime, I had not heard back from Ilario about who owned the property. Marco the agent was of no help; he claimed his friend who was listing it was the owner, but was on vacation in the Maldives. I thought that this might be a good time to start looking in Lunigiana—why not? Just in case the Vineyard House fell through. I needed to keep plugging along. Patience in Italy was good, but covering your ass was even better. On to plan B.

CHAPTER 22

Love Is Hard Work

I called Rupert and said, "Okay, you win, let's look in Lunigiana." We had been at this for a while in Alassio and maybe it was time. Rupert was thrilled, because he felt there would be many more possibilities in northern Tuscany where he and Reynaldo had their country house. We both scoured the internet, but Rupert had an ace up his sleeve. He had a real estate agent that he really trusted, Federico, who had sold them their house. He was a nice, decent man—a good egg— and he would help us find our house, Rupert was sure of it. Problem was, it was time for me to return to Atlanta for a few months.

Every day back home I would spend all morning online looking at properties. I made this my job. I would email agents with little or no response. But one day I got a lovely email from a woman working in the area we were searching. Paola and her partner, Tiziana, owned a small agency in Aulla, a small town located near Carrara and Lucca. It was an ugly, industrial town that had been rebuilt after it was bombed to the ground in World War II. Aulla's claim to fame is that it had a bomb factory—the actual reason it was bombed during the war. The agent wrote that she wanted to see if she could help me find a house. I had inquired about one of their properties and she had actually responded, how about that? I was thrilled. I told her that I would be back in Italy in March and we should definitely meet then. I told Rupert about her, and he volunteered to go to meet her the next time he was in Aulla.

After their meeting, Rupert reported back to me. He said Paola and Tiziana were very nice, and that we were going to go see a few properties with them when I arrived.

I arrived in the middle of March, the rainy season in Lunigiana. But I figured if I liked a property in the rain, I'd really love it in the sunshine. I arranged to stay with Rupert for a couple days while we looked at properties.

Paola and Tiziana greeted us with handshakes when we met, and we promptly sat down in their office and looked through the photos of houses they had selected according to my specifications. They seemed efficient. They had printed off some photos of homes, including the one that I had found on the internet that had started our conversation via email. I put the ones I liked in the "yes" pile and discarded the rest. I liked three properties. We all gathered around the big monitor on her desk, while Tiziana made us shots of espresso. Paola explained location and a little about the area to us, pointing at the monitor. I was familiar with Lunigiana because Rupert had shown us the area in hopes we would by something when we were on the hunt for homes the first time around. I knew he was disappointed when we ended up in a flat in Alassio. But he was really excited to be on the hunt again in Lunigiana.

We threw back our espressos and decided that we could look at the house I had found on the internet that morning, and we would make appointments for the others. The house I found was an abandoned stone building owned by one family. Paola told us it was their summer house when they were children. One brother lived in the area and another brother lived in Milan—and they were both set on selling it. This was good news. We all jumped into Tiziana's Fiat Punto and off we went at breakneck speed. Rupert looked at me, terrified, and latched his seat belt, and said, "This is going to be interesting." I also latched my seat belt and held on for dear life. We drove for about forty minutes to a beautiful town called Villafranca.

"This is one of my favorite towns," said Rupert. We drove down a country road, which then became a long driveway. The summer house was standing in front of us at the end of the driveway on a rise—it was really beautiful. Like the Vineyard House, it was a very square, stone, Tuscan-style house; like the Vineyard House it did not have many embellishments but was a simple a solid design. The sun had come out, so the scene was very tranquil.

Paola headed towards the front door, but the keys would not fit. I thought *Are you kidding me? What's up with the key situation and real estate agents?* I did some deep breathing, then looked at Rupert and made the gun-to-my-head sign. He laughed and suggested we look around. The property was a good size, and although it was in a valley, it had a beautiful vista of trees and mountains in the distance. "I say we come back tomorrow. Let's add this to the list," said Rupert.

"Good idea," said Tiziana. We got back into the car and drove back to Aulla just in time for lunch. It was Friday, so Rupert promised we would drive around the next day with Reynaldo to see if we could find anything for sale. I loved that idea.

The sun was shining Saturday, and we awoke to the sound of birds singing. We dressed and headed to the bar for a brioche and espresso, then headed towards Villafranca, which was where the summer house was. We wanted to show it to Reynaldo. Plus, we wanted to look around the area to see if we found any *rustici* (stone rubble that might be for sale). Reynaldo drove my Fiat 500—he was a great driver and loved to drive. We flew down the road and, as we approached the town, we all spotted a great looking abandoned stone barn up a hill. Reynaldo screeched on the brakes, did a quick 180, and parked in the field below the barn. We all looked up and said "WOW;" this looked amazing. There was a rudimentary driveway overgrown with grass that was knee-high. I was wearing flip-flops, as was Rupert—not exactly ideal hiking footwear, but we managed. When we got to the top of the knoll there was the most beautiful stone house. Yes, it was in disrepair, but it was stunning all the same. Upon closer inspection, we noticed that built on the right side of the rubble was a brand-new garage. It was made of metal and was locked up like Fort Knox. We all collectively walked to the structure to have a closer look. On even closer inspection, it just looked like some sort of storage. But for what?

We peeked into the falling-down structure—again no roof—but there was a small fireplace in one of the rooms; most likely this would have been the kitchen. It was a lovely house, with a great position on the property and beautiful front lawn that sloped towards the road. Reynaldo was already heading to the back of the property on the left side of the building. Rupert was a few paces behind him, and as he looked back to see if I was following behind, he jumped about two feet into the air and ran towards me screaming, "Snake, snake, snake!" He was flailing his arms and running in circles; it was a hysterical sight, seeing this large, manly man running around like a silly girl and screaming so dramatically. At the same time Reynaldo heard the screaming, he motioned to be quiet, putting his index finger to his mouth. He pointed to the backyard and then again brought his index finger to his mouth. Rupert, mouthed the word, "W H A T?" Reynaldo pointed again and started fast walking towards us, and when they both reached me we started running. Of course we could not help but laugh as we ran—between Rupert leaping and waving and screaming, and Reynaldo silently gesturing, the scene was right out of a sitcom. We ran to the car, jumped in, and laughed so hard no one could speak. It seemed this abandoned house was not abandoned at all; there was a fully functioning garden in the back and people working it. The garage was most likely for gardening supplies, tractors, and power tools. Nothing to see here, just a normal Italian family using their land, and that was it. After lunch, we headed to the summer house to show Reynaldo and see what he thought. He loved it—especially the property and the position of the house. We tromped around for a while and then headed back home. It was a really fun day. These were the good house-hunting times.

On Monday we were to meet the ladies from Aulla to see new houses. Paola looked great in her black outfit with a brightly patterned silk scarf tied around her neck. Rupert gave me a look to indicate he was not a fan of Tiziana, who was less into fashion and wearing a shapeless frock. We piled into Tiziana's Fiat Punto and, wheels squealing, headed to our first appointment.

"We are seeing a beautiful villa above the hills of Villafranca, then we go to a more rustic location," Paola informed us. "Also, we will go again to the one you liked on the internet—the summer house. I have the right keys." I nodded my head, all while hanging on and praying to myself. Tiziana was a terrible driver. Rupert was pale and unresponsive at this point.

"*Eccola* [here it is]," said Tiziana finally. We looked up and saw the most beautiful stone villa, in a very picturesque village—but yet another *borgo*. We walked up the stairs and entered through a doorway at least nine feet high. The hand-carved wooden door was in pretty good shape. The front room was grand with blood-red wallpaper and the remnants of gold leaf trim. We stepped into the next room, and it was even bigger and had frescos on the wall—a seascape with boats and the rolling waves and seashells. We walked back through the foyer and into another quite stately room that looked like it could be the dining room. Behind the dining room was a kitchen; it was not much. Next to the kitchen were the stairs that led up to four rooms in all four corners. This floor had a very different vibe—it was much more rustic, with the lighting streaming through. Everything had been ripped out of the space and all that was left were bare wood floors and brick and straw and mortar. It needed a complete overhaul. The work would be massive, and at the end you would have a beautiful villa, but in a village with no land and a pretty unimpressive view. It was a "no" for me. On to the next one on the list.

We entered a small hamlet about ten minutes from our last location, and turned down a narrow road into pasture. I was about to ask where we were, but we sharply turned onto an extremely narrow road, and when I looked down my side of the car there was about a hundred-foot drop-off; we could have easily plunged to our deaths. I closed my eyes until Tiziana hit level ground. In front of us stood an old farmhouse. We entered from the back and the stench hit us as soon as we opened the door. I could barely stand it. I made it through one room and had to abort the mission. "I'm out," I said. It was clear to me this was a big NO.

We got into the Punto and hit the same hill going up at lightning speed, fishtailing and almost careened off the edge. "STOP," screamed Rupert. "STOP STOP STOP!!!!!" Tiziana could not hear him as she was revving the engine to gun up the hill, but the car was too light and just threw up gravel and dirt and was sliding left and right. This time Rupert said it loud enough for her to stop: "STOP, GOD DAMNIT. We're getting out. This is too dangerous." As we walked up the steep hill, he looked over at me and said, "She's an idiot." When the car reached a safe part of the road, we got back into the backseat, buckled in, and headed to the next property on our list.

The next property on the list was a barn, not far away, that I had seen on the internet. Paola had not seen it in person, and it was not vetted, so we all had our doubts. We rolled up to a pasture with a large hay barn made of stone and concrete on the left. It had a small house to the right of it with a narrow driveway in between. The barn towered over the house. The rest of the property was very flat. I wondered what had been planted there, as we parked in the field and walked towards the barn. The barn was clearly for animals, with a cement trough running on one side. Rupert was walking on the property some distance away from the barn, so I walked out to meet him and we headed to the far side of the property. We stopped and we both looked down into a very large dry bed. He looked at me and I said, "Water." "Yep," he repeated. "Water." This entire field was on a huge flood plain. Obviously this was another big no, so we headed back to the car and scratched this one off the list.

The next house on our list was the one we had seen the week before in Villafranca, the quaint Summer House I liked. We drove down the narrow winding road to the long drive and the house on the rise of a hill was even more enchanting that day. I swear there were fairies and nymphs hiding in the woods. The grounds were spectacular. In fact, at one point Rupert lay down on the sun-soaked ground and rolled around like a happy dog. "Great poker face," I said as he enjoyed his romp. "I don't think they can tell you like it."

"I love it," said Rupert. "I really, really do."

This really was a proper summer house, with a large kitchen and four bedrooms, and a great room and hay barn at the far end that had a separate entrance. There were three *cantinas* below, perfect for studios and a commercial kitchen, and the hay barn would make a great master bedroom. We were already designing the spaces in our heads. We walked down the hill on the right side of the house to a small lake, and beyond it were woods with fruit trees and chestnut trees. In front of the house were more fruit trees, and rolling hills and a terraced area. We climbed on top of one of the hills and looked back at the house. "I love it," I said. We walked down the hill and I promptly got stuck in the mud, and my sneaker came off in the muck.

"Oh, jeez," said Rupert as helped me out of the hole. "There must have been rain; the land is still soaked." We laughed and headed back to the house. As we walked in and out of the *cantinas*, which had no doors and were like caves at the bottom of the building, Rupert and I both noticed that there were some large cracks in the stone walls.

"Earthquake damage?" I wondered.

"Not sure," said Rupert. "But it would explain the large crack in the floor in the main house above. We will need to check it out with the geometra." We got back into the car and returned to Aulla, then said our goodbyes to Paola and Tiziana and promised to be in touch. At lunch we both agreed that we would have the house checked out to see if the price was right. Once again no mention from the agents how much it cost—they would ask the brothers. Typical.

I headed back to the states, Rupert back to Genova. We would continue to search the internet and, in the meantime, we were still waiting to hear about the Vineyard House in Alassio. "No news was good news" was the way we handled the wait. But the truth was no news was just no news in Italy; anything could happen.

While cruising the internet, I came upon what looked to be a really great house; it had an amazing view and from what I could tell, it was not far from Rupert's house. I sent the link and Rupert wrote back immediately that he knew the house but had no idea if it was for sale. But he seemed excited and said he would ask around and get back to me. About a week later I got an email from Rupert saying that his real estate agent knew the sellers and he would love to show it to us, as it was in fact up for sale. We arranged to see it the next time I was in Italy.

I had been in the states for six months, and was happy to be back in Italy by May, and ready to once again look for our house. It had been two years since we had begun the house hunt and I was optimistic. I was holding my first workshop in Alassio, teaching photography and styling, and I planned to welcome everyone in June. Frank would be coming in June as well.

Rupert had arranged a visit to the house with a view that I had found on the internet, and Federico had a few other houses booked for us to see, too. I got to Rupert's the night before our house tour. I always loved visiting Codiponte; it was such a charming village and his home was warm and welcoming. He greeted me with a G&T, a nice selection of charcuterie, and of course a bowl of potato chips, which Rupert called his medicine. If he had a bad day, a G&T and a few chips solved everything, as far as he was concerned. He regaled me with a few stories about his village and all the latest gossip. I admit I love hearing village gossip!

His first story involved his nearest neighbor. He had lent one of his apartments to his neighbors below who were in the midst of renovation. The neighbor was an older woman who lived with her grown daughter and four-year-old grandson. They were staying in his apartment together while the work was going on.

One weekend, the Nonna (grandmother) and her grandson were visiting relatives in the nearby town. Since the daughter had no alone time, she took the opportunity to invite her boyfriend, over to the house for a little sex romp. Because it was cold that day, they built a fire in the living room fireplace and had sex on the rug in front of the fireplace. They kept feeding the fire until it was so hot that it caught the chimney on fire. At 3:00 a.m. Rupert awoke to the sound of screaming and his neighbor's daughter pounding on his door in nothing but a scant nighty. Rupert scaled the roof with a garden hose in his rubber boots and pajamas and kept the flames at bay until the local volunteer fire department showed up. I laughed at the thought of the ridiculous scene.

"Are you mad at them?" I asked.

"No, poor things, here in Italy every adult child lives with their mother so it's hard to have alone sexy time." He said. "That's why everyone is down deserted roads in their cars all weekend. It's terrible. The economy here has forced people to such extremes when it comes to shagging." He laughed, "Insurance paid for everything, it's okay." What a story.

The next morning we began the usual routine—espresso and a brioche. After we downed our breakfast we met Rupert's real estate agent Federico at his office. That's where I met his brother Marco for the first time. Marco, the local *geometra*, shared an office with Federico. Marco reached out and shook my hand—and he was a much better-looking man than his brother. Dark and sexy, with a small build and a Roman nose, I quite liked his look. He said hello and nice to meet you in a quiet voice; I liked his demeanor and could see myself working with him. Federico sold the houses and Marco renovated them, how perfect. We said good day to Marco, and we were off to see the house with the view, but there were a couple more that Federico wanted us to see after as well.

We drove out of town, on to a local road that dumped at the bottom of a winding mountain road. We headed up for about five minutes, winding our way up until we stopped at a freestanding house with a terrace (the house with a view I had seen on the internet). It had a small outbuilding that was falling down in front. The front of the house looked rather stoic with a dark wooden door and lots of heavy stone on

the facade. It had somber entryway steps with thick concrete steps leading to the wood door, and a small bridge led the way to the main house.
We walked in and were greeted by two men, the owners, who were
brothers. We would find everyone in Italy did business or owned property with their relatives, sisters, brothers, parents, grandparents, aunts,
and uncles. It was *normale*. Federico did the introductions, and we were
off for the house tour.

One of the brothers, Alex, lead the tour. I could tell that he was
the more outgoing brother, an architect, while his brother Davide was
more reserved. We found out that Davide was doing the actual manual
labor on the renovation alone on the weekends. The main floor had two
bedrooms (one with a fireplace), a kitchen, and a small room that was
both dining and living room—It could not have been bigger than ten
by fifteen feet. The kitchen was down a small hallway and there was a
full bathroom on the far end of the kitchen; it was an odd configuration.
The top floor was pitch black. It had no windows and a wet black tarp
on the floor of two rooms—a small one and a larger one. There was a
small door with glass in it that led outside to an unfinished terrace. I
could not see much, which in hindsight I was grateful for, because the
floor was flooded and there were bats flying around. "Um, wow," I said
to Rupert.

We headed back down and out the front door, over the bridge and
down the stairs to the ground floor…or what I thought was the ground
floor. I was totally confused. Usually I could nail a floor plan, but this
was a very large and very confusing plan. From what I could tell, the
upper floor was not connected to the lower floor internally. When we
got inside, there were half-built walls as we walked through. "What is
this?" I asked.

"This is going to be guest rooms. We are building a B&B."

"Oh," was the only response I could muster up. When we exited, to
the right there was a free standing building; it looked like a storage barn.
There was an incredible wooden rolling barn door, which I quite loved.
Alex opened the door to a narrow staircase that led to the floor below;

I almost fell down it. "Wow, this is interesting," I said, when what I really meant is "Why the fuck would they put this here? People will kill themselves." The barn was stuffed to the rafters with all sorts of things: furniture and building supplies and equipment. It was like the Italian version of an episode of hoarders. "Great building," I said to Rupert. "It would make a great studio space." The truth is my heart skipped a beat when I saw this barn; from what I could tell, the light was amazing.

We walked back out to what could be a great terrace but was being used as a parking lot and building supply area. The view of the mountains and the village below was incredible. We walked to the other side of the terrace and descended down a ramp covered in tall grass and trash to a door below. It, too, was completely filled with building supplies. We followed Davide into the space through a packed room to another room, where we found the staircase from above. A lovely wood ceiling had been recently installed. To me there was no rhyme or reason to the renovation. "This will be the *cucina* for the B&B," Davide explained. Even though it was a mess, I got great energy from the room and said, "Yes, it would be a perfect kitchen." It was perfectly proportioned.

We headed out to the back of the building and descended a crumbling set of stairs to the ground floor of the building. Much to our surprise, we saw that the back of the building looked like a fortress, with an enormous tower. It was much taller than I had imagined—the building was four stories tall! Davide showed us the *cantina* on the ground floor at the very bottom of the tower; it had a gorgeous barrel ceiling and was a big beautiful room, all stone, and again filled to the brim with building materials and old doors and windows and railings.

I finally broke the silence, "What was this originally?" I asked.

"It was a defensive tower and fortress," said Alex. "We think that it is originally from the twelfth century and was inhabited over the years by the military. We think a priest lived here and farmed here with his family after it was no longer the property of the military. It likely belonged to the church, because on the fireplace mantel the date 1600 is carved along with the priest's family name. I have all the plans. I can show you," he offered. "We bought this in 1998, and we have been renovating it by ourselves since then. But now we do not have time to work on it anymore, so we sell it," he continued.

I thought, *Wow, you've been renovating for sixteen years and it is barely finished!* I started to get wary of buying such a huge project. My thought was that it was just too big. Even though it had an amazing story, it was just too much.

We went back up to the main house for one more look; with the light coming into the main room, I took out my phone and took some photos of the ceiling and the floor. The ceiling was beautifully appointed with antique wood. The wood was from an old ship that they had resurrected and repurposed to cover the ceiling. The floors were antique *cotto* (terracotta), beautifully laid in a traditional Tuscan herringbone pattern. I loved the materials that they had chosen for the finishes. I kept thinking that I was scared to undertake such a daunting project. One thing that stuck in my head was that they had at least picked pretty finishes and had not messed up the interior or exterior like so many Italians did when they took on a renovation. They clearly had good taste. So that was a plus; we would not have to rip anything out they had already completed…well…except those insane stairs in the studio—the "stairs of death." I left thinking I loved it; something about it stuck with me, but for now we would leave it.

We thanked them and were off to view the next property. I posted the photo I took of the fortress herringbone floor with my shoes pictured on Instagram and got immediate comments from all my interior design friends. The comments were that it was gorgeous, and I had to agree. I will never forget the caption I wrote on Instagram: "I love this house." Of course, I've said that before, right?

Federico headed back through Fivizzano and down a big road. There was a house on the left that looked interesting and had a for sale sign on it. He drove too fast for me to say anything, but I made a mental note to come back. We drove to a small village that had a house with a courtyard for sale. I felt bad because as we exited the car, I knew it was a no. It was a very sad and small house, and even though it had a barn on the other side of the courtyard, the whole thing lacked charm. No view and the village was a not for me. I looked at Rupert; he knew this was a no. I was not even interested in going inside. Rupert was polite and acted like he was interested and went inside with Federico. They emerged and Federico announced, "That's it for today."

Luckily, we drove back on the same road. I thought, *Oh good we will pass the house that was for sale and I can jot down the number.* Just as we were just about to pass it, I yelled "STOP." Federico slammed on the brakes—poor thing, I think I scared him. "Here," I said. "Right here, this house." The house was a big stucco villa, more modern than the houses we had been looking at. Rupert asked Federico if he knew the owners. Of course he did: "Yes, yes, two families, two sisters own it." Of course they do, I thought. "I will call and make an appointment," said Federico. So with that we headed back down the hill and agreed to wait to hear about the next viewings from Federico. In the meantime, Frank was arriving, and I headed back to Alassio.

Frank arrived in June; the weather was great and we spent most of our days reading at the beach, swimming, cooking, and eating. We walked into town for *aperitivo* every night. It was heaven. He left after ten days. Then I was busy teaching my workshop. I loved teaching almost as much as styling. I loved mentoring, and this was a great way to share my knowledge and talk creativity in my happy place, Italy. Let's face it, there was so much inspiration here and the light…the light was perfection.

We had a great time at the workshop, everyone was lovely, and we put the students up at the B&B one of my friends owned in Garlenda. It was a great set-up. We had eight women of all ages—a couple bloggers, a photographer, a graphic artist, an interior designer, and even an architect. It was a marvelous group. The photographer was an old friend and co-worker, Deborah Whitlaw Lewellyn, who had photographed my first entertaining book, *Picture Perfect Parties*. She was a wonderful photographer and we worked well together. We bought all sorts of produce to style still lifes. We styled, shopped, photographed, cooked, and ate and drank for five glorious days.

I started thinking about making sure that I had a studio space to teach when we looked for houses. That went on to the list of house requirements. Most of the places we liked did have spaces for a studio, so maybe in the back of my mind I had known I wanted this all along. I wanted to incorporate the shift in my career with house hunting. Finding the right home would take effort and purpose. Buying a house really was like dating, finding the right one and falling in love, but for real. I discovered that love is work.

I did not even stop to think about the seminary house in Garlenda, or the Vineyard House outside Albenga, or the summer house in Villafranca. I just enjoyed June. July would be here soon enough.

CHAPTER 23

The Real Deal

In July 2014 I went back to visit Rupert and we had many appointments lined up with Federico. We were back at it. Around that time, I got a call from our *notaio* about the Vineyard House—it had been months. He had given the research to his daughter Adrianna, who was also a real estate lawyer. I had met her when we closed on the flat in Alassio. Adrianna was lovely, spoke perfect English, and was very professional. She had taken on the task of finding the owner of the Vineyard House as a pro bono project. They were now intrigued by the property and the mystery of who owned it. The agent Marco was of no help; he had disappeared after our last viewing and never answered my emails.

I discovered that Adrianna was also Reynaldo's goddaughter. The fact that Reynaldo was so close to Ilario's family was something I only learned in passing one night at dinner. I had known Ilario for at least eight years and had no idea. As I knew by now, Italians are not big on information, so it was not a big surprise when this important piece of information was revealed to me. Everything in Italy is about connections. I call it "turbo juice." If you have the right connections, you're golden in Italy—the world unfolds before you; if not, you're shit outta luck and you have to figure it all out yourself, which is painful and endless and unfruitful. Once Adrianna had her answer, she called and told Rupert the owners were from Genova, but unbelievably Rupert and Reynaldo—even Adrianna and Ilario—did not know them. The vineyard was indeed a business and would have to be converted to a residence. That was all they knew right then. If she got more information, she would let us know. "Well, at least we have a name," said Rupert. "We can worry about the rest later."

We had a full schedule of house-hunting booked. We met Federico at the usual place and drove off with him on a beautiful summer day. We stopped at the top of a hill, parked, and got out. "Watch yourself, Annette," said Rupert. "There are ticks and snakes."

"Oh, thanks, Rupert. Now I am really stressed," I said.

"Well, my dear, you will be living in the country now, so you better get used to living with N A T U R E." He emphasized the word to make his point. The truth was that I always wore sneakers or boots when house hunting; well, except that one time where Rupert and I wore flip flops, and he stepped on the snake. I chuckled to myself recalling his running and screaming down the hill at the abandoned semi-house in Villafranca.

We walked into a big field of long grass and up the hill to a formation of stone houses. In front of us was a series of stone buildings all in various stages of falling down, with a stone barn in pretty good shape in the distance. Federico explained, "This is about twenty-five acres, with five buildings and a barn. It is for sale and would be a great B&B or artist compound."

We walked from building to building—it was beautiful. This grouping of houses was most likely a family farm. We walked up the hill to the barn and, much to our surprise, there was a white horse living in the barn. He had water and food and was just standing there. It was obvious that someone was taking care of him. The scene was just magically bucolic. Of course I took a million photos of him.

"What a lovely horse. You think he's lonely all alone?" I asked no one in particular.

Federico said, "No, there are more horses here—they are just out in the pasture." All of a sudden we saw more horses walking towards the barn, with a man walking behind. We all said *buongiorno* to the man and he tipped his hat. Federico knew him and told him we were looking at the property to buy. I asked if he came with the property—him and his horses. He smiled and said no, this was his place, and if he sold it they would have to move. Of course I immediately thought they could stay if I bought this place, but that was really putting the cart before the horse, literally speaking.

I walked over to one of the larger buildings where Rupert was looking around and walked inside. "This is pretty amazing," I said. "Incredible," he agreed. "But it's in bad shape; it would need everything. This is really a ruin, Annette."

I had a sad feeling in the pit of my stomach, but it would be a fortune to outfit this place—not to mention the cost of basic landscaping. It would take twenty years to make it right. It was an impossible dream project, at least for us. Sometimes you just have to admit you love the idea but not the reality. We both walked down to where Federico and the man with the horses stood talking. We looked at the view and both sighed in unison. The sigh then turned into laughter; we were such suckers for the romance of renovation. Serious sickos.

Rupert's phone rang. "*Pronto,*" he said, answering the phone the typical Italian way. "*Si, si, si, si, certo okay, a domani.*" He turned to me. "Annette, tomorrow we can go see the house in Villafranca again—they have a price—but they want to meet at their offices in the morning first. They have another house for us."

"Okay, sounds good," I said. Everything dealing with real estate was a covert operation, veiled in mystery.

Our next stop was the stucco villa—the one I had seen from the road on our last visit. Federico filled us in on the details about the house, "These sisters have the house. They want to sell because their children do not want the house. It is a summer home and the children prefer the seaside." We rolled up the gravel driveway on the side of the villa. When we got out, there was a woman walking up the drive from the road.

"*Buongiorno, signora*," said Federico. "*Come stai?*" Then he said to Rupert, "This is one of the owners." We walked towards the woman and shook her hand. She was wearing a house dress—a dress with flowers typically worn by women in Italy of a certain age. Rupert and I called them muumuus. She walked us in front of the villa; there was an expansive terrace and three *cantinas* off the terrace at the bottom of the building. Each of the *cantinas* had a lovely, carved wooden door.

This house was more formal than the ones we had been looking at. I stopped in my tracks when I saw the most incredible kitchen garden. I remember thinking that I needed a garden like this in my life. We entered a side door into what was the most charming kitchen. The *signora's* husband was sitting at a table, eating his lunch. *Buongiorno*, we all said. Federico apologized for disturbing his lunch. We walked through the kitchen into a main hall; off the hallway were four rooms, a dining room, a living room, a bedroom, and a bathroom. I was trying to have an open mind as this was a more modern house. We were about to start up the stairs and the *signora* stopped us. "You must wait to see upstairs," she said. "It is the house of my sister."

"The story is that the house is divided in two parts," explained Rupert. "One sister owns the lower floor and one sister owns the upper floor."

"Ah, oh," I said. "Are we sure the other sister wants to sell it?"

"Yes. Federico has already asked and they both want to sell it." *Remember, the first rule of buying a house in Italy is to ask who owns the house.*

"Okay, so, how do we see the second floor?" I asked.

"She is on her way to show us her floor. She should be here in a few minutes," Rupert said. So we waited, and while we waited we toured the rest of the grounds. It was really a beautiful place, located right above Fivizzano. It would be convenient for groceries, the pharmacy, and the open market. It had a lot going for it. It had a certain charm. When house hunting in Italy, there are always compromises that have to be weighed. You would never find the perfect house; there were always drawbacks and positives. I always kept this in the back of my mind. It took me two years to figure this out and once I did house hunting became easier. I could sort out the pros and cons and decide to pursue a house or not. This pros and cons list helped eliminate the seminary house in Garlenda, we could never get rid of the neighbors peering at us through their window on our terrace. I was still interested in the vineyard house near Albenga. I was very interested in the summer house in Villafranca at this point and this villa was a contender as well.

The other sister walked down the road as we were cruising around her garden. "*Buongiorno, signora,*" said Federico. "*Buongiorno,*" she replied. She walked over and shook hands with all of us, and we headed in behind her—through the front door this time—and up the stairs, where we came to a locked door. Of course, we all pretended that this was not totally weird. The door opened to a hallway and, just like the floor downstairs, it had five rooms off of it: a very cute eat-in kitchen and three bedrooms that were worn but charming. One of the bedrooms had the most gorgeous vintage wallpaper in a rich golden yellow, and antique twin beds with a picture of Jesus above them. There was a super cute vintage bathroom with aqua tiles that were to die for, and a living room with a fireplace. It was pretty charming and would be easy to renovate. At this point I felt like I had seen a hundred houses and was growing weary, but I soldiered on.

The next day we woke up, had our espressos and brioche, and off we went to see the real estate girls in Aulla. We met them in front of their office, and this time we drove our own car. Rupert and I agreed we had had enough of Tiziana's driving. We followed them to the Summer House in Villafranca. We got out of the car and walked all over the property, this time discovering a river that ran along the right side of the land. The lake was really magical and would be a great place to do photography during workshops. It was perfect and went up high on my yes pile.

We walked over to the ladies who were talking on the front terrace. "So what's the price?" I asked Paola, "Did the brothers agree?" Paola smiled and said, "Yes, they agree. The house is five hundred thousand euros."

I thought to myself that the house was not worth more than 375,000 euros at the most, but we could negotiate later. I wanted to get a *geometra* in here to look at the place and give us an estimate on what it would cost to renovate. I had a feeling that the cracks in the *cantina* and in the house were serious and I wanted an expert to take a look. Rupert and I thought it would be wise to have Marco come have a look and give us his take on the cracks.

At that point Tiziana piped up. "You better hurry with your bid because there is another family looking at this house." That is when I decided that I, too, was not a fan of Tiziana's, because she was clearing making this up. Paola looked uncomfortable, but she refrained from speaking.

"Well," said Rupert, "we will see what happens then." You do not want to get on Rupert's bad side, believe me. Tiziana was walking on thin ice with Rupert at this point. We agreed that we would have Marco check out the house and we would be back once we had his take on the house. Tiziana was clearly not happy that we were not making an offer today.

We met Marco at the Summer House in Villafranca at the end of the week. Rupert's friend, Heike, decided she wanted to tag along, which was fine. The more the merrier. Plus she had looked at so many properties that she was an expert in her own right, according to Rupert. It was a beautiful day, and I was happy to show her around. Heike was unique—she was the combination of a sexy German babe and an Italian construction worker, clearly in touch with her masculine side, and she smoked like a chimney. I cannot picture her without a cigarette hanging out of her mouth. She was attractive, but years of smoking and the last couple years of manual labor living in a deconstructed ruin in Italy had taken a bit of a toll. She always wore her heavy suede buckle-up boots, whether it was winter or summer. She had her signature look: tight jeans and either a white sleeveless tank top or a t-shirt. She looked like she had just rolled out of bed, and oddly this look worked for her. She had lots of opinions, some good and some not so good. But for the task at hand of assessing this house, she might be helpful.

Heike and her husband Reinhold were true pioneers; they owned a property high on a hill surrounded by an olive grove, which they harvested themselves every year to press oil. She did give me a great tip about house hunting. She told me how she started taking photos of all the things in each property that were not pretty and needed to be fixed—leaks, broken tiles, peeling wallpaper. "The ugly bits," as she said. "Take photos of those so you can remember." We have a tendency to remember all the great stuff and not the bad stuff; this was great advice.

At the end of the week, as scheduled, we all rolled up to the house in Villafranca, followed by Marco in his big black pickup truck. He walked towards us with a notepad in hand. Marco spoke no English, but I could understand most of what he said. Still, Rupert would need to explain the technical parts of the conversation. We all listened as Marco spoke, assessing the house. He went right to the crack in the foundation of the building—the wide crack in the ceiling of the middle *cantina*—and he ran his hand up and down the crack. Then he looked at the two other *cantina* rooms on either side and proceeded to the interior of the building. He looked at the barn and the top loft of the barn. All the while he walked, he was asking Rupert and me questions about what we were thinking of putting where. We all wandered to the front yard and walked to the lake and to the river. The one thing that was strange was that the front yard was still soggy in areas. There were low points where water was standing. At the end of our tour, Marco pointed out the soggy parts and the cracks and said that he thought that the cracks were not from an earthquake but from water. He thought it would be wise to bring a geologist out to survey the property to see where the water was coming from. He gave us an estimate of what this would cost. He told us that it would be worth it to know what was really going on here. We thanked him and said goodbye. We walked around the property again with Heike in tow. She liked the place, but she, too, thought that we should do due diligence and hire the geologist as Marco suggested.

We got a call the next day from Paola saying she had a couple houses to show us. Tiziana was not going to join us, but Heike wanted to tag along. I was due to go back to Alassio, but postponed until the next day to see these two new properties.

It was raining and we met at the first location at the top of a narrow road. Paola was there and so was the owner of the house. We were in my little Fiat 500 and Paola suggested we climb into the owner's car; it was wet and the road was not great and the owner knew the road well. We all agreed this was a great idea. We got into the owner's SUV, with Paola, Rupert, Heike, and me in the back seat. We started down this danger-ously narrow road and I started to panic—our little SUV was sliding and the rain was really starting to come down hard. Heike looked at me and she could tell I was frightened. Rupert mouthed the words "We are going to D I E." Rupert and Heike smiled and did not say a word. Then we got stuck in the mud—it was only a second before we got free—but it was enough to make me bury my head in Heike's lap for the rest of the ride. Finally, after what felt like an eternity, we arrived at the house. The thing that I kept thinking about was that we had to drive back out on the same road. For me, that road was a deal breaker; it was a no for this house and I hadn't even seen it.

"Rupert, there is no way to change that road, right?" I asked.

"Most likely no," he said.

"Then forget it. I cannot live with that piece of crap road," I said.

Heike laughed. "You're such a baby, Annette," she said. Rupert insisted we look at the house now that we were here. I was outnumbered.

There were two buildings: one was a house, completely ready to move into, and one was a rustic, a ruin ready to renovate. It was pretty, just not for me. We politely looked around and then the inevitable came:

we had to drive back down the road. Luckily, it had stopped pouring rain. We took our seats, and off we drove down the bitty road where my life flashed before my eyes once again—twice in one day. At the bottom, I jumped out of the car, quickly shook hands with the owner, jumped back into my car, turned the key, and almost took off without Rupert and Heike, I was so ready to bolt.

Paola knocked on the driver's side window and asked if I would like to see the next house. I rolled down the window and said, "Okay, lead the way." We followed Paola for about forty minutes on a fairly wide paved road, which was great considering my panic attack an hour earlier. We parked on a narrow road outside what looked like an abandoned village. In fact, we found it *was* an abandoned village. There was one building that looked like a commercial building in the village.

"I know this place," said Heike. "I buy bread here. It is amazing bread." I looked over and saw that Heike was right: it was a bakery. I was pretty excited about that, and we walked inside. The owner, an older lady, smiled at us and cut off a slice of bread for us to try. *How unexpected*, I thought, *and how lovely*. Well, at least I knew if I bought a house here, I would live in a place where the mornings would be filled with lovely aromas.

Poor Paola, she was on a mission and we had hijacked her plans. Paola came into the bakery to find us. "I lost you," she said and smiled.

"Oh, sorry, Paola," I said, as I was scarfing down delicious warm bread. We could not help ourselves! "Shall we go?" she said. We bought a couple loaves and headed out the door, saying we would be back. We walked down the tiny walkway to a large, newly-built house with a courtyard and free-standing barn. The barn was old, as was a part of the house connected to the new part. It was a weird-looking house. Rupert immediately said, in an affected English accent, "Englishpersons," which meant that it was owned by English people. It always made me laugh when he said this because it meant that the inside of the house would be badly decorated. Of course, he was right. It was a pretty house, not very Italian on the inside—more like a country manor in the English countryside. It was not for us, but worth looking at...if only for the warm bread. The house was nestled into the side of a mountain, so the effect was that one was looking straight up the face of the mountain. It was like an enormous wall pressing down on me, and it made me feel very claustrophobic. Besides the bad décor and the abandoned village, this wall made it a definite no. I headed back to the States having some prospective houses in mind but again nothing definite.

Rupert got a call from Marco when I was already back in the States. Marco had arranged for the geologist. It was September and everyone was back to work after the August holidays. "They are going to the house on Thursday. I will let you know." "Sounds good, talk soon," was the gist of our quick conversation. I went back to work and did not think much about the Vineyard House, the Fortress with the View, or the Summer House on the knoll. Buying a home in Italy was a long process, and I was much more concerned with selling our flat. I had to start thinking outside the box, as clearly I was not going to get any help from the local real estate agents. It was now fall and I wrote an email to the developer of our building. He was a wealthy man from Milano, an elegant man. I asked again if he might want to buy the flat for his kids. He said he would think about it. I just wanted him to know it was still for sale. I told everyone that would listen about our flat being for sale. I was on a mission.

I got a call from Rupert with news about the Summer House on the knoll in Villafranca. Marco had met with the geologist, and they had done the survey. Rupert started with, "You're never going to believe this, Annette. Simply put, there is an underground river running right under the property, right under the house, and the house is sinking," he said calmly.

"You're kidding me!" I replied.

"No, I am afraid not," he said. "It's sinking, and that is why there are such large cracks—the house is literally splitting apart."

"So how did the real estate agents not know what was going on with the place," I asked.

There was a long pause, and Rupert said, "Well, I thought the same thing, so I went into the office to confront them. Tiziana was there. I asked her point blank if she know the house was sinking. She said 'Yes, but you can fix it.'" Rupert was sounding more and more furious as he went on. "I then asked how in good conscience could they show us the house, give us pricing, and expect us to just buy it? Tiziana did not have an answer. I was so mad, Annette, that I had to leave the office before it got ugly. The bottom line is that these ladies are not ethical and I will be spreading the word about them."

"I am not surprised, honestly, Rupert. I knew that there was something serious going on with that house. Although it was magical, it had some fatal flaws. Oh well, now we move on," I concluded.

I was back in Alassio in May 2015 and planned to lead workshop in June. I was excited to spend the summer at the beach and looking at a few houses, but mainly I was trying to work on selling the flat and enjoying what might be one of my last summers on the seaside in Alassio. Rupert and Reynaldo came to dinner one night and we talked about the houses still in the running—the Vineyard House, the Fortress with the view, and the sisters' villa that was still a possibility. I really needed a house for our workshops, so I had to start really thinking about what we needed. We could host our students at the house with the view, which made that location a top contender. Although, if we got the Vineyard House, we could continue to use the B&B in Garlenda. And the sisters' villa had the lower level *cantinas* that could be guest rooms and a studio space.

I really needed to think about what needed to be on our list going forward. Since the workshops had begun, our needs had really evolved. During dinner, Reynaldo asked if I had heard from Adrianna about the Vineyard House.

"Yes, she found the owners and the classification of the property. I am going to work on it this summer," I said.

The next day I was having dinner with Monica, and I mentioned the Vineyard House and asked if she had any thoughts about how I should proceed now that I knew who the owners were. Marco, her friend, had disappeared from the scene, so I thought maybe she could help me. "I call Marco," she said, "but also you should have my *geometra*, he knows everything in the area. He will know about this house."

I said this was a great idea. Monica was a smart cookie.

"You send me the information and I will send it to Pietro, my *geometra*; he is the best," she concluded. In the meantime, Marco the real estate agent reemerged—I guess Monica convinced him to get to work. He called me and asked if I had decided on the hospital. I grinned at this question. "I think it is a no on that, Marco, but I am still interested in the Vineyard House. Please price it without the vineyard—just the house." Frank and I had decided that we did not want the vineyard, thinking maybe reclassifying it as a residence would be easier that way. It was worth a try.

"Okay, I get the good price for you."

At the end of summer I still hadn't made any progress on buying a house. I headed back to the States and back to work, continuing to cruise the internet for possible houses in the Lunigiana. One day I stumbled upon a house that looked so familiar. Then I realized it was a house Frank and I had seen with Rupert twelve years earlier, shown to us by terrible real estate agents that essentially ruined the Lunigiana for us, much to Rupert's dismay. They had shown us the most miserable houses in the area. But this one was very special, the only one we liked. In fact, it was a house in Casola. We were not interested at the time because it was a big renovation undertaking for us. Since we were newbies in Italy then, a giant renovation project was not what we had in mind. But, I thought, as seasoned veterans, we might just be ready for it now if it was still available. I sent Rupert the link and asked him if we had seen this house many years ago. He immediately emailed me back and asked, "Did you just find this?"

I replied, "Yes. It looks like it's still for sale." That's the thing in Italy—everything in real estate moves very slowly, so it was quite possible that it was still up for sale twelve years later. Granted, it may have gone on and off the market several times.

"Shall we go see it?" Rupert wrote back.

Of course I agreed. Twelve years ago we were looking for a small summer house, and now we needed something that had a few rooms to house guests attending my teaching workshops. I remembered that I loved this space, but it was very big. I remembered the incredible kitchen and the beautiful light and the hay barn. The mere fact that it was seared in my memory was a good enough reason to visit again, as far as I was concerned. Rupert put the house in Casola on the list and planned to research who the owners were and make a date to visit when I returned.

It had been three years of house-hunting, and we still were not even close. There were contenders, like the Vineyard House, or the Fortress House with the View, or maybe the Sisters Villa. But none of these made my heart beat faster. This was dating, with no end in sight. I really wanted to commit to something, but the right something had not come along.

Frank was coming to Italy at the end of May. Rupert and I made a plan to meet at the house in Casola without Frank, and then maybe take him to the Fortress House with the View. Rupert had found the owners of the Casola house—the son from Milan was going to drive down to show it to us. The day we arrived, they met us at the gate to let us in, and suddenly it all came back to me—I remembered it well. It was a u-shaped building with a grassy courtyard in the middle. It had at one point been a school, most likely a religious school for nuns or priests—the owner's son Paolo was not sure—but he told us it was definitely a school, that his great-grandfather had run the school, and when it closed, he bought the building.

Paolo was a small, wiry man that seemed nervous and anxious, and he was accompanied by his father, the owner. His dad was probably in his seventies and was very chatty, talking non-stop from the moment we said hello—which I found super annoying. Having the seller walk the house tour was something I just could not get used to in Italy; it made looking at a house very unpleasant, not to mention awkward, for me.

We entered the main building into a gorgeous foyer, which honestly I did not recall. Then we wound our way to the giant kitchen that had a magnificent built-in hearth. This I remembered vividly. "Ah," I said. "I love this kitchen."

"Yes, I remember you said that the last time," said Rupert.

The old man proceeded to give us the history of Casola, which I only half listened to, as his yammering was getting on my nerves. His son said nothing. We climbed to the top floor where the bedrooms were. The light in the place was simply divine—this is also what I remembered. We walked into every room. The place was not lived in, but it had reminders everywhere that it had once been a warm and pleasant place to dwell. There were old beds, chairs, and loveseats wrapped in rich velvet and damask fabrics, all serene and lovely. It would have been the perfect tour, if the old man would have stopped talking.

"When was the house last lived in?" I asked Paolo.

"Ahh, probably in the summer when I was a child, maybe thirty years ago," he said.

"So no one lives here now?" I went on to ask.

"My father, he lives in the other part," said Paolo. I could literally hear a clank in my head as I thought, *Well, that's a hard no*. I could not imagine renovating this enormous house and all the while listening to Paolo's dad's opinions and having him visiting 24/7, plus trying to live and work in the same space.

In Italy there are two tactics I use when wanting to tune out and still seem polite:

1. Pretend I don't understand Italian.
2. Say "Ah" and nod my head and smile.

Worked like a charm. We continued our tour. We walked across the yard and entered the most gorgeous barn, and my heart sank because I knew it would make the most amazing studio ever. But, unfortunately, a family living next door was a deal-breaker. Everything else we viewed that day made my heart ache. The back formal garden, although unkept, was so beautiful. The façade of the building was so lovely; there were tons of large windows that looked out to a beautiful courtyard. The house was painted a pale yellow and patinaed—I would not touch a thing about the outside of the building; it was perfect. It was an elegant house. Although the barn added a rustic touch, it was beautifully appointed. It was two floors of a good scale. It was a school at one time, so would tick off the boxes of a workshop space. There was a gated courtyard that would provide ideal parking for us and for our guests. There was a beautiful view from the terrace. But it was a no, because the communal living situation would be challenging in the end. That was the day I came to the conclusion that we needed a space that was freestanding.

We thanked them and headed to the car. Paolo walked us to the car and very aggressively asked, "Are you going to buy the house?" Rupert and I were taken aback. Paolo's demeanor was desperate and urgent. "You don't even know how much the house is," he explained. Rupert looked Paolo straight in the eye and calmly said, "We are not interested, but thank you."

"Why?" Paolo cried, close to tears.

"Because it is too big, and there is too much work," said Rupert. There were times in our relationship I truly loved Rupert, especially when it required him telling it like it was. Paolo was quiet for a minute. We said goodbye again and started to get into the car. That was when Paolo went from desperate to mad. He started telling Rupert that we had wasted his time and that he had driven down especially from Milan to meet with us. He thought we were serious. Typical Americans, he said.

That was what flipped Rupert's switch—he got very calm, which was actually alarming, then he got very close to Paolo's face and said, "I know you are a gentleman so you will step back and let us get into our car and drive off. Do you understand?" Paolo understood, and he turned and headed back to the house.

We hopped in the car and sped off. Even though it was noon, we were ready for a cocktail, so we headed straight for the bar. With the Casola house sadly eliminated, we were running out of choices. In Italy, things present themselves. Just like that guy in the corner at a party that you don't want to talk to. You start chatting with him at the bar and figure this is a nice guy and you end up talking to him all night. That's what buying property in Italy is like. You may have met the one, but you don't know it yet. Had we already met our house, I wondered?

Frank arrived and we had a lovely time; as usual, it was pure bliss. Then, one afternoon, I got a call from Monica. "Can you come to the office? I want to talk to you. At seven o'clock, please," she said.

"Of course, we will be there," I said. We arrived at her store, said hello to her mother who was minding the cash register, she was a fixture in the store and helped out when she could, and made our way back to her office. Monica was sitting there with a good-looking man wearing a neat buzzcut, and all black.

"Annette and Frank!!!" Monica rushed toward us kissed and hugged us. "This is Pietro the *geometra* I told you about. He knows everybody. I asked Pietro as a favor for me to look into your Vineyard House. I let him tell you everything."

Pietro spoke English pretty well, which was great. Frank and I pulled up a chair to hear what he had to say about the vineyard property.

"I know this property," he said. "It is very nice area, with many vineyards. This vineyard is owned by a family in Genova. They have it for many years. The family business has not paid taxes on the property for thirty years, so this is a problem. Now they owe fifty thousand euros. They want to sell the house to pay for the vineyard taxes." Frank and I were following so far. He continued, "I think that they sell the house and they pay the taxes. But that is not the problem. The problem is that the house is considered a ruin, and the classification of this ruin is that it is uninhabitable, and you will not be able to turn it into a residence ever, but if you get permission you can tear it down and then get permission for a new house so you can live there. It is complicated and could take many years. You will not own the vineyard, the family from Genova will own it. You will buy the small bit of land around the house only. The family will work the vineyard, and most likely you will need to build an access road for them to bring trucks and tractors to the vineyard. That's it." He concluded with, "My advice is to move on, look for a more simple project."

Wow, we thought. *That was a lot of information.* Monica chimed in, "This is not a good project; you should find something simple."

Frank and I looked at each other. Frank said, "I like this guy, Annette. He communicates like an American. No bullshit." We all laughed and shook his hand.

Frank said, "How much do we owe you?" Pietro smiled and said, "*Niente* [nothing]. I do it for Monica. She is great, okay? No problem." I found this very interesting. "Good luck to you, and let me know if you need me again." With that, he left. We all looked at each other. I almost burst into tears as I hugged Monica, "Thank you, thank you so much, you're a wonderful friend, I love you."

"I love you too, my dear." She had a big smile on her face as she said, "Now we drink." We headed off for *aperivito*, then dinner, then more drinks. I love beach life and I loved that Monica had saved us a lot of work, money, and heartache. It is so important that one has Italian friends to guide them through this daunting process and we were so grateful to her. I also felt that she was happy because the little castle fiasco was still on her mind. She most likely felt bad about the experience with her landlords and the castle house high in the hills that was not theirs to sell. She felt she had redeemed herself, and honestly I felt the same. She had saved us a lot of time.

With the Vineyard House eliminated, Frank and I headed to visit to see the Fortress with a View that weekend, with Rupert and Reynaldo in tow. I was excited to show it to Frank. Even though it was very big, it was very interesting and had a view that was to die for. Federico met us in the piazza and it was nice to finally have Frank meet him. We hopped in the car and headed to the fortress. Davide, the quieter brother, was there to meet us.

Frank and I walked all over and I got a better sense of the place and the floor plan the second time around. The fact was that this house was probably the most perfect for our purposes—a place to hold workshops, a huge terrace, and enough rooms to host all of our workshop attendees with ease. There was an outbuilding that could have even more guest rooms and a downstairs area that was already fitted for a kitchen. The main house could serve as our residence. I asked Frank if he thought he liked the house, and he thought it definitely had potential; it just depended on the price, because there was a hell of a lot to renovate. "Let's see what they want for it," he said.

Frank headed back to the main house after our tour. He had his good poker face going. Rupert and I stood outside in front, talking to Davide, when we heard Frank yell, "WE ARE DEFINITELY BUYING THIS HOUSE!" Lucky for us, Davide did not speak English or Frank would have blown everything. Rupert and I both rushed into the house.

"Are you insane?" I asked. Frank was in the bedroom, pointing at something and smiling. "That stays, right?" he said. Frank had gone into a bedroom that looked like one of the brothers had moved in. What he had found and what had convinced him that we were buying this place was a ten-foot floor-to-ceiling mirror on the other side of the bed.

"You're such a pervert, Frank," I laughed.

Back outside on the front stoop, as Rupert liked to call it, we began to conduct business. "How much do you want for this place?" Rupert asked. I loved his bluntness, but Federico seemed uncomfortable. He was an agent, but did not want to talk money. Only in Italy! Davide looked at me, then Frank, then Rupert. He smiled and said, "I will get back to you about that. We are not sure we want to sell it now."

I thought, *What the hell? Are you kidding me?* What was up with Italians and selling their houses? Could they not bring themselves to sell their stuff? I was totally confused and felt like a big door had been slammed in my face. Frank looked and me and mouthed, *W H A T?*

Since he spoke no Italian, he was in the dark. I whispered that I would tell him in the car. We said our goodbyes and headed down the hill, all of us pretty confused.

"Rupert, what happened?" I groaned.

"Oh, they are either for real and undecided about selling, or they are fighting because one wants to sell and the other doesn't. I would bet that Davide does not want to sell and Alex does. Alex is the money guy, and I suspect they have run out of money, but Davide does not want to throw in the towel. They will come around. In the meantime," Rupert asked, "Frank, what did you think about the house?"

"I like the house, but it's a very big project. I need to think about it, and it depends on the price, of course," Once again, the saga of the Fortress House began. Another mystery, another adventure. Frank and I tried to forget about it and enjoy our time together before he had to return to Atlanta.

When I returned to Atlanta in the fall. I was a bit deflated for the first time. It was now going on four years and still no house. Our flat was not moving. I felt like I was at a standstill. I was depressed, and even searching the internet for houses—always one of my favorite pastimes—was not making me feel better. The only thing that kept me going was that I knew that there was the perfect space out there for our workshops and the workshops were really doing well, so my vision was clearer. Rupert and Federico sent me links to a few houses, but none of them made my heart go pitter patter like the Fortress did. We had heard nothing from the brothers about the Fortress price, which was not a good sign, as far as I was concerned. Rupert told me to "have faith and remember that in Italy these things went *piano, piano* [slowly, slowly]."

Around November 2015 I got a call from our developer that his friend was interested in our flat and ready to make an offer. I was thrilled and immediately put him in touch with our *notaio*, they knew each other since we had all done the closing of our Alassio flat together. It was good synergy. Our *notaio* was happy to take care of everything.

Rupert was happy as well. After three and a half years we had sold our flat; correction, I had sold it.

I occupied myself with the holidays, Thanksgiving and Hanukkah. I was working, styling and producing and writing. In January, I got an email from the developer of our flat in Alassio. I will never forget it, because I was working on a photo shoot, and I looked at my emails when we broke for lunch. The developer wrote that his friend wanted to close and could I please email him?"

I called Frank and, of course, he was thrilled, but also a little skeptical. He was not a huge fan of the developer, but I assured him it was all going to be fine. I wrote back to the developer and said that it was great news, and that I would be back in Italy in March 2016 and we could have the first closing then. He quickly replied that this was a good plan. I still was not sure about buying a house, but that was not the point. I could finally check one thing off the list; I was over the moon. I called Rupert the next day and told him about the closing. He was really excited and said that we could buy a house now. "Yes, we just need to find one," I said. I had convinced myself not to put too much hope in getting the Fortress.

I finally heard from my *notaio* that we would in fact have our first closing March 2016 and I flew over for the *compremesso*. The buyer lived in Lugano, she hired the developer's *notaio* in Milan. Our first closing would be there. It all went smoothly, the buyer seemed nice, and the developer was charming, as always. We cruised through the closing in three hours.

With renewed faith and a new attitude, I started cruising the internet quite frequently. My mood was much better. It was at that moment in time Paola sent us a message that she had split with her partner, the awful Tiziana, and if we were interested she had a few more houses to show us. I always liked and trusted her, so why not? Rupert and I made a date to meet her. We also made another date with Federico, who seemed excited to show us an interesting property he had. I arrived back in Italy in May and headed straight to Rupert's house. He met me at the bridge—a beautiful old village bridge that we enjoyed crossing when walking his two dogs. Rupert had two Weimaraners, one old dog, Rosco, and one rescue dog, Shelly. They were gorgeous and lovely dogs and I loved walking them around the neighborhood.

After our walk, we headed off to an appointment to look at a property. Rupert was familiar with the property, so we planned to meet Federico at the house this time. We drove deep into the countryside, down a long and winding road, and stopped at what looked like a village filled with stone buildings, completely abandoned.

"Oh, I love this!" I exclaimed.

"Yeah, well, let's have a look around before we fall in love, shall we?" Rupert said. Sometimes he was the voice of reason.

"Is the whole village for sale? Does anyone live here?" I asked. I pointed to the corner house; it was a square, beautiful stone house. It was a rustic *borgo*, an old village that had long been abandoned Federico told us. "I love this one. Can I just buy one of the houses?" I asked. The house I loved was not for sale—of course it wasn't. I thought, *That's always the way*. But the rest of the houses were for sale. The entire village was for sale. "Should we buy a village?" I said in a moment of insanity to Rupert.

Rupert laughed and said, "Now that would be ambitious but I am up for it if you are." I like to think I dream big, but the idea of telling Frank I was buying a run-down village did not sound like a good idea. We walked all over the village. There was a blacksmith and a small church at the end. It was truly spectacular; Federico had not let us down. The specifics of what was for sale and how much it cost were not on the table. Those loose ends would have to be sussed out. So typical, and so frustrating.

We walked in and out of the small buildings. Some were connected and others were free standing—not your typical village, but still simply charming in every way, and every one had its own story. We ended our tour at what seemed like a printers. It was a gorgeous space with old wooden beams and floors, stone walls, and lots of windows. It was gorgeous. Fair to say this was an awe-inspiring project. Rupert and I headed out and thanked Federico; he promised he would be back with pricing and specifics.

As we drove back up the hill, I said to Rupert, "That was amazing, right?"

"Yes, Annette, but that is a project and a half, so this is something you must think about long and hard. It is quite abandoned here, with no one nearby, and being out here alone is something to think about," he concluded. He was not wrong about that, and I knew this one was a pass, too.

We got a call a few days later from Federico, who had gotten word that the brothers owning the Fortress were ready to sell. They had formally listed it with agents in the area. "Wow," I said. "Shall we go look at it again?" Rupert agreed and we made a date while we still had Federico on the phone.

It was a Saturday and Reynaldo was with us. Rupert had also made an appointment with his neighbor for us to see an available house in his neighborhood after lunch. I was curious about this place since I had seen it on my last trip. I was doubtful about buying a house in the same neighborhood as Rupert—too close for comfort, I thought, and I'm sure he agreed. We shared a lovely lunch prepared by Rupert in his courtyard, and then walked over to the house to have a look. The owners, a husband and wife, were there. He was a smarmy-looking character with black dyed hair smashed onto his forehead. His wife was wearing the traditional muumuu floral *nonna* dress. She was a pleasant-looking woman, whose only makeup was red lipstick. We exchanged greetings, and the husband explained that the house was a summer B&B, a retreat for company employees, which was a popular thing in the '60s and '70s. They ran it until the early '90s and then wanted to hand it over to their kids. But the children were not interested in running the business, so they just left it empty. It seemed like an odd business decision to me, but that was their story and they were sticking to it.

"Okay, we go," he said in broken English and handed the key to his wife to lead us. He motioned that he would wait outside and smoke a cigarette. The house was long and skinny—it was like a train car—with room after room off a hallway, none of them connected. It seemed like a camp or a motel. It had been heavily damaged in the earthquake a few years earlier. Since it had not had earthquake protection, it was a mess, with huge cracks—some so big it was dangerous to enter the rooms! We quietly went through the entire place and were more afraid than impressed. It was pretty awful and it seemed that tearing it down was the only way to go it had no redeeming architectural features that needed to be saved as far as I was concerned. We walked back to the front garden and Reynaldo looked relieved when we showed up. "Well," said the owner. "Would you like to buy it?" Clearly he thought I was a stupid American, because what he said next was absurd. "It is five hundred thousand euros." Being a polite person, I did not laugh. I quite calmly looked at everyone and said, "No, thank you. Very nice to meet you. Good luck." With that, I was out and down the road in a matter of seconds. I never looked back, and surely Rupert was relieved as well. I would not be his neighbor after all.

On Monday we had an appointment to look at the Fortress once again. This time we met Federico there, along with the brothers. We shook hands and exchanged pleasantries, and I asked to look around once more. I did the tour and this time I filmed it; then we met at the front of the house to see what the brothers had to say.

Alex spoke first: "We are selling the house. It is with a heavy heart. We love this place, but we cannot finish it." He added with a smile, "That's all." I loved it—such a heartfelt, dramatic confession. So Italian. Such tragedy. But, of course, no talk of money. So Italian.

After a pause, I said "How much?"

"We don't know yet. We need to discuss it," Alex said.

"Okay then," I said "Call us when you know." Honestly, I had had it with trying to buy a house. It was a theater of the absurd. I was heading back to Alassio and we had one more appointment with Paola, so I was ready to go. We met Paola in Fivizzano for coffee. She pulled out her computer and showed us a few houses, but I was not interested and I did not want to waste her time. Rupert and I agreed that if she found something really great, we would love to work with her. But for now I needed a break from all of this. I had to get back and sort out the final closing for the flat.

I kept thinking about a conversation Frank and I had in the US. One night Frank and I were having a glass of wine in the hot tub and I was lamenting about not finding the right Italian house for us. Frank consoled me and said this: "Annette, why don't we buy the fortress? Yes, it's big, but I'd rather have a little bigger place than have to deal with adding on to a house in Italy. It's the best thing you've seen, and if your only hesitation is that it is too big, then forget that and put an offer in on that house." I was both shocked and thrilled—that was the best advice ever. It was the right place; we could enjoy the countryside, host our workshops, and the kids could visit with their friends. Yes, it was a big renovation, but I was up for the task. I was excited to move forward and finally make a decision. I believe we had made the right one, thanks to a little push from Frank.

With that advice in mind, I called Rupert and said let's put an offer in on the fortress and see what they say. Rupert agreed it was the best house that we'd seen and that we did keep coming back to it. In Italy they say, "*You don't find the house, it finds you;*" maybe the fortress was trying to tell us something. And now we were listening. "I think it's the one," I said to Rupert. After all this time, I couldn't believe those words were coming out of my mouth.

Like it was meant to be, that week Fredrico called Rupert and had finally got a price on the Fortress from Federico, and the timing could not have been more perfect. The price was good; however, I wanted to think about it and make a fair and final offer when we went to meet with the brothers. I was excited and nervous. One never knows in Italy, but I felt confident that this was the one, and the house wanted us to buy it. I know that sounds crazy, but that is truly how I felt.

Rupert and I arranged to visit the fortress house with the view and make an offer, the brothers were waiting for us outside. They looked a little tentative, but they smiled and we shook hands. After the niceties were out of the way, and we had an espresso that Alex insisted on making us, we got down to business. I made them my offer and I told them that we were serious, that it was all cash, and that we would be able to close quickly. Sometimes in Italy you are allowed to skip the first closing and go directly to the last one, but only if the sellers are willing to do this. My thought was that we would coordinate the last closing of the flat with the single closing of the Fortress. Frank felt that if I did this it would be a feat beyond measure. He told me, "Annette, this just can't be done. This has never been done in Italy." Very funny. When we made the offer, I proposed one closing, and Davide was keen on it. So it looked like they would accept our offer, but I knew not to prematurely celebrate until everyone had signed everything.

CHAPTER 24

Everything Worth Having Is Worth Waiting For

In June 2016 I finally got the call about the closings—the final closing on the Alassio flat and the Fortress would close within a week of each other in July 2016. Our *notaio* was a genius. That meant that I would close before I left in August and would have some time to start the renovation plans with Marco and Rupert. We would hire Marco the geometra ASAP and start the renovations in the fall.

I read the email confirming the July closing while I was on the street in Alassio leading my June 2016 workshop group in shopping for props, and I started to jump up and down in the middle of the sidewalk. All my students looked at me, wondering what on earth was happening.

I called Rupert to confirm it was true we bought the Fortress with view, and when I hung up the phone and told everyone, "We just bought a medieval fortress in Tuscany." I was so excited, the rest of the day was a blur. We got the house, we got the house, the hunt was over. I was doing my happy dance all over the streets of Alassio that day.

Rupert said the brothers wanted us to come over to celebrate as soon I could get there. Also, we had to sign a paper stating we had made an offer and it had been accepted. I had power of attorney, so Frank would not have to come to do all the closings. I needed to finish the workshop, then I would be down right away, I told him. Our *notaio* had a lot of work to do as the fortress was classified as an *agriturismo*. He assured us it would be easy to change the classification. We had to give Davide and Alex a check for the earnest money and sign the piece of paperwork, and the rest would be set into motion. Frank was thrilled, I was thrilled, and we officially hired Rupert to be the project manager, so he was thrilled.

I got to Lunigiana on Tuesday. It was going to be a good Tuesday indeed. Rupert and I drove over together. When we arrived, the brothers were in the storage space off the terrace. They waved to us and headed up to greet us, all smiles. In the living room, Rupert and I sat next to each other on a small, antique love seat. The brothers busied themselves in the kitchen and arrived with a plate of Parma ham and a wedge of *Parmigiano* and a bottle of white and a bottle of red wine. It was very sweet; I did not expect this, but it was really lovely. Rupert said "*Grazie*," and took a glass of the white wine. I took the white as well and we cheered with a hearty "*Salute*!"

"Oh, this is delicious," I said. "Lovely wine."

"We make it," said Alex. "Over there." He pointed with his left hand towards the window.

"Where, what town?" said Rupert. "Where is the wine from?"

"Oh, it is from our vineyard here on the property," he said.

I instantly became flushed; I think my heart even stopped a second. *Did we buy a working vineyard?* I thought. I looked at Rupert. Could it be true? Rupert very calmly asked them, "Does this house come with the vineyard?"

They both laughed and Alex said, "Yes, of course you knew this. We will introduce you to Manolo the vintner; he is hoping he still has the job with the new owners. We hope you consider keeping him."

I could not speak—a first for me. This was the best news ever! It was so Italian never to mention that the property had its own vineyard. Federico arrived then, and they gave him a glass of wine and we all toasted each other again. This time I really cheered like never before— we owned a vineyard, we owned a vineyard!!!! Hooray! I could hardly believe it! I was married to this place forever.

The best phone call came later when I told Frank we owned a vineyard. With his usual wry sense of humor his response was, "Wait, so they were selling a fortress with a vineyard and told no one? Italians are so great at marketing." But we were always amazed at the lack of day-to-day communication. Surely Federico knew there was a vineyard but never mentioned it, we marveled. But in this case we were super happy, because it was as if we got a special gift that day.

We closed on the flat on a Tuesday and on the fortress on a Thursday in July, and I was packed and ready to move that Sunday. I would move all my belongings into the main house of the fortress and stay with Rupert for a few weeks while we got started on the plans for renovation. Leo was sad, but he agreed to help me move and borrowed the company van from Monica. Monica was sad, and we had a little farewell gathering that weekend, knowing full well it was not goodbye. I was only moving two hours away.

We drove down to Lunigiana and unloaded the van. Leo stayed the night at Rupert's house and then headed back. I had very few things to move as the buyer of our flat wanted everything included. So moving was not a major undertaking. Compared with what was about to come, it was nothing at all.

Rupert and I did our first official walkthrough on Monday. When we got there, nothing had been moved out. We had agreed with the brothers they could slowly move out by the end of October. By November we hoped to start the renovation. We had a look around and took an inventory of building materials they were to leave. The first order of business was to collect everything they were leaving us and put it all in the *cantina*, the barrel-ceiling room at the bottom of the fortress.

We met with Federico's brother Marco and started the plans for the renovation. Marco the *geometra* would be in charge of hiring the construction company. He also had a great network of sub-contractors. He would help us arrange the scaffolding. We needed a lot of scaffolding, as the entire building was stone and the exterior walls were at least a hundred feet high. All the mortar was to be removed and then reappointed—it was a massive undertaking. Everything was included in the contractor's bid except the scaffolding. Marco explained that we would need to pay the scaffolding company in cash and told me the amount needed.

"That's a lot of cash," I said. Marco gave me a look that said "Start collecting the cash." And Rupert and I knew what he meant. They were not to be messed with; you were to do what they said. They were most likely part of organized crime, the mafia. We never talked about it again, and they got their cash. I will say the scaffolding company was a dream to work with, with on-time installation and great service.

The first two weeks were filled with signing contracts and going over plans and the budget. Marco was amazing and organized and precise. I know people have certain concepts of an Italian renovation being slow and disorganized (based on how they do most of their business), but I have never found that to be true. In fact, quite the opposite—I am impressed with the level of professionalism and the beautiful work they do. With everything signed and planned, I prepared to head back to the States and leave it in Rupert's hands.

We visited the site one last time and on that day I met Ciro, who would be the foreman on the jobsite. He was a ruggedly handsome man in his fifties. The fact that he was easy on the eyes was a plus for both Rupert and me. We nicknamed him the Marlboro Man, because he was quiet and good-looking, and, ironically, he was one of the only workers that did not smoke. When we first laid eyes on him he was on the upper terrace securing the railing. We looked up and he waved. I will never forget Ciro's lean figure silhouetted high up against the deep blue sky. This image will forever be seared in my memory; not only was it the very first step to renovation, it was the very first step a new love affair with *La Fortezza*, our new home.

Rupert and I did daily updates on Whatsapp. There seemed to be about a million decisions to be made every day. Frank and I were committed to recycling as much of the leftover building supplies as we could. This involved scouting the property that was littered with everything from doors to iron rails to stone to terracotta tiles. The brothers moved out very slowly, and they waited until the last minute to clear out the barn. It was stacked to the ceiling, and when it was finally cleared out, Rupert sent a photo to show me just what an incredible space it was. Somehow I knew it would be perfect as a studio and I was right! The light was beautiful, soft, and golden; it would be a great place to photograph food and still lifes. It needed work, but the bones, now that we could see them, were incredible. Rupert proposed we build a bathroom and I thought we needed a big sink. The renovation was going to consist of three phases. We were on a roll.

Phase one:

1. The Main House. This was where we would live, and it was the most finished space of the entire property. We reorganized the floor plan so that the kitchen was enlarged, and the living room and dining room would be bigger. We added a full bath to the original bedroom on the main floor; this would become our guest room—the room with the floor-to-ceiling mirror (that left with the brothers, thank goodness). Upstairs we put a new ceiling and, with that, a new roof and a new terrace. We made a master bathroom and a master bedroom out of the two existing spaces that we once called the Black Hole of Calcutta. We decided to keep one blackened beam for remembrance of the bats and the water and the darkness.

2. We reappointed the entire façade—about 100,000 linear feet of stone. This required all the old mortar be removed and new

mortar reappointed. It took six months of skilled laborers to finish this project; it was really something to see.

3. We renovated the Barn/Studio. We cleaned all the beams and reinforced them. We stuccoed a few walls and painted them white to serve as backdrops for photography. We laid terracotta floor tiles. We added lighting and a bathroom.

4. We added earthquake beams to protect against earthquakes. This was something now required by the Italian government.

5. All the buildings needed plumbing and HVAC and lighting.

6. Every window and most doors needed to be replaced.

This was the main focus to rebuild *La Fortezza*. We also named the property during this period. All houses in Italy have a name. This property had always been known as *La Prugna* (little prunes), and the story goes that little prunes grew along the river on the property (another discovery during closing—we had a river!). But it's such a large building we thought that it needed a more substantial name. So we named it The Fortress, *La Fortezza*, simple yet fitting. The folks in town were tentative about calling it a new name. But we felt they might come around slowly and they did.

Once the first phase was finished, we would continue with phase two and three. But for the time, phase one was plenty. We began the renovation in November and hoped to be finished with phase one by the end of May 2017, as my first workshop would be held there in June. Frank and I arrived to check the progress in February. We stayed with Rupert and arrived on the second day of our return to Italy at *La Fortezza*. I had pretty much seen all the progress thanks to Facetime and Skype and photos via Whatsapp every morning from Rupert. They were working furiously, and it showed. The walls were up; our new floor plan worked great. The kitchen was beyond amazing, fitted with exposed copper piping; I thought it would add an interesting visual effect and it did. Our plumber Nicola was an artist. The counters were Carrara marble, and the recycled Carrara marble sinks made for a nice touch. The cabinets were simple, painted a pale grey. The showpiece, my French blue Lacanche range with copper fittings, was the perfect punch of color. Ciro was there to greet us and do a walkthrough. He was quiet and thoughtful about the update. It was a pretty seamless process so far.

Rupert was doing an amazing job. We had appointments to pick out various finishes, and we were going to look at lighting as well—a busy week ahead of us. I had made an appointment to meet a local chef, as I decided we needed one to cook for our upcoming guests. Our guests would not be staying with us on this first workshop, as our guest rooms and commercial kitchen and student lounge area were part of phases two and three. But we would feed them. I arranged for them to have rooms with a Dutch couple, Mickie and Doobie, who owned a B&B near Rupert. Rupert had introduced us the year before. Mickie and Doobie were a nice couple with one teenage daughter who was sweet and awkward. I liked their B&B, although it was a bit primitive for my tastes; however, it was the best one in the area. It would work nicely. I hoped our workshop crew would like it. Rupert had been friends with them for a long time so I trusted they would do a good job.

Frank and I returned to Atlanta after a week's stay with Rupert, satisfied that everything was going well. I had sorted out the chef, a handsome, classically-trained chef from Tuscany named Leo whose parents ran a B&B up the road. I had emailed his mom to see if she knew a chef I could hire in the area, and she offered up her son Leo. He would split his time between his parents' B&B and our place. Our guests would bunk at the rustic B&B about twenty minutes away with the Dutch couple.

In April 2017 I returned and stayed two weeks with Rupert until our place was ready to move into. We would go to *La Fortezza* every morning, or go shopping to buy fixtures, antiques, and various items for the place. Rupert knew every flea market in the area. I soon began to know them, too, and the owners started to recognize me. We bought all sorts of lovely things. We bought an amazing iron bed, and ordered an iron table and chairs for the terrace. I bought all the plates and glasses and flatware and linens from the flea market. I was amazed at all the beautiful things I could buy there! I bought props for photo shoots for our workshop classes. I saved some prop shopping so that our attendees could also shop for props to fill the shelves of the studio. All told, my favorite part of the process was discovering new vendors and incredible found objects that we could upcycle on the property.

I had to start thinking about the grounds surrounding the fortress. We met with the gardener, Gianluca. He had been working for the brothers. We needed to go over the garden plan; that, too, would be done in phases. Phase one included a kitchen garden below the terrace. Below the terrace there was a very strange ramp. It was thigh-high with grass, then there was a pad that I thought could eventually be a patio, and then an old garden that had been long forgotten. My plan was to revive it to be the kitchen garden and make it like the one I saw at the fighting sisters' villa. Although the villa was not for us, I had never forgotten that garden.

Our gardener, Gianluca, was a slight man, I remember thinking when I met him that he was too delicate for the heavy work he did. But he was excited to work on the land, as he had only been cutting the fields for the brothers. He had lots of ideas and we were excited to hear all of them. We assured him that he was to stay, he had a job here, and that he would have lots more work. Gianluca seemed both relived and thrilled. I was new on the scene and nobody knew me, so everyone wondered what "*La Americana*" was like. I was gung-ho on hiring everyone that had already worked there—and more. The economy in Italy is awful, so the more Italians I could hire, the better. They were happy and I was happy. Nothing like a win-win plan to help welcome you to the neighbors.

The same week we met with the vintner; he would stay on and manage the vineyard. Rupert had asked him to meet us at the house and he arrived after lunch. We were standing outside when a Range Rover Defender pulled up and Manolo jumped out, wearing a tight t-shirt and a pair of camouflage short shorts with boots. He had long, curly, sandy-blond hair and a handsome tanned face. He was small, but very fit. Rupert and I looked at each other as he walked up the steps towards us and shared a look that said "WOW." My first thought was, *Are you kidding me? This hot guy is my vintner?* He reached out to shake our hands and it seemed all in slow motion, like a sexy Italian movie. Then he very formally introduced himself in the best formal Italian. That made him even more sexy! Lucky for me I could not speak Italian very well, because at that moment I could hardly speak English.

After the introductions, he talked about the vineyard, his basic needs, and what we could expect of the yield. Once he was done he said he had to go, he'd be in touch, and then he said goodbye. He left and Rupert and I were still not sure that we did anything but nod at whatever he told us. I thought, *well, that was wonderful.* I swear we were both flushed. Making wine was going to be fun.

The work progressed quickly for phase one. I was so impressed with Rupert's attention to detail and his non-stop devotion to getting things checked off the list. I was able to move in early May 2017. I had asked my housekeeper from Alassio to come down and help me move in. I had bought a bed for the master bedroom, and Rupert had found an incredible floor to ceiling gilded mirror in Parma for Frank to replace the one the brothers had took with them. It was funny because when Rupert sent us a photo from the Parma antiques fair on a Sunday morning, Frank did not care how much it cost, he just said, "Buy it!" Very out of character for Frank. It made me laugh.

It was all hands on deck, so Rupert helped move me, too. He wanted to assemble our closets. We had decided that Ikea would be a good idea to outfit the closets. Anyone who has bought anything that needs assembly at Ikea knows that sometimes it's extremely challenging. This was the scenario for these Ikea closets. Rupert labored for two days, insisting on finishing them himself when I offered to hire someone to help. He was up for the challenge. After forty-eight sweaty hours, the closets were in. They turned out great and I am forever in his debt. Rupert's moods were unpredictable, but sometimes he was nice.

Meanwhile, my housekeeper and I plodded on with the unboxing. We were very surprised that a family of mice (to this day I think it was rats) had taken up residence in our stored suitcases. It was all hard shell luggage and they still managed to gnaw through and set up house-keeping in our clothing. We were completely grossed out and ended up throwing most of our clothes away. There were a few things we could salvage, but not much. Of course, we were so freaked out that we ended up washing everything—all the dishes and kitchen items I brought—with scalding hot water bleach, wearing rubber gloves.

The house was still filled with dust and pieces of mortar from the stone walls. I had never been so exhausted in my life; I truly thought I was going to die moving into that place. Everything hurt. I did have my copper tub that I bought in Marrakech. Since I had conducted a few styling and photography workshops there, I had made some great shopping connections. I found an amazing personal shopper, Mary, who offered to help with anything I might need for the house. I bought lots of things, but the most beautiful of all was my copper tub. I was sure that having one made to fit the house would be difficult, but it was easy. I just gave Mary the dimensions and she had it custom-made, and it was affordable—even with the delivery cost! The thing that is cool about shopping in Marrakech is that delivery to Italy is easy. The Moroccan drivers have family in Italy, so they bring wares and deliver them when they come to visit over the weekend; then they head back to Morocco. So it was easy to get deliveries, and the tub arrived without any problems.

I loved that tub. I would fill it every night to soak my aching muscles. To my dismay, it was always filled with concrete dust and fine gravel while the renovations were going on, so I never felt clean and the bottom of the tub scratched my butt. But after a week of cleaning and moving and assembling and washing and putting everything in its place, I was sort of moved in and my tub was all I hoped it would be.

One morning, about a week into living in my new house, I walked downstairs in my pajamas, blurry-eyed, and saw a brown blob on the dining room chair. I thought at first it was a bird; maybe it flew into the chimney and down into the house. But upon closer inspection, there was a bat sitting on my dining room chair. I had brought Vivi our Italian mini Dachshund with me this time, but she was of no help—she did not even see the bat. I was freaked out and ran upstairs, got under the covers, and waited for the construction crew to arrive. Once they arrived, I tiptoed down the stairs, went outside still in my pajamas, and motioned to Ciro to come in. I mouthed the words *"pipistrello."* It means bat. He came into the house, looked at the bat, and looked at me and smiled. He gave me the thumbs up, and with that I walked back upstairs and said let me know when it's gone. Without a sound he evacuated the bat—I think he most likely threw the bat out the window, but I did not want to know what became of it. I was just happy he got rid of it for me. I came downstairs, made us an espresso, and carried on with my day. But I feel like I bonded with Ciro that day a little more.

I had two weeks to get the Studio in order for the workshop attendees' arrival. Rupert and I had outfitted the studio from his flea market finds in Parma at the fair in March. We bought a shelving unit and a large wooden table and chairs. I had bought some amazing industrial lights, and those were hung from the beams.

It was quite a feat, getting this all in place before everyone arrived. I had to buy a printer. Our terrace furniture was delivered, so we could dine outdoors. It was a whirlwind of work and I had never been more grateful for my many years of producing large projects. Everyone pitched in, including all the construction workers on site. It was a harmonious thing.

I was so happy when Frank arrived with Levi during the installation of the studio and terrace to help out with the last-minute details before the workshop began. Everyone was working, doing last-minute finishing touches on the construction. The studio looked amazing with big vintage industrial lights and a giant wooden table. The large green industrial shelf was loaded with wonderful props. The studio was ready to welcome attendees. Frank and Levi and I bought a projection system for lectures and for watching movies on the terrace in the evening. And a speaker to play music while we dined on the terrace. The terrace had a built-in banquette and we placed two very large tables in front of the banquette seating and had beautiful wrought iron chairs around the perimeter of the table. It would be beautiful when it was all set for dinner. We also bought a wood slat table that would serve as a buffet table for *aperitivo* and dinner service. It was starting to shape up.

There was one spot on the terrace that had no railing, and I was very concerned that it would be a dangerous spot. If you fell off, it was a fifteen-foot drop. In Italy there are no building codes, from what I can tell, so this spot would just be left open unless we specified we wanted a railing. I had an idea that we could use one of the temporary construction fences as a fix for it. I told Rupert to ask Ciro to pull one of the fences over and place it in the open spot where the rail was supposed to be. Rupert flat refused to do it, and an argument ensued. I thought he was just joking around but he was not. "Why would we do that?" he asked.

"Because we have guests coming and photographing and walking around and I do not want someone to step off the edge and have a terrible accident," I replied.

"Not doing it," he said. Now I was getting mad. I rarely yelled, but I was on the verge of screaming at him. He started walking away and I said, "RUPERT, WHAT THE HELL?!" He stopped, gave me the pissed-off look, and continued to walk away, toward the main house. I assumed he would gather his things and head out.

I yelled again, "RUPERT, PLEASE TELL CIRO TO PUT UP THE FENCE BEFORE YOU LEAVE." He stopped and looked down at me from the bridge. His face got bright red and I can't remember much of anything after that, just the screaming. I was so shocked at the level of his rage and a little afraid, to be honest. At that moment, Frank came out and said, "What's going on?" Rupert was silent. He went inside, gathered his things, and went home. Quietly.

All the while Ciro, who had heard the argument, had been attaching the fence I had asked for. It was obvious that he understood what

I had wanted him to do. It was not a big deal, but for some reason for Rupert it was. This was the first, but not the last, of his hissy fits. It was odd, but not unexpected since his moods were unpredictable.

CHAPTER 25

Love Is Work, Part Due

N ow that I had moved in, it was time to start my styling and photography workshops and see if the fortress was everything I hoped it would be. The workshop attendees arrived. We had six attendees and a photographer joining us. I now had a chef; Leo was great—he was organized and cooked amazing food. We had a few challenges at the start. The first day of the workshop, he was to arrive at noon to prep and to cook the welcome dinner for our group. He arrived three hours late and was not replying to texts. Needless to say, I was freaking out. When he walked in the door, he smiled and started hauling in the groceries. Before he started cooking, I did pull him aside and asked what happened and why he was late.

"Late?" he said in his Italian accent, smiling. "Annetta, I was notta late. It is Italian time, R E L A X-A, I am a professional." I was not amused. I did not know this person and this cheeky millennial was telling me, his boss, to relax. I was not having it. (Although to this day it is our inside joke and every time I run into him he tells me to "relax, he is a professional" and it makes me laugh.) But in his chill way he smiled again and headed into the kitchen to work. He was wonderful in the kitchen, clean and efficient, and I was impressed. He brought his girl-friend to assist, and she was a wonderful help. They managed to crank out some gorgeous meals for the five days of our workshop; and that day it commenced like clockwork. The serving was a bit challenging with the walk from the main house kitchen to the terrace with the food, but Leo made it work—I was very thankful to have him. Even Rupert joined some suppers—he got over his angry spell quickly, for which I was grateful. We invited the Dutch couple as well to join us for the fare-well dinner. It was a great first effort and I was grateful that it all went off without a hitch. People even seemed to like their accommodations, which I was very happy about. But I couldn't wait for the next phase of renovation so that I could house the students in the fortress.

We conducted another Styling and Photography Workshop in July. I was not teaching this one; I had hired a woman from Denmark, Sip, to come teach—someone I knew from Instagram that came recommended to me when the original teacher I had hired became ill and could not make it. This instructor seemed nice; she was a little ditsy on our Skype call, but I shook it off and we planned her stay with us.

Sip arrived by car the day before her workshop. As soon as she arrived she threw her things down and said, "Let's go shopping." So we hopped in my car and headed to the grocery store. She was going to be photographing, cooking, and styling. The car ride was about thirty min-utes to my favorite grocery store. She talked nonstop on the way there, and was a bit manic as she shopped at the store, talking while tossing things into the cart. We were in the store for over an hour and a half, and she never stopped talking. I was a bit concerned, but she seemed nice enough so I just listened. She told me that she was super famous in Denmark, had written twelve books, and was a very well respected photographer. She told me about her kids, her failed marriage, again how famous she was, and about how everyone in Demark loved her so much. She was a bit ridiculous, honestly, but she was funny at the same time. I had never met anyone like her. We headed back to the house, unloaded everything, and sat on the terrace for some nibbles and wine.

She talked and I listened. Finally, it was time for her to head to Mickie and Doobie's B&B. The next morning she came and prepared her class. The students arrived and she picked them up. They all appeared at *La Fortezza* for the welcome dinner and we were off and running.

The classes were great, and the students loved her energy. She was nonstop and talked from 7:00 a.m. until 2:00 a.m. I know this because one of her students had told me that lessons continued after they left to go back to the B&B, and she was exhausted from lack of sleep. At one point this student asked me if she could take a nap on my couch. I was concerned, but everyone else seemed super happy.

At the farewell dinner I once again invited Rupert and Mickie and Doobie from the B&B to join us; they brought their daughter as well. One of the students ended up staying with her husband at Rupert's apartment, which was across the street from the B&B. They were a young couple; the husband had come along for the ride and was occupying himself by day.

The night of the farewell dinner, Sip and her group were running late. Rupert had arrived on time and asked me where they all were. "I have no idea, but they will get here eventually," I said. But Rupert seemed very agitated about their tardiness, and started complaining to me about how rude they all were. I said, "Rupert, this is their vacation. They can arrive when they like, and why are you so upset? You're a guest here. It's my dinner party and I am fine with it." These were the times I was perplexed by Rupert's grumpy mood swings. *Jeez*, I thought, *have a drink and lighten up*. That's exactly what I did—I made him an extra-large G&T and handed it to him and told him to try to enjoy the evening. Thank goodness everyone made an appearance and we had a lovely dinner. Mickie and Sip had really hit it off and talked all night on the terrace. I felt I had had a successful workshop season. Or at least I thought we had, until I got a call from Rupert the next morning. He sounded very upset, shaken actually. He said that he had given Sip a piece of his mind that morning. Wait. I was a little confused. "When did you see her in the morning?"

He told me that he was so upset with the young couple staying with him from my workshop that he hiked up Mickie's hill and wanted to talk to them about their behavior during their stay. "What behavior?" I asked. Apparently the couple had not spoken to Rupert and this upset him.

What?! I thought, but I let him continue. "She's a horrible person— so fake and so full of it. And that couple were pigs, throwing all their towels on the floor of my bathroom." I thought, *I throw all my towels on the bathroom floor to signal that they are dirty when I stay somewhere*, but I did not say it for fear of more yelling. He was really upset and said that he gave everyone a good talking to.

Oh my God, I thought. *Is this really happening? Right before everyone left—are you kidding me?* I truly did not know what to say, I was gutted. My workshop attendance depended on the guests enjoying their stay. It was a vacation as well as a learning situation, and I knew I would depend on good reviews and recommendations. "Okay," I said. "Let's talk later, once you calm down. Don't worry, Rupert."

I had no idea why I was consoling him other that I was hoping it wasn't really as bad as I thought it was. Surely I would talk to Mickie and she would say it was fine. I got a call from Mickie mid-morning after she got everyone on their way to the airport. She told me that Rupert had walked up to the B&B while everyone was enjoying breakfast and reminiscing about what a great time they had. First, he called the couple staying with him "rude" and "pigs." She went on the say that he then proceeded to call Sip a fake and said he hoped he would never see her again. Mickie was in the kitchen and came out and asked him to please leave. She spent the rest of the morning consoling everyone; some of them were crying. I was speechless. Needless to say, the rest of the day was horrible. Here we had put all this work into this beautiful space and he had ruined it in one mindless moment. Why had he sabotaged it? Why?

I did not speak to him for a couple days. I needed to think about what to do next. I spoke to Frank and he gave me good advice. He told me to take a timeout as I was heading back to the States soon, and it would all calm down. Of course, I called Sip and emailed the entire workshop with my sincerest apologies and offered everyone a deep discount if they came back. Everyone was very empathetic and kind and told me it was not my fault and not to worry; they loved their stay. I was happy that one incident would not affect the group, but I was still worried that it would affect my business in a negative way. I had a pit in my stomach for a long time.

I finally got a vaguely apologetic email from Rupert after I had sent one saying that I was so sad that this was how he behaved. He responded and, as we always did, we swept it under the carpet and got back to work. I did not think that I would ever figure him out, and knew it was not worth trying. This was how he was—unpredictable and moody and sometimes volatile—and until the next time he went down that road, we decided we would move on and that he would begin work on phase two. We were a bit stuck in some ways, because he was great at his job 90 percent of the time. But he was not great at being a friend. Frank and I are of the thinking that people are flawed, but we're not perfect either, so we forgive and carry on.

Rupert moved on to phase two.

Phase two:

1. We would build out the guest quarters, those rooms located below the main house. It would consist of three bedrooms with en-suite bathrooms, a kitchenette, and a washer/dryer.
2. We would build out a commercial kitchen and the student lounge below the terrace. Having another kitchen would allow us to not only cook and serve guests more easily, but it would also be a great place to shoot photographs.

3. We would create another terrace next to the kitchen garden, located on the same level. It would be the perfect sunny spot for breakfast in the morning, and *aperitvo* at night while the sun set over the incredible vista.

Back in the US, Frank and I were gathering and filling out paperwork for the daunting task of tackling our residency in Italy. In order to stay in Italy for more than ninety days at a time, we had to do this. It would insure that I could conduct our workshops spring, summer, and fall. If you don't have this, then you must leave for a 180-day cycle before you can return—ninety days in Italy and 180 days out before you can enter the country for another ninety-day cycle. I know it sounds complicated, and it is, and that's why we wanted residency. If you're a resident, some things like banking and utilities are easier and less expensive, so there are lots of benefits. First stop would be Miami to start the initial application process at the Italian consulate. We booked a flight for January 2018, as timing was imperative to the entire process. We would be back in Italy in February to continue the process.

February rolled around and we arrived at *La Fortezza* for a week to check on the progress of phase two. Like before, Rupert and I had been in constant contact. Rupert and the team were doing a great job. Ciro was not the foreman on this phase, because he had had health issues and was recuperating. So the second in command, Leo, was in charge. The commercial kitchen level was a disaster. Once the bats evacuated, they found thousands and thousands of old terracotta roof tiles that occupied the space. The crew had moved them outside onto the property—piles and piles of them. They were old and brittle and would crack and break if we installed them, so were unusable. Anyway, we had bought new tiles for the roof. I offered the old tiles to Heike since she had seen them and mentioned that if we did not want them she would take them.

Rupert and Marco got to work insulating the floors. Italians have great solutions to solve the problem of humidity, since stone houses tend to be humid. They devised a system that circulates air and takes away the humidity. They used what are called "igloos"—they literally look like little plastic houses—that are spaced so air can move through, and then a subfloor is placed on top to cover and the tile is installed on top of that; this keeps the air moving under the floor so no humidity can build up. Once all the igloos, subfloors, and floors and stucco and stones were reappointed and finished, we moved ahead with the décor part of the project. My favorite part.

One day I woke up early, called Rupert, and asked if the antique tin travel tub he bought in Parma was in the *cantina*. Rupert answered, "I think so. Why?"

"I have a great idea. Have the guys bring it to the commercial kitchen when they arrive," I said. We had an appointment with the lighting guy that morning, so I wanted to see if my idea would work. Rupert showed up about a half hour after our call. The guys had brought the tub upstairs, and I was about to tell them what I wanted when Rupert walked in. Everyone smiled and said hello. They were all standing around the antique tub waiting for instructions, and they all looked a little confused.

"I want to make a chandelier out of the tub," I said, "for above the dining table. I want to see if it will work. Do you have your tape measure on you? If we invert it and hang it upside down we can retrofit it with light bulbs. I want to paint the interior white so it reflects light and shines on the table. Like a big light box." I explained.

Rupert thought it was an interesting idea, and Frank, who was also standing there, began smiling and nodding. "I think it's genius," he said.

"Thanks, honey," I said. "You know that guy at the lighting store can retrofit anything. Do you think he would do it?" When I said this, I could tell Rupert was starting to get the idea. "Yes, I think he can; I think it would be rather simple."

We agreed to ask him that day, if we saw him in the store. With that, the guys turned the tub upside down and held it above our heads: it was the perfect scale above our large table.

"This will work," said Rupert, after a little measuring. I thanked the guys and they loaded the tub in our truck and off we went. At the lighting store, we explained the tub to the *maestro* retrofitter, and he loved the idea, so we were good to go. Oh, and he said he could do it for 150 euros. *Fantastic*, I thought. And it would be done in two weeks' time!

As were heading to the finish line, the commercial kitchen was looking great and Rupert was excited about the custom tiles we had painted: a scene of giant blue fish hanging from hooks; it was a fun illustration and it looked great. There was lots of open shelving and the tub light had been finished and installed. I moved into the kitchen and the guest quarters in a week's time and we were ready to roll.

We did about a million errands that week, but the most important one was the residency appointment. First we went to the post office to get our residency forms. The forms were for *Permesso di Soggiornio* (stay permit). We filled them out, and bought a specific stamp that was to go on our form, a *marca da bollo* that we purchased from the *tabaccherie*. Then we returned to the post office to turn everything in and pay for processing. We were then given a random date to show up for our appointment to turn in our other paperwork. Lucky for us it was a month away, and Frank and I would return just in time to meet this appointment.

We returned for this *Questura* appointment in March 2017. We paid Rupert to come with us to help sort out anything we didn't understand. We arrived with a three-inch-high stack of required paperwork and our official photos, plus our new visa from the consulate. We waited in line outside the *Questura*—the police station—with about thirty other people from all over the world, in the rain. Again, the Italians were surprisingly efficient, and when it was finally our turn, Frank went to one window and I went to another. They took our paperwork, and that was it. They handed us a reference number so we could look online to see when we could pick up our residency cards. You could only pick up your card on Saturday between 9:00 a.m. and noon, they informed us, and we were off. After all the hard work, it was a bit anticlimactic, I must admit. We received residency cards, just as they said, in June.

Frank and I had a few more things to take care of on that trip; one big item was the truck arriving from Morocco. I had been on a buying trip with Oma to Marrakech in February. I had bought rugs, chairs, and various decorative pieces for the guest room renovation in phase two. They arrived in a truck from Morocco, and two men who spoke no English unloaded all my goods into the studio in the pouring rain. It was funny when they pulled up, because Frank had thought everything in the truck was ours and started to panic. What he did not realize is that vendors load goods into trucks heading to Italy and then guys drop them off along the way, just like our moving vans in America.

Frank left and I stayed on. Rupert and I made a quick trip to Parma for the antiques fair and picked up a few things for the kitchen, a dining table and chairs, and a couple of vintage leather club chairs for the student lounge.

Phase two was coming along well. Everything was going smoothly, which was wonderful. Decorating the guest quarters was easy and fun and they looked amazing. I bought antique beds and wonderful French white linens.

I had dear friends, Steve and Jill, come stay for a few days. They were in Italy for a wedding, and since I was moving in and decorating, they volunteered to help me. You know how you have some friends that say they want to help you and then you have friends that actually help you? Steve and Jill were the latter. They were amazing—so thoughtful and kind. I was touched that they came and rolled up their sleeves and helped finish up the décor. They were super easy and they were able to understand how stressed out I was to finish in time for our workshop season. I loved having them, and they really eased my mind and my workload. When they left for the wedding, I was sorry to see them go. But they would be back because Steve would be teaching a painting course at *La Fortezza* in September and then doing a stint as our first Artist in Residence in 2019.

CHAPTER 26

Redos and Rescues

The second season of *La Fortezza* Workshops was wonderful. I learned so much. I had been teaching, and was now having students stay on the grounds. This made it a whole different ballgame. Our first attendees at the fortress were great; they loved the guest quarters and were very happy. I had bought antique beds that could be put together to make a single room and then pulled apart so students could share a room. We had an onsite chef, a local woman, Teri, who was funny and prepared all sorts of local dishes and homemade breads and cookies. She made breakfast, lunch, dinners, and snacks, and went shopping and touring with us some days. We dined *al fresco* on the terrace while sipping wine from our vineyard; it was all dreamy. We conducted lectures and had hands-on styling classes in the beautiful light of the studio. Everything was humming along and it was all working; I could not have been more pleased. Once we had more guest rooms in the dependence (the outbuilding), which would be phase three, this place would be even more amazing than I imagined.

Phase three

1. Outfit the dependence with three guest rooms with en-suite bathrooms.
2. Build another gravel patio outside the outbuilding.

Phase three got off to a rocky start. Rupert and I planned to meet Marco in the square in Fivizzano; this was just to be a numbers meeting, something brief, since we had already designed the spaces. It was one of those days when Rupert was not in the best of moods, and as usual I didn't know why but suspected what happened before we went in to Marco's office did not help.

Earlier in the day, in front of the Ricci bar, Rupert and I got out of the car and, at that moment, Leo the chef drove up in his van and stopped and said *ciao*—he was sweet and cordial. Rupert kept walking. Leo said bye and to say *ciao* to Rupert. "Will do," I said, and he drove off. Rupert was waiting at Marco's door. He opened the door and I said, Leo wanted me to say *ciao* to you. Rupert looked at me as if I'd said Leo wanted me to tell you that he wants to kill you.

Rupert had the weirdest reaction. He said, "Leo doesn't give a shit about me." "What are you talking about?" I said. "You heard me," he responded. This shook me up. He was seething mad at me! We said hello to Marco, then the strangest thing happened; Rupert asked me to conduct the meeting by myself in Italian, and he just sat there, mad as hell. I had no idea what to think and asked him what was going on with him. I think Marco could sense something was up. Rupert was just silent. He just sat in the chair, super pissed off.

"Okay, Rupert, we are ready." I smiled at Marco to try to calm the stress level in the room.

Rupert looked at me and said in a tone that frankly scared me, "Go ahead, Annette." I had no idea what he wanted, and we sat there in silence for what seemed like an eternity. Then he said, "Would you step out of the room? I want to talk to Marco alone."

With that, I stood up, left the room, left the building, got in my car, and drove home. When I got home, I poured myself a glass of wine and sat on the terrace. I had never been treated like that in my life. There was no going back. I was beyond furious. Not only were we Rupert's friends, but we were his clients. I would never think to treat a client like he had just treated me, much less a friend. What was wrong with him? The truth was that I had no idea what was going on with him. I wish I could have come up with a rational explanation for this behavior, but it was just nuts. Maybe it was jealousy, maybe it was him hiding things, keeping things from us, maybe it was insanity. I really had no explanation. His mood swings were unpredictable and frankly, I was at the end of my rope. I was trying to be nice, but even I had my limits.

I sipped my wine and tried to calm down. In the meantime, I emailed an apology to Marco for wasting his time and explained that I would be in touch. He was very gracious—after all, this was not the first time he'd seen Rupert come unhinged. Rupert called about two hours after the meeting, and asked to come by; I said sure. He sat on the terrace with me. He really had no explanation. He told he was sorry for acting badly, and I told him that I was embarrassed that this all happened in front of Marco, who was a consummate professional. I said I was embarrassed for him. Then I fired him. I fired Rupert! Boy, that really got his attention. I was serious, and I was done; he had bullied me long enough and it was not worth it. He asked me to reconsider and that he would promise to behave better. I said I would talk to Frank. He left. We were not starting the new phase for a few weeks, so Rupert had time to regroup and apologize, which he did. We started on phase three with him as manager, but for me it was never the same; I was on guard, and I knew this would happen again. It was a pattern too hard to break.

Leo was going to continue as the foreman, but Ciro was working on another job site. I was a bit sad and would really miss Ciro. He very briefly consulted one day on the guest quarters. He was so happy to see me that he threw his arms around me which, for Ciro, was way out of his comfort zone; normally he was the very reserved Marlboro man.

The outbuilding, which we called "the dependence," was quite simple compared to all the other projects and it could be finished in a month, since all the heavy work had already been finished with phase one. We simply needed to tile the floors, and we would barely touch the stone walls. I wanted it super rustic, like the stable that it had once been. I had already bought all the beds and some of the furniture in Marrakech, so we could feasibly make this happen quickly—and we needed to, because we scheduled full workshops in September.

We had Gianluca our gardener work on the new patio. He was clear on what we wanted and had no problem making it happen; I think he was excited to do a big construction project. One day, we all met on-site to sign off on the patio plan. Marco was there as well for a walkthrough of the dependence. First we met with Gianluca, so Rupert could explain to him how he wanted the retaining wall constructed. Gianluca had another idea how to do it that he explained to Rupert, and I agreed with Gianluca's plan. Rupert became very angry and started talking down to Gianluca.

Now, there was not a nicer person on planet Earth than Gianluca; he was an angel as far as Frank and I were concerned. I told Rupert to stop it. "Stop talking to him like that. You're not understanding what he's saying." Rupert turned to me and told me I did not know what I was talking about. Instead of engaging with him, I decided to deescalate the situation and head into the house and let them work it out. I will never forget looking over at Marco and the workers as they watched in amazement. Rupert left after the meeting and we never talked about it. I did apologize to Gianluca for Rupert's outburst. I told Gianluca to do his own plan; that I was fine with it. Rupert would come look at the progress, but he visited less and less after that incident.

The floors were down, the interior was being painted, and the bathrooms were about to be installed. One morning, a day before the bathrooms were to be installed, I sat straight up in bed and looked at Vivi and said, "I think we might have a problem." I quickly made myself an espresso and walked out to the dependence to see if I was right. I had a distressing thought first thing in the morning that the floors were not slanted towards the shower drain, and with a wet room this is a huge problem. I don't know why, but in my mind they were level. I walked into the upper loft room and looked, and my first thought was, *Shit!* They were not slanted. They were level. All of them were level. My fear was true—all the floors would have to be ripped out. We were so close to being finished—the deadline was a week away.

I called Rupert and told him to get Marco and come over. "Houston, we have a problem. Just come over and I will show you." They were both there in a half hour and I showed them. Marco just shook his head, then he called the contractor and the plumber. Our sweet painter Antonio showed up to touch things up. He immediately realized that we were at DEFCON-1.

The plumber showed up and then the contractor, and then it started—what I like to call the "Italian meeting of death." This is a meeting that goes round and round, with lots of talking, then drawing, then phone calls, then the blame game kicks in. It can take hours and hours, sometimes days. I was out after about an hour. I figured that eventually they would all agree that it needed to be redone.

At one point I was standing outside as they were all talking, and Antonio the painter walked by and said to me in a low voice, "They are going to have to rip it all out and do it over again." "No shit," I said, and we both smiled.

After three solid hours, Rupert said to me, "Let's go up to your house and I can explain what we are going to do." It was noon and, quite frankly, I was over it. But I agreed, and the plumber, Marco, Rupert, and I all went into the house.

"Aren't they going to just fix it?" I asked. Rupert said "Let me explain this to you." All I heard was "Let me *mansplain* it to you." He was very condescending, and I had promised myself no more. The plumber started to mansplain it as well, when he saw my frustration. At that point I said, "NOPE! Rip it out, redo it, and everybody out!" I kicked everyone out of the house. They all left. Leo showed up after lunch with a jackhammer. He carefully pried off the tiles, neatly stacked them in the yard and then jackhammered the subfloor for the rest of the afternoon. Rupert called me and told me that Ciro would be there the next day to reinstall the subfloor—properly this time—and re-lay the tiles. Ciro to the rescue; all was good. I was very happy to see Ciro the next day. He was happy to see me, too, although we both thought it a shame that no one caught the mistake and it all had to be redone. But let's face it—things were going too smoothly. I should have guessed something would go awry.

CHAPTER 27

The Best Boyfriend

On the day Ciro finished the dependence, I was on the upper terrace on a phone call with a client. I looked down and saw Ciro was walking to his car; I'll never forget it. It was the end of the renovation of *La Fortezza*; it was finished. I knew it would be the last time I would see him for a while and he did, too. I waved to him; he smiled and then he did something extraordinary—he blew me a kiss. The scene was unmistakably full circle: now I was the one on the terrace where I had first seen Ciro's silhouette against the deep blue sky when he waved hello on the very first day of renovation. We were waving goodbye from the exact same spots—only reversed. The moment was not lost on me or on him. It was bittersweet; we were finished. I poured myself a glass of wine and quietly celebrated what was both an end and a beginning.

We greeted our final groups of 2018 in the fall. Since I had been granted residency, I could stay longer and thought it would be fun to have a few fall workshops. We photographed and cooked in the new commercial kitchen with my Ferrari of stoves—my massive Lacanche with eight burners and two ovens—and lots of counter space for making handmade pasta, plus plenty of room for everyone to photograph. Our chef Teri had left so I hired a stylist chef from Atlanta, Philip, who spoke Italian and acclimated well. He had gone to culinary school in France and spent lots of time in Italy; he loved all the local food and foraged our kitchen garden every day to feed our groups. Everyone loved him. He was handsome, friendly, and knew his way around our newly-built pizza oven. We enjoyed our guests, the season, the wine, and the beautiful food and memories we created and documented in photographs. I made new friends: a woman who lived down the road, whose family owned the local pharmacy and made a local *amaro*. Federica was a beautiful person and I loved getting to know her and her family.

Giovanna, who had befriended me on Facebook, was now talking to our workshops about local foods of the region—she, too, was becoming a part of our curriculum at *La Fortezza* workshops.

On the day before I was headed back to the US, Rupert and I parted as friends. I had cleaned out the fridges and given him all the leftovers and fresh produce, like I always did. We hugged and he said that he was really going to miss me, and I think at that moment he meant it. I think, though, that we both realized that it was over. We had done a great job together on a massive renovation. We were both happy and sad it was over. I told him I would miss him, and I would be back the next March.

My impression was that Rupert was very torn between the lines of friendship and business. This is something I do not struggle with in my line of work—all my clients usually become friends. I think I am good at separating the two…but actually, not always. I think Rupert is more strictly business. With that in mind, Frank and I decided to hire Rupert as the property manager; it seemed to make perfect sense as there were still things that needed attention, along with a small punch list. Rupert thought it was a great idea. That way we could still work together. For a variety of reasons, though, it ultimately didn't work out. I realized that every time we ended a phase, there had been an emotional blow-up. For me, this was the last one. "I need space," is what I told Rupert, but the truth was I needed infinite space. Some things end as they begin. Some things never change; but for me, this particular friend was gone. Some boyfriends just don't work out and that's okay.

Walking around before I departed, with everything completed, I was filled with a great sense of accomplishment. I took this time alone to collect my thoughts and really take it all in. All the great memories, eating and drinking on the terrace with friends and workshop attendees, harvesting from our garden every day, watching Vivi run gleefully all over the property. Cooking in the kitchen from what we had gathered from the garden. These were all perfect moments. As I locked everything up to head back to the US, I caressed every surface, put things away for the winter, and took great care to take my time and relish every piece of this place. *La Fortezza* was the perfect boyfriend after all. I could hardly wait to return and see what would lie ahead—a new page, new adventures, and a new life. Just like the best of all forever romances.

Epilogue

Never did I imagine that my adventures in Italy would be so deep. When I first set foot here, I couldn't have fathomed the love I would have for this place. The inspiration of the light, the food, the people, and the history would seep into my soul over the years to come. How could I even remotely know the intense effect it would have on my heart? When people say that everything led me to this point, I now know what they mean. It has been thousands of days—with the help of hundreds of people—that have gotten me to this juncture. My family has supported this love affair and happily come along on the adventure. I owe them so much.

Waking up in this beautiful place is overwhelming and humbling. Yes, I have worked hard to achieve my goal: the perfect place in the perfect setting with the perfect light. But it still blows me away when I walk to the vineyard with Frank and Vivi and think how this place is ours.

If I have one piece of advice, it is to dream big. Chase that boyfriend, because with hard work and laser focus you can have it. You can. Over the years we will continue to entertain friends, host people, and inspire beauty. I hope you have the *buono fortuna* to join us at *La Fortezza*. I have created this place for our family to gather and for all of us to meet, eat, drink, and be inspired. This place is my peace and my heart.

Acknowledgments

I have to thank my husband Frank, who always trusted my vision no matter how crazy it may have sounded at the time. To my children who truly were my travel guinea pigs and endured Italian cornflakes and no sugary fruit loops for most of their youth.

Thanks to all of our guests no matter what transpired during your visit…yes thank you, although some names have been changed to protect the innocent, you know who you are. Mainly thank you to all my sweet Italian friends who made an effort to include me and take me in, and a special thanks to Leo who was and has remained so kind and helpful over the years. Thank you once again to Janice Shay, my mentor, advisor, and great friend, you have been so helpful and supportive in all my writing endeavors. I owe you a million Aperol Spritzes.

About the Author

Photo by Kate Blohm

nnette Joseph lives half of the year in Italy and is an expert on entertaining, cooking, and styling. She regularly appears on NBC's *Today* and Martha Stewart Living Radio. Her recipes and party ideas have been featured in *Better Homes and Gardens*, *Epicurious*, MSN, *The Huffington Post*, *Southern Living*, and *Woman's World*, among others. She is the author of two cookbooks, *Picture Perfect Parties* and *Cocktail Italiano*, and is currently working on *La Fortezza Cookbook* out in Fall, 2021.

Currently Annette conducts creative retreats and workshops at La Fortezza, teaching styling, photography, painting, and food-centric workshops. La Fortezza is a medieval fortress in northern Tuscany she and her husband painstakingly renovated for three years. On twenty-seven acres, the property has a large kitchen garden, rose garden, and vineyard, as well as a newly-planted olive grove.